easy paleo meals

150 gluten-free,
dairy-free
family favorites

KELLY V. BROZYNA
from The Spunky Coconut

VICTORY BELT PUBLISHING INC.

LAS VEGAS

First Published in 2015 by Victory Belt Publishing Inc.

ISBN-13: 978-1-628600-85-8

This book is for entertainment purposes. The publisher and author of this cookbook are not responsible in any manner whatsoever for any adverse effects arising directly or indirectly as a result of the information provided in this book.

Photography: Kelly V. Brozyna
Design: Yordan Terziev and Boryana Yordanova

Printed in the U.S.A.
RRD 0215

table of contents

how it all began

When I was in elementary school, we put on a play where we dressed in leotards and wore animal masks of our own making. I can still remember the way I looked in the photo from that play: slim-figured, but with a *huge* round belly. I had stomach pain to go with the bloating, and I was always constipated. The doctor told my mom to give me prunes, which unfortunately did nothing whatsoever to help.

In high school, I hunched my shoulders and wrapped my arms around my waist to try to conceal how bloated I was. In college, I decided that my enormous belly was fat, so I dieted like crazy in an effort to get rid of it. Although it was less noticeable when I lost weight, I was as constipated and unhealthy as ever.

Until I had children, I thought I was normal. I thought everyone pooped only once a week. I often looked like I was six months pregnant. That's how everybody is, I thought.

I was misdiagnosed twice. First a doctor thought I had a stomach ulcer because I was having horrible pain followed by vomiting. (Vomiting was not a regular symptom of mine.) A year later, a different doctor thought I had a parasite. He gave me mega-doses of antibiotics (which I took), and then he found out that it wasn't a parasite after all. "Just keep taking the antibiotics," he encouraged me. "Whatever's wrong, it can't hurt to take them." (Currently slapping my palm to my forehead.) That time I lost around forty pounds in two months. I looked like a skeleton.

The pain, bloating, and constipation continued, but I just lived with it, and my weight fluctuated.

When my oldest daughter, Zoe, began eating solid food, she stopped growing and gaining weight. When my in-laws came to visit, I wished that they wouldn't take her photo, because she looked so unhealthy. I went from doctor to doctor trying to figure out what was wrong. Then an osteopath suggested that I go see a nutritionist. The person he recommended, Cheryl Diane, turned out to be a family friend. Sometimes the person you need is right there all along!

Cheryl told me about EnteroLab, the laboratory that I still recommend for gluten testing. We found out that Zoe is gluten and dairy intolerant. I removed gluten and dairy from her diet and, *for the first time in a year*, twenty-four-month-old Zoe gained weight. She gained five pounds immediately. Not only that, but she transformed into a different child. Her behavior had been crazy: She would run away from me, right into the road. She constantly scratched my face so that it looked like I had been clawed by a cat. The minute I stopped feeding her gluten and dairy, all of that stopped.

At first I blamed Zoe's condition on my skinny husband. "You can't gain weight," I said. "The gene must have come from you." So Andy was tested and found to be intolerant of gluten and dairy, like Zoe.

Could I be gluten and dairy intolerant, too? No way. After all, I was normal, right?

My denial went on for a few more months, but I refused to make six meals a day: one meal with gluten and one gluten-free meal for breakfast, lunch, and dinner. No, thank you. So we all went gluten-free at home, and I cheated when I was out. Oh, baby, that hurt. Literally. I insisted that it was a coincidence, until one night it hurt too much to deny anymore.

I sent my samples to EnteroLab, and guess what? I have celiac disease, an autoimmune disorder that leads to intestinal damage, nutritional deficiency, and other serious health problems when gluten is consumed. Back then, in 2004, it was a real bummer. No one, except for medical specialists and professional bakers, knew what gluten was, nor had they ever heard of celiac disease. There wasn't a plethora of gluten-free recipes in books and online or a wide variety of prepared gluten-free foods on grocery store shelves like there is today. What's more, I wasn't an avid home cook at that time; I relied quite a bit on prepared foods and dining out, both of which, to be on the safe side, would need to be eliminated. Simply put, I didn't know how to eat without prepared foods, and I worried about how I would live without them. Cheryl told me to bake with almond flour and coconut flour. Do what, now?!? But I trusted her, so I bought almond flour and coconut flour. I also bought the book *Cooking with Coconut Flour* by Bruce Fife. And that's how it all began.

At first, we weren't consciously trying to eat grain-free, just gluten-free. For the first several years I used buckwheat flour occasionally, and we ate quinoa, both of which are considered pseudo-grains. I don't remember ever thinking that buckwheat and quinoa were causing us issues, but my second daughter, Ashley, and I did react to brown rice every time we ate it. A few times a week we would have brown rice pasta or stir-fry with brown rice, and we would get painfully bloated and gassy.

My friend Shirley Braden, creator of the blog *Gluten-Free Easily*, encouraged me to prepare grain-free meals to see if it would make a difference for Ashley, but I was reluctant. Then one day in 2010, after Ashley ate a big bowl of brown rice noodles, she sat down on the couch and just stared at the wall for an hour. It freaked me out.

So that was it—no more brown rice or brown rice pasta. I even cut out pseudo-grains just to be safe. We were officially Paleo. We became Paleo because it was necessary, but I tell you honestly: we have never eaten such delicious food in our lives! If someone told me that I could go back to my old ways of eating tomorrow, I would have to say, "That's okay, I'm good!"

Ashley's story

Though eating the way we do—gluten-free, grain-free, and dairy-free—has helped all of us thrive, its effect on Ashley, my second baby, has been the most dramatic by far.

When Ashley was four months old, she began having sudden seizures that lasted for two hours. Over the following week, her head increased 20 percent in size and developed bulges here and there. At the children's hospital the staff performed a sonogram on the soft spot on her head to look for an accumulation of fluid in her brain. When that proved negative, the doctor wrote down "head growth spurt" as an explanation in her records.

From that night on, Ashley stopped developing. She also became intensely fearful. When she was a year old, we had her evaluated through our state's early intervention program. The team found her level of development to be that of a four-month-old.

At eighteen months, Ashley was not only terrified all the time, but also banging her head on the floor and walls, flapping her arms, screeching, and "stimming" (engaging in self-stimulating repetitive behaviors). A developmental pediatrician diagnosed her with global delay, sensory processing disorder, hypotonia (low muscle tone), and autism.

Ashley had a lot of physical and occupational therapists because she was so delayed. One therapist in particular liked to talk about all the things Ashley couldn't do at the end of each visit. The moms in my support group discussed an alternative approach: the power of positive affirmations. After a particularly upsetting visit with that negative therapist, I decided to let her go.

I took a piece of pink construction paper and cut it into a big heart. Inside the heart I wrote a note to Ashley:

"I know you can walk. I know you can talk. I know you can eat. I love you so much and I'm so proud of you."

I put the positive affirmation on the refrigerator. Every day I would carry her over to the fridge, read her the note, kiss her, and smile.

When we put Ashley on a gluten- and casein-free diet when she was around twenty-two months of age, most of her symptoms disappeared. (Casein, the protein in dairy, is very similar to gluten on a molecular level and can affect behavior in a similar way.) On her second birthday, she took her first steps and ate her first bite of solid food. It was an epic birthday.

We continued to focus on biomedical treatments for Ashley. After interviewing a few different doctors, we found one whom we adored. This doctor started working on Ashley's health. She ordered a blood test to look for a genetic mutation of the MTHFR gene, which is considered a predisposition for autism. The MTHFR genetic mutation is estimated to be present in 50 percent of people. When "turned on" or "triggered," the mutation leads to all sorts of problems, like autism, pulmonary embolisms, fibromyalgia, miscarriages, schizophrenia, severe depression, and cancer, to name a few. What does the mutated MTHFR gene do? Simply put, it makes it very difficult for the body to detoxify. (To learn more, listen to Balanced Bites podcast episode #178: "The Autoimmune Solution with Dr. Amy Myers"; in the podcast, Dr. Myers explains how the MTHFR mutation can make it very hard to get rid of mercury, for instance.)

Ashley was found to have the MTHFR mutation, so we did another test that looks for markers for heavy metals. Ashley was burdened with high levels of aluminum, arsenic, lead, mercury, and other metals. Her markers were off the chart—the highest her doctor had ever seen. It would take many years of working with her doctor to pull out the heavy metals and other toxins that Ashley was holding. To this day we are still working on it.

Although Ashley's symptoms are minimal, she is still extremely delayed from the seizures and brain damage that she experienced when she was a baby. She is eleven years old now, but cognitively more like a toddler. I brush her teeth (it's a struggle), wash her hair (also a struggle), prepare and cut her food for her, help her get dressed, clean up her accidents (she's still toilet training), and do everything one would do for a two-year-old. I don't know if that will ever change, but I adore her the way she is, so I don't really worry about it. No one is more loving and affectionate than Ashley. She makes me so happy, and I am grateful to have her.

It took catharsis, positive affirmation, skilled guidance from qualified practitioners, and lots of perseverance to keep my perspective positive and Ashley's health progressing. But by seeking a healing diet and lifestyle for Ashley and Zoe, our entire family was put on a path to health and happiness.

♡ Kelly

about this book

Going Paleo is about improving the quality of your life. Though a huge part of that is about maintaining better physical health by being more selective about what goes into your mouth, it also is about simplifying and enjoying life. I've learned over the years that when you get organized, plan your meals, and keep a list of what your kids like to eat, life becomes easier, less stressful, and more enjoyable. Eating lots of leafy greens and making your own yogurt (page 182) and broth (page 131) also contribute to a healthy Paleo lifestyle, and it's so much easier to do than you might think. It's all about the planning. This book will guide you through the process of doing just that so that you can enjoy life and be healthier at the same time.

Part 1 covers the ingredients and kitchen tools that are fundamental to the Paleo diet, including all the key ingredients needed to make the recipes in this book. For those of you who are new to Paleo, the "Eliminate" and "Enjoy" lists on page 16 will show you at a glance what is and is not included in the diet (don't worry, there's lots more of the latter).

In Part 2, I show you how to get organized, stock your pantry, and use meal plans as well as share helpful meal-planning and kitchen tips and menu ideas.

Part 3 is packed with more than 150 recipes that will take you from breakfast to dinner and beyond to dessert to satisfy your sweet cravings. Several of the recipes are made with homemade base recipes, such as my baking mixes (pages 132 and 133), used in everything from bagels (page 160) and crackers (page 282) to pancakes (page 158) and more, and my "cheese" base (pages 110 and 111), a sort of sauce that can be thought of as an updated, Paleo version of that all-purpose mid-century recipe binder: cream of mushroom soup. It works its magic in several recipes in this book, from Creamed Kale (page 219) to Fettuccine Alfredo (page 264). Once made, these base recipes make getting healthy meals on the table go quickly and seamlessly.

For those of you who are allergic to eggs and/or nuts, I've marked those recipes that are free of these common allergens with egg-free and nut-free icons. And if you regularly cook for children, I've marked those recipes that are especially kid-friendly with the Kids' Favorite icon. Just look for these symbols throughout Part 3:

At the back of the book, in the appendix (beginning on page 379), you will find natural living tips and guidance on how to live free of toxins. Though eating real, unprocessed food is central to going Paleo, adopting clean-living habits in other parts of your life, outside the kitchen, will help contribute to an overall healthier lifestyle.

Whether you're just beginning to cook Paleo meals or you have been eating this way for some time but are looking for new fresh and easy meal ideas, plus strategies for being more efficient in the kitchen, you are sure to find something of use within these pages.

why paleo?

I want my family and myself to be healthy. We eat Paleo because it provides us with optimal health, and I believe it can do the same for you.

Paleo is the closest term I know of to explain how my family eats. We don't eat grains, refined sugar, vegetable oils, or processed foods, all of which contribute to an unhealthy gut and are excluded from a Paleo diet. Dairy is considered to be okay by some people in the Paleo community—if it does not affect your health and you consume only the highest quality dairy (whole, grass-fed, raw). However, most forms of dairy are detrimental to the health of my family, which is why we exclude it from our diet. On a molecular level, the protein in dairy, called casein, is very similar to gluten, the protein in grains. We have successfully treated a number of issues by eliminating gluten and casein: celiac disease (yours truly), attention deficit disorder (my sweetie pie), and growth problems (Zoe, our firstborn). Ashley, our middle daughter, has autism relapses when she eats gluten or becomes constipated. Eating this way isn't optional for us, but we are so *far* from deprived.

Paleo is about eliminating foods from your diet that are detrimental to your health and replacing them with foods that are nutrient-dense. The key to eating Paleo is to focus on what you *can* eat rather than what you can't. When people ask me how I manage to eat on a restricted diet, I always say that the truth is, I don't feel restricted! You'll see what I mean when flipping through the recipes in this book or in other Paleo cookbooks (see "My Other Publications" on page 400 for a list of my previous books). Happy Paleo eating!

Health issues in my family that we have successfully treated with Paleo: autism, MTHFR, attention deficit disorder, failure to thrive, celiac disease

part 1:

paleo ingredients & kitchen tools

If you're new to Paleo, the first order of business is to learn what is off-limits and then to focus on the enormous amount of real food you *can* eat. If you don't have a lot of cooking experience, chapter 2 will get you fully equipped with all the tools you will need to make the recipes in this book; some are required tools for any kind of cooking, such as a good-quality chef's knife, and others are darlings of the Paleo community, such as the nifty spiral slicer, indispensable for making noodles from all types of vegetables. Then you can get to the fun parts of organizing and stocking your pantry and developing a meal-planning strategy (see Part 2, beginning on page 34) and cooking all the delicious things there are to eat (see Part 3, beginning on page 104).

chapter 1:
Paleo Ingredients

For you Paleo beginners, the simple "Eliminate" and "Enjoy" lists on the following page will get you started. At a glance, these lists will tell you which ingredients or foods should be included in your diet and which should be discarded. A short primer on why the "Eliminate" ingredients do not grace Paleo tables follows the lists.

Eliminate

Gluten/Grains:
wheat, barley, rye, spelt, oats, corn,
brown rice, other grains

Dairy:
milk, butter, cream, fresh and aged
cheeses, cultured dairy products such as
sour cream and crème fraîche

Refined Sugars:
corn syrup, high-fructose corn syrup,
barley malt, brown rice syrup,
white/cane sugar

Artificial Sweeteners:
aspartame, saccharin, refined stevia
(see page 20), sucralose

Additives:
preservatives, nitrates, artificial colors
and flavors, anything you
can't pronounce

Man-Made & Processed Foods:
Avoid all so-called "foods";
eat only real food.

Man-Made Fats & Refined Seed Oils:
canola/rapeseed oil, corn oil, rice bran oil,
soybean oil, margarine-type products

Enjoy

Meat & Poultry:
grass-fed, free-range, organic

Eggs:
local and pasture-raised if possible;
otherwise free-range and organic

Seafood:
wild-caught and low-mercury*, such as
anchovies, salmon, and sardines

Vegetables & Fruits:
non-GMO and organic

Healthy Fats & Oils
for Cooking & Eating:
bacon fat, ghee**, avocado oil, coconut oil,
olive oil, olives, chocolate, coconut butter,
shredded coconut, nuts, seeds,
nut and seed butters

Nongrain Flours/Meal:
arrowroot flour, almond flour, cashew flour,
coconut flour, flax meal

Natural, Unrefined Sweeteners:
dates, honey, coconut sugar, natural stevia

Unprocessed Drinks:
homemade drinks (see chapter 7) or
mineral water, such as San Pellegrino
or Gerolsteiner

*Find out why my family avoids mercury on page 226.

**Ghee, though made with butter, is casein-free and therefore can often be consumed by people who have celiac disease or who are intolerant of gluten or other forms of dairy. For more on the relationship between casein and gluten, see page 18.

why are gluten, casein & more eliminated?

Gluten is a protein found in grains that creates inflammation throughout the body and affects the brain, heart, and joints in addition to the digestive tract. *The New England Journal of Medicine* listed fifty-five "diseases" that can be caused by eating gluten. Although gluten is conventionally considered to be a protein found only in wheat, barley, rye, spelt, and contaminated oats, you may be surprised to learn that all grains contain a protein that potentially can cause the same problems. To learn more about gluten, I recommend that you watch Dr. Peter Osborne's video "Gluten Sensitivity Vs. Celiac Disease Vs. Gluten Intolerance" from Glutenology on YouTube (www.youtube.com/watch?v=cv5RwxYW8yA).

Casein, the protein in dairy, is very similar to gluten, the protein in grains. For this reason, if you are gluten intolerant, I suggest that you remove dairy from your diet as well.

Refined sugars are the most common forms of sugar. The refining process removes natural vitamins and minerals, leaving the sugar depleted of nutritional value. To correct this imbalance, our bodies pull vitamins and minerals from within. Calcium is pulled from bones and teeth to protect the blood. Over time, the digestive tract and every organ in the body are harmed. It is also well established that excess sugar causes hypoglycemia and leads to obesity, diabetes, and high blood pressure, which increases the chances of heart disease. A diet high in sugar can trigger autoimmune disorders like allergies, asthma, arthritis, and multiple sclerosis, as well as feed yeast and the growth of cancer cells.

Man-made fats and refined seed oils can't be created naturally, unlike coconut oil. Rapeseed, for instance, must go through a multi-stage chemical process and then be deodorized in order to make the resulting "canola oil" palatable. Furthermore, these man-made fats and refined seed oils are typically made from genetically modified seeds that are treated with high amounts of pesticide in the field. As if all that wasn't reason enough to avoid them, they are extremely detrimental to your health. (Shocker!) To learn more about the negative effects of these sorts of oils, I recommend that you read the post "Why You Should Never Eat Vegetable Oil or Margarine!" published on the blog *Wellness Mama* (wellnessmama.com/2193/never-eat-vegetable-oil/).

essential paleo ingredients

Once you've made it through Part 2 of this book and cleaned out your kitchen cabinets and pantry (at which point you'll be feeling pretty awesome), you will want to restock your cupboards and fridge with high-quality ingredients. Here are some of the must-haves for nutrient-dense healthy eating.

grass-fed, free-range, organic meat & poultry

One of the qualities that I admire the most about the Paleo community is the emphasis it places on consuming healthy, humanely treated animals, who lived the way they were intended to live, outdoors.

Meat from grass-fed or pasture-raised animals is nutrient-dense protein. It's full of amino acids, B vitamins, iron, and more.* Gelatin, collagen, and homemade broth (or stock) are also essential to the health and healing of your gut and give you a healthy glow. In this book, you will find many meat dishes (see chapter 14), as well as recipes for homemade broth (page 131), collagen smoothies (pages 142 and 144), and gelatin-based gummies (page 170).

produce

Have you heard that people who follow the Paleo diet eat nothing but meat? Not so. Actually, my family eats *more* plants than we ever did in the old days. We eat spiral-sliced plant "noodles" in place of pasta and pile our plates with veggie sides—broccoli, cabbage, carrots, cauliflower, zucchini and other types of squash, leafy greens, and so on—instead of grains and bread.

Vegetables and fruits are incredibly nutrient-dense. By eating a greater proportion of them, you will improve your health. Consuming fermentable fiber (fiber from vegetables and fruits) and fermented foods (like yogurt and sauerkraut) is important to create and maintain a healthy gut. In addition to beets, lemons, and turmeric (to name a few), dark leafy greens are among our most important allies for supporting the liver. The only trouble I have with plants is keeping enough of them in the house to feed my family of five!

Pesticides and genetically modified organisms (GMOs) don't belong in our bodies. The phrase "you are what you eat" comes to mind. For the health of my family, I buy organic, non-GMO vegetables and fruits, and so should you.

* To understand the importance of eating meat (and fat), I recommend reading the book Eat the Yolks *by Liz Wolfe (Victory Belt Publishing, 2014).*

natural sweeteners

Coconut Sugar

Coconut sugar is rich in vitamins and minerals, as opposed to refined sugars, which have been stripped of their nutritional value. Coconut sugar has a caramel color and flavor and can be substituted in equal amounts for other kinds of granulated sugar.

Dates

My nutrition mentor always says, "Eat foods as close to their original state as possible." If it's possible to create a recipe using a whole food, such as dates, as opposed to a processed food, such as refined sugar, then it's best to do so. Dates are not only delicious, but also contain small amounts of fiber, vitamins, and minerals. Dates are the sweetener I use in my ice creams (see my book *Dairy-Free Ice Cream*), puddings, and often pies.

Honey

I use small amounts of honey in baking to add moisture as well as sweetness. Raw honey is not necessary for the purpose of baking but is preferable for no-cook uses because of the added health benefits, such as boosting the immune system. If your honey is solid, gently melt it so that it's runny enough to measure and blend into the other ingredients in a recipe.

Stevia Extract, Natural

Consuming large amounts of sugar is very harmful to your health, and artificial sweeteners such as aspartame, saccharin, and sucralose are even more frightening. Combining stevia extract with another natural sweetener (such as coconut sugar or honey) allows me to keep the total amount of sugar in a recipe to a fraction of what typical recipes call for. For instance, my coconut cake batter (page 338) contains only 2 tablespoons of honey and ⅛ teaspoon of liquid vanilla stevia, while typical coconut cake batter contains 2 cups of refined sugar.

Stevia is a perennial herb that is native to northeastern Paraguay. In the wild it grows to be about fifteen inches tall, and it blooms with small, primarily white flowers. The sweet leaves of the stevia plant have been used in Paraguay for at least 100 years.

Like vanilla extract, liquid vanilla stevia tastes terrible straight from the bottle. However, you won't even notice the stevia when you use a fraction of a teaspoon in a cake.

I don't buy chemically processed or genetically modified stevia brands. I recommend only the SweetLeaf, NuNaturals, and NOW Foods brands of liquid stevia extract.

To read about the misconceptions surrounding stevia, including the FDA controversy, check out my husband Andrew's article "Stevia Extract, the Healthy Sweetener" on my blog, *The Spunky Coconut*. Go to the FAQ section, scroll down to the question "What is stevia and is it safe?", and click on the link to the in-depth post.

good carbs

Carbohydrates provide fuel for the body. They are particularly important for growing and athletic bodies; kids especially need carbs and fruit unless there's a medical reason to avoid them, such as diabetes, obesity, or biomedical treatments. Good sources of carbs include all types of root vegetables and winter squash. Recently, white rice has been added to the Paleo community's list of good carbs (see the sidebar below).

Personally, I rarely eat white rice because I get enough carbs from root vegetables (carrots, sweet potatoes, white potatoes, and so on) and squash (such as pumpkin). In addition, my baking mixes (pages 132 and 133) contain arrowroot flour or tapioca flour, both of which are sources of carbs since these flours are made from starchy root vegetables.

white rice

In January 2014, I noticed people in the Paleo community talking about white rice and calling it a "safe starch." Initially I thought this was some kind of rebranding, as if everyone wanted to deny that white rice is a grain. So I asked my friends Josh Weissman of the blog Slim Palate *and Stacy Toth of the blog* Paleo Parents *to explain it to me. They told me that the protein is removed from white rice, making it safe for people who react to gluten. (All grains contain a type of gluten, but only certain grains receive the gluten label. To learn more, watch the video "Gluten Sensitivity Vs. Celiac Disease Vs. Gluten Intolerance," by Dr. Peter Osborne, at www.youtube.com/watch?v=cv5RwxYW8yA. It will amaze you!)*

I decided to test myself with white rice and see if I reacted to it the same way that I react to brown rice (which makes me bloated and gassy). Sure enough, I didn't have a reaction. Then I let my daughter Ashley have some, and she didn't have a problem with it, either.

So here's what I think: If you or someone in your family needs more carbs, like a growing child, an athletic adult, or a person with a high metabolism, like my husband, then white rice might be a viable solution.

flours

Almond and Cashew Flour
Almond and cashew flour, like almond and cashew butter, should be refrigerated, because nuts will go rancid at room temperature. You can use these two flours interchangeably.

Arrowroot Flour
Arrowroot is a starchy root. This flour makes baked goods chewy. You may substitute tapioca flour if you prefer.

arrowroot   coconut   salt   flax

Coconut flour is approximately 20 percent protein and 30 percent fiber (more fiber than any other flour), and it contains 5 percent iron.

I used to think that you had to sift coconut flour because it clumps together. Then one day, while I was working on a previous cookbook, I decided I was going through my coconut flour fast enough that it didn't need to be refrigerated. And I found that when coconut flour is kept at room temperature, it doesn't clump. If your room-temperature coconut flour is clumpy, or you simply prefer to keep it in the fridge, then you should sift it before adding it to your recipes.

Golden Flax Seeds

Flax seeds give baked goods elasticity. Unlike brown flax seeds, which are usually labeled just "flax seeds," golden flax seeds are virtually invisible when ground and used in baking. You may purchase golden flax meal if you prefer not to grind the seeds yourself; just make sure to keep it refrigerated in an airtight container because it will go rancid faster than whole flax seeds (which also must be refrigerated).

Psyllium Husk Powder

Psyllium husk is 100 percent fiber. I use this powder as a substitute for gluten and gums in baking. Recipes that call for it will not work if you leave it out.

cashew

baking soda

psyllium

oils and fats

For a long time, all oils and fats were demonized. It's such a relief that studies now show the real problem: hydrogenated vegetable, canola, and soybean oils. In fact, good fats, like the ones listed here, are crucial to the health of your brain and gut, the regulation of hormones, weight loss (yes, weight loss), and much more. I credit our high-fat diet with helping my family overcome our health issues. I also attribute my high-fat diet before, during, and after pregnancy (while nursing) to my youngest baby Ginger's success.

Have you ever felt hungry half an hour after eating a meal? This happens to me whenever I eat a meal that doesn't contain enough fat. Fat is satiating, which helps prevent overeating. My fellow fat-loving friend and keto expert Leanne Vogel of the blog *Healthful Pursuit* explains, "Fat loss and the maintenance of a lean physique are much easier if hormones are balanced. Eating a greater proportion of fat allows for hormonal balance of androgens such as testosterone and estrogen."

Consuming fat reduces blood sugar and insulin levels, balances your metabolism, and encourages normalized cholesterol. A deficiency of fat and cholesterol in the brain leads to lower levels of the neurotransmitter serotonin. (That's the one that makes you feel good.) Finally, fat contains vitamins that are great for your nails and skin. Therefore, eat fat for beauty, health, and happiness!

Avocado Oil

Avocado oil is good for high-heat cooking. It has very little flavor, so it's perfect for cooking eggs and frying foods.

Bacon Fat

Being a part of the Paleo community has enabled me to meet some amazing people, like my friends Stacy Toth and Matt McCarry of the blog *Paleo Parents*. I asked Stacy for a quote about bacon fat because she and Matt are the authors of the book *Beyond Bacon* and are experts on all things pork.

Stacy explains, "Bacon fat, like all pork fat, may surprise you as a healthy fat for cooking—but it is! In addition to having a fairly high smoke point, which reduces the risk of oxidation, it is also one of the best food sources of vitamin D available. It is mainly made up of healthy monounsaturated fats, like oleic fatty acid. Pastured pork also contains a good deal of omega-3 fatty acids, essential for reducing inflammation and maintaining health. Of course, it's extremely tasty with a luxuriously creamy mouth-feel hard to find outside of butter—so it's a great replacement for those avoiding dairy and processed seed oils!"

Coconut Butter/Cream Concentrate

Made from dried coconut meat, coconut butter/cream concentrate (also known as coconut manna) is mostly fat but also contains protein, fiber, and minerals. It can be purchased raw or not raw. You can also make coconut butter yourself. Alexa Croft of the blog *Lexie's Kitchen & Living* has a great tutorial for making it (search for "How to Make Coconut Butter" on her site, lexieskitchen.com). I buy Artisana (coconut butter), Nutiva (coconut manna), and Tropical Traditions (coconut cream concentrate).

Olives, 80% dark chocolate, nuts and seeds, and nut and seed butters are good sources of fat for snacking.

Coconut Oil

At about 7 grams per tablespoon, coconut oil has the most lauric acid of any component of the coconut. Lauric acid improves nutrient absorption and digestive function and regulates blood sugar. The medium-chain fat in coconut oil is easy to digest and is converted to energy rather than stored as fat in the body. Coconut oil actually increases your metabolism while protecting against bacteria and viruses. Like avocado oil, it is good for high-heat cooking and tastes wonderful in baked goods.

Ghee

I use ghee made from grass-fed butter. Dairy is problematic for people with celiac disease (like me) because casein, the protein in milk, is almost identical to gluten on a molecular level. Ghee is free of casein, lactose, and unhealthy oils like canola oil (which are found in butter substitutes). Most people who don't tolerate casein or lactose do well with ghee. However, in the recipes in this book, I always give an alternative to ghee for those of you who need one.

Olive Oil

Cold-pressed organic olive oil is my favorite healthy fat for making homemade salad dressings (pages 120 to 125). It's best consumed raw rather than used in cooking, because heat damages its fats.

miscellaneous

Agar Powder
Agar powder is an algae that is often used as a substitute for gelatin. It can be used to thicken yogurt, but I mostly use it to give structure to pie fillings.

Apple Cider Vinegar
My vinegar of choice, apple cider vinegar with "the mother" has multiple health benefits. It helps regulate blood sugar, supports immune function, improves digestion, and balances pH levels. Apple cider vinegar adds a pop of brightness to recipes and encourages baked goods to rise when combined with baking soda.

Applesauce, Unsweetened
I often use applesauce in baking to add moisture and a little sweetness. Make sure that the applesauce you buy is organic and free of added sugar.

Cashews, Raw
Cashews are the perfect whole food for creating creamy dairy-free dishes. I use raw cashews to make dairy-free salad dressings (pages 120 to 125), to create mock ricotta cheese (used in my lasagnas on pages 260 and 262) and cream cheese (used in my Cheese Danish, page 166; Pumpkin Bread, page 274; and Black-Bottom Cupcakes, page 328), and to make the "cheese" base (page 110) that is used in many of the recipes in this book, from soups to quiche.

Chocolate
Dairy-free dark chocolate (such as 80% cacao content) is a great source of good fat. It's important to buy organic chocolate. Chocolate is treated with more pesticides than any other food crop—that's not something you want in your body! Also, there is a real problem with child slavery on cacao plantations in Africa. Always look for the Fair Trade or Rainforest Alliance Certified symbols on your chocolate packaging. Learn more about chocolate in my book *The Paleo Chocolate Lovers' Cookbook*.

Coconut Aminos
Coconut aminos is a great substitute for soy sauce (which contains wheat) and tamari (which is also made from soy), and I adore the flavor that it adds to recipes. Additionally, coconut aminos has greater amounts of amino acids, the "building blocks of protein," than its soy-based counterparts.

Collagen, Powdered
Most people are familiar with gelatin—it's the stuff used to make Jell-O. Collagen hydrolysate, as the brand Great Lakes calls it, or collagen peptides, as the brand Vital Proteins calls it, comes from the same part of the animal but is processed differently. Powdered collagen is great for smoothies because it is water-soluble and won't gel or clump. Both of the brands I mentioned are grass-fed, and either will work in my recipes. I even have a Lemon Breakfast Cake recipe that uses collagen on my blog, *The Spunky Coconut*. You've probably heard that collagen is great for your hair and nails, but it also is a good source of protein, supports joint health, and is very healing for the gut.

Dried Fruits (without Added Sugar or Preservatives)

Besides dates, which I puree and use as a sweetener, my family's favorite dried fruits for snacking and using in recipes are apricots, cranberries, figs, plums, raisins, and sour cherries.

Flax Egg

Flax eggs can be used in place of real eggs in some recipes, for an egg-free option. To make a flax egg, grind enough flax seeds to get 1 tablespoon of flax meal. Place 3 tablespoons of hot water in a small bowl, then stir the flax meal into the water. Let the mixture rest for 5 minutes, then use it in your recipe. *Note:* If one of my recipes does not list a flax egg as an option, then a real egg is required.

Freeze-Dried Strawberries

I love using ground or crushed freeze-dried strawberries in scones (page 176), N'Oatmeal (pages 180 and 181), and cookies (pages 344 to 349). They provide a concentrated strawberry flavor without the moisture of fresh strawberries. Finely ground freeze-dried strawberries are also really pretty sprinkled on cupcakes and semifreddo pie, as seen in my book *The Paleo Chocolate Lovers' Cookbook.* Organic freeze-dried strawberries are sold in health food stores and on iHerb.com.

Naturally Fermented Foods

Consuming homemade yogurt (page 182) and other naturally fermented foods is important for gut health. You can make your own sauerkraut (there is a recipe on my blog) or buy a naturally fermented brand of sauerkraut, pickles, and pickle relish, such as Bubbies.

Mayonnaise, Paleo-Friendly

There are plenty of great recipes for homemade Paleo mayonnaise in books and on blogs. While I admire people who make their own mayo from scratch, I've never gotten into the habit. I buy Sir Kensington's or Primal Kitchen brand mayo, available online and in some grocery stores.

Shredded Coconut, Unsweetened

Mostly good fat, shredded coconut also contains protein, fiber, and a tiny bit of iron. I use it for easy, healthy porridge (page 178) and N'Oatmeal (pages 180 and 181), and occasionally in treats. I buy it organic and sulfite-free.

Sun-Dried Tomatoes

One approach to easy, flavorful cooking is to keep a stash of pantry items on hand to boost the flavor of dishes, such as anchovies, olives, and sun-dried tomatoes. I use sun-dried tomatoes in salad dressings, dips, quiche, pasta dishes, and quick breads.

Tomato Products, Jarred

To avoid BPA (bisphenol A), a chemical found in some plastics and other food packaging, such as cans, I recommend buying products in glass jars. Because of the acidic nature of tomatoes, buying tomato products in glass containers is particularly important. I purchase the Bionaturae brand at my local health food store; their jarred strained tomatoes and tomato paste are organic and have no additives (like sugar or preservatives).

chapter 2:
Kitchen Tools

This chapter reviews the appliances and tools that I feel are the most crucial to own—the ones you will turn to again and again when making the recipes in this book. This list is not exhaustive, however: It doesn't include the most basic tools or those items for which quality is not particularly crucial, such as wooden spoons, spatulas, tongs, measuring cups and spoons, and a vegetable peeler. I assume that you already have most of these everyday implements.

For a more in-depth list of the appliances and tools that I use in my kitchen, visit the Tools section on my blog, *The Spunky Coconut,* which also includes links to purchase these items.

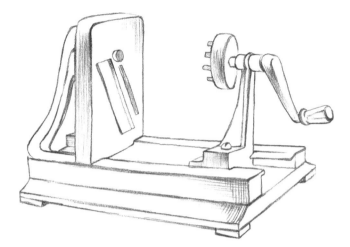

Kitchen Scale

A kitchen scale will make your life easier by shortening the time you spend cooking. And, because measuring dry ingredients by weight is way more precise than using cups, your recipes will turn out perfectly every time. Plus, a scale is inexpensive (under $20) and super simple to use. It's a no-brainer. Get a scale; it will increase your happiness. In this book, I have supplied the gram weights for ¼ cup and greater amounts of dry ingredients used in baking recipes that benefit from precise measuring, such as flours, sugar, cocoa powder, shredded coconut, and baking mixes.

Knives

It's important to have a good-quality chef's knife, serrated knife, paring knife, and honing steel for sharpening. I often encounter people who are afraid of chef's knives (which have blades that are 8 to 10 inches long) or any sharp knife. The truth is that a sharp chef's knife is much safer and easier to use than a small and/or dull knife, which requires you to apply more pressure.

The chef's knife is the knife you'll use most frequently for slicing and dicing meat, vegetables, and fruits. Buy a quality chef's knife and it will stand the test of time. Because it gets the most use, it's important to keep it sharp by running the honing steel down it every day. It's also good to have your knives professionally sharpened once a year. You can usually find people providing this service at a farmer's market.

The serrated knife is ideal for slicing bread, which is why it's often referred to as a bread knife. However, this knife is also good for cutting through waxy surfaces like tomatoes, watermelon, and citrus; the teeth on a serrated knife are better (and safer) at cutting those slippery skins than a smooth chef's knife. Just remember that a serrated knife is for slicing, not chopping.

Finally, the smallest knife: the paring knife. I use it mainly for slicing strawberries and removing the insides of tomatoes and peppers. A larger knife would be awkward for these types of tasks. Again, it's all about safety.

Heavy-Bottomed Pots, Small and Large

You need at least two heavy-bottomed pots: one 2- to 3-quart saucepan for making porridge, jams, and sauces and one 4-quart (or larger) pot or Dutch oven for making yogurt, soups, and more. My brand of choice for pots is Le Creuset. Their pots not only look beautiful, but also last forever, and they can be used in the oven as well as on the stovetop. In December, you often can find Le Creuset pots at discount home stores like Marshalls, T.J.Maxx, and HomeGoods. Just look for the Le Creuset name on the lid.

Slow Cooker

Whether you're feeding two people or four or more, the bigger the slow cooker, the better. Because who doesn't need leftovers? My family of five will eat a whole chicken in one dinner, but two people can eat chicken twice! And after the whole chicken is cooked to melt-in-your-mouth perfection, you can turn around and make broth with the bones (see page 131 for my recipe). I use my 7-quart slow cooker every week, all year long.

Spiral Slicer

Spiral-slicing is so easy; you're going to love it. It's a great way to make grain-free "pasta" and eat more vegetables. I've used the Benriner Turner Slicer for many years, and it has stood the test of time. However, it does not secure to the counter, so my arms get a workout while I use it. (Is that necessarily a bad thing?)

Blender

A professional, high-powered blender like a Blendtec or Vitamix is ideal, although most of my recipes can be made with a regular countertop blender.

Mini Blender

A mini blender, such as a Magic Bullet, is handy for pureeing small amounts, like salad dressings (pages 120 to 125) and dairy-free cream cheese (pages 166 and 274).

Food Processor

My favorite use for a food processor is finely chopping vegetables, as seen on page 56. I also use my food processor to make dips (pages 236 to 238), meatballs (page 266), puddings (pages 358 and 359), and more. Mine has an 11-cup capacity.

12-Inch Stainless-Steel Skillet

I use my 12-inch stainless-steel skillet every day. It's perfect for making my Best-Ever Pancakes (page 158), Perfect Crispy Potatoes (page 184), and pasta recipes (chapter 12). Make sure that the skillet that you buy comes with a lid. I have two skillets so that I can make double batches.

10-Inch Cast-Iron Skillet or Pizza Stone

I use a 10-inch cast-iron skillet or pizza stone (I have both) to make pizza. Both of them make the crust dry on the bottom and chewy on top.

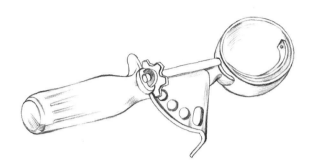

Stainless-Steel Muffin Pans and Rimmed Baking Sheets

To prevent aluminum from transferring to our food in the oven, I use only stainless-steel muffin pans and rimmed baking sheets.

8½ by 4½-Inch Glass Loaf Pans

I adore these loaf pans. They are narrower at the bottom than they are at the top, which gives you a slightly taller bread, and they're made of glass as opposed to aluminum, which transfers to your food in the oven. I also use them to roast garlic since I don't use aluminum foil for the same reason.

My daughter Ashley has the MTHFR mutation, which severely limits her body's ability to detoxify. We are especially concerned about avoiding toxic metals and synthetic chemicals, like those found in aluminum baking sheets, nonstick pans, and plastic containers. For optimal health, I believe that removing as many heavy metals and other toxins as possible is a worthwhile effort for everyone, not just for those with the MTHFR mutation.

Scoops with Levers

When you're short on time, every minute counts. That's why I always use a ¾-ounce (size 40) scoop with a lever for making meatballs and cookies: It's so much faster! For ice cream, donuts, and fish patties (like my Fish-n-Chips on page 312), I use a large ice cream scoop with a lever.

1-Gallon Glass Cracker Jars

I use these jars for my baking mixes (pages 132 and 133) so that I can make a lot of mix at one time. This way, I can make a mix once and use it for weeks. Baking during the week is so much faster because I don't have to measure two or three flours, baking soda, and salt. And my mixes have been great for getting my husband and kids to bake more often. What a bonus!

2-Liter Glass Jug

When you don't drink soda, it's nice to have a big pitcher of herbal or green tea on hand. My kids are obsessed with tea: jasmine, chamomile, rose hip, and hibiscus (page 150) are their favorites. I often make a 2-liter jug in the morning and keep it on the counter (rather than chilling it), and by the end of the day it's all gone.

have food, will travel

Toxin-free stainless-steel and glass food and beverage containers are better for you and for the environment. They also hold up better than plastic and save you money in the long run, since plastic bags are disposable and plastic containers stain, hold odors, and need to be replaced as they break.

Lunch Boxes

The amount of waste from school lunches is so sad. From plastic bags to individually wrapped snacks and juice boxes, a lot of waste ends up in landfills. In addition to helping you avoid toxins, reusable lunch boxes are better for the environment. I like LunchBots lunch boxes (which are made of stainless steel) and Laptop Lunches (which are BPA- and lead-free).

Reusable Water Bottles

They are heavy, but my kids love the Lifefactory glass water bottles with the flip caps for taking herbal tea or lemon water on the go. We have had the same bottles for a couple of years now. For a lighter-weight solution, I recommend a stainless-steel water bottle, like a Klean Kanteen.

Stainless-Steel Condiment Containers

I'm obsessed with these little containers from LunchBots. I use them for dips and dressings in packed lunches. I bought extras, because they're also great for packing cream and deodorant to take on an airplane.

Some of my favorite recipes to pack for lunches on the go include Apple & Jicama Sandwiches (page 300), Chicken Nuggets (page 302), and dips (pages 236 to 238). When I pack our lunches, I check that I've included protein, fat, vegetables, and fruit for balance.

part 2:

a strategy for easy paleo meals

Since I've written several cookbooks and maintain a food blog, you might logically assume that I love to cook, but I don't. I love to eat. (Was I not supposed to say that?) This may be an "everything cookbook," but I'm not going to do a little bit of everything. I'm only going to give you my favorite family recipes that I've crafted over many years of testing. Why would someone who doesn't like to cook spend years testing recipes? Again, because I LOVE to eat. And because I'm very picky about ingredients: They have to be really healthy. My family's health issues require it (read "How It All Began" on pages 5 to 8 to learn more). And I may or may not be obsessed with coconut. But that's another story.

To make my life easier, I realized that I needed:

1. organization

2. kitchen quick tips

3. meal plans and menus

Equally important are my baking mixes, which can be found among the staples in chapter 6. I knew that if these things made my life easier, then they would make yours easier, too. And that's how this book came to be. In this part, you'll find my top tips for making the very best use of your time in the kitchen.

ranch
orange & almond
russian

pancakes & muffins

chapter 3

How to Get Organized, Stock Your Pantry & More

Imagine you just moved. All your boxes have arrived at your new place, and you're eager to get them unpacked so you can feel at home. You put the appliances, bakeware, and dishes away neatly in the cabinets. Next come the pots and pans, silverware, and storage containers. Finally comes the food: the flours, oils, sweeteners, spices, extracts, bottles, cans, and jars.

You think it looks organized, and for a while it's not bad. But then bags become half empty, and they keep multiplying. Without meaning to, you buy more flour and dried fruit, thinking you had run out. Bags of who-knows-what are filling the cabinets.

We've all been there.

This happens to me every time I move, and recently I decided that I'd had enough. Inspired by some photos of beautifully organized kitchens on Pinterest, I set out to organize my kitchen. It was really fun, and it changed my life. I highly recommend it. This chapter shows you how it's done.

I used to think that having tons of clear glass storage jars was just about style. Functional, maybe, but not really necessary. Pretty, yes; essential, no. But now that I've seen what it's like to have glass jars meticulously organizing my ingredients, I've completely changed my mind. Storage jars help keep me organized, and that makes my life easier.

Here's what I mean: Before I switched to glass storage jars, life in my kitchen was like looking at an *I Spy* book: "Where's the cocoa powder? Oh, there it is. No, wait, that's the green tea powder; the bags are so similar. Cocoa powder . . . cocoa powder . . . gotcha! Nope, that's coconut sugar. Cocoa powder . . . where are you?!?" And since the move to the pretty glass containers? Well, let's just say that *I Spy* and I have broken up for good. It's such a relief. Here's how you can get organized, too.

how to get organized

step 1:

Shop

See, it's fun already! The first thing to do is go to Target, Marshalls, Ace Hardware, or any other store that sells storage containers and buy a whole bunch of them. I prefer clear, narrow boxes for keeping smaller items snug and large metal baskets for bigger items and bulk. Wide-mouth glass jars are also a must; I use them for flours, cocoa powder, and other dry goods in the pantry.

Buy more containers than you think you'll need. Make sure to keep your receipts, because some containers won't work out, and then you can just return them.

step 2:

Empty

This step can create a mess, so to make it less stressful I suggest that you empty one cabinet or pantry shelf at a time. If you're like me, you will likely find half-empty bags of flour and random packaged items that you didn't like and never finished. Throw away those things that you don't want or need, and then group like items together.

When the first cabinet or shelf is nice and neat and all the like items are grouped, move on to the next cabinet or shelf and repeat the process.

step 3:
Organize

Use your nifty storage containers to organize each group of like items. If emptying the pantry was not exactly your idea of a good time, then I hope organizing similar items in matching storage containers will be fun for you. Trust me, it's going to be worth all the effort.

I'll be honest with you: It's going to get worse before it gets better (at least it did for me), and it might take you a few days. But in the end your life will be so much easier, and that's what it's all about!

Here are some tips for success:

- Transfer frequently used items, like flours, to wide-mouth glass jars so you can find them easily and know at a glance when you're running low.

- Refrigerate all forms of nuts and seeds to prevent them from turning rancid. This includes whole nuts and seeds, nut and seed flours, and nut and seed butters.

- Do not refrigerate coconut butter, coconut oil, or ghee.

- Opt for glass food storage containers. As compared to plastic, glass containers don't hold stains or odors, last longer, are often oven-safe, and they are a better choice for the environment.

step 4:
Fine-tune

Now it's time to take a step back and admire your work. Then, over the next couple of weeks, make adjustments as needed. Are you constantly reaching for something that you put on a high shelf, requiring a step ladder to get it, or that's located at the back of a shelf, making it hard for you to grab? Move those items down or to the front of the shelf to make them more accessible. As you begin working in your newly organized kitchen, you'll undoubtedly want to make several small adjustments until it functions like a well-oiled machine. The most important point is to make sure that the organization you choose is what works best *for you.*

The following photos offer a peek into my kitchen cupboards and freezer to give you an idea of how I organize my kitchen (plus a bonus tip for storing fresh herbs!).

Hanging baskets are a great way to keep fresh produce off the counter. Check regularly to see if pears, avocados, and other fruits that can bruise are ripe. Transfer ripe produce to the fridge to store for several more days. I highly recommend gorilla hooks for hanging baskets. They make the tiniest holes and can hold up to 40 pounds.

A Berkey brand water filter (seen on the counter on the right) is a great way to purify water. These filters can be found online.

From left to right:
Top shelf: natural remedies, coffee grinder, whole coffee beans.
Middle shelf: natural remedies, cake decorating supplies, natural food coloring.
Bottom shelf: mini blender, extracts, liquid measuring cups, ceramic Bundt pan, juice press.

From left to right:
Top shelf: dark chocolate bars, glass loaf pans, sustainably sourced palm shortening.
Middle shelf: Pizza & Bread Mix, dairy-free dark chocolate bars, plantain and potato chips.
Bottom shelf: canned goods, dried fruit.

From left to right:
Top shelf: empty storage containers, sugar, salt, collagen protein, cacao butter, jasmine green tea.
Middle shelf: Everyday Seasoning, Salt Blend, Easy Taco Seasoning, onion powder, ghee, honey.
Bottom shelf: psyllium husk powder, matcha powder, cacao powder, carob powder, white rice, arrowroot flour, coconut flour.

It's hard to reach anything stored in the cabinet over the refrigerator. Utilize that space by removing the cabinet doors and arranging some your most frequently used cookbooks in a rainbow across the open space. If there is a gap between the refrigerator and the cabinet, use it to organize items in trays purchased at a craft store. We use our trays for the kids' arts and crafts supplies: construction paper, crayons, pastels, pencils, tape, scissors, etc.

To cut down on clutter, use magnetic clips to hang one large focal piece on the fridge. I'm crazy about this print by Valerie McKeehan (lilyandval.com).

Ever open the freezer and have to duck as a bag of frozen cherries flies out? We've all been there. This freezer redo was as easy as buying a few storage containers at Target. These containers have held up perfectly and keep me organized.

From left to right:
Top shelf: coconut milk frozen in BPA-free trays with lids, fruit, ice cream bowl, homemade ice pops, peas and other veggies.
Bottom shelf: ice in BPA-free trays with lids, Cappello's pasta, meat.
Door: dips, grass-fed butter.

From left to right: Fresh herbs planted in miniature pails, fresh herbs in water, green onions growing back in water.

fun tip:

Green onions will grow back if you place the roots in a small jar of water. Cut the green onions an inch above the root end and place in just enough water to cover the roots. Tie a rubber band around them to help them stand up. Keep them on a windowsill and change the water every other day. They will be fully grown in about a week.

Knowing how to store produce to keep it in pristine condition for as long as possible is part of smart kitchen management, and it reduces shopping trips to replace ingredients that are past their prime. The best way to keep parsley and cilantro fresh is in a jar with water touching only the bottoms of the stems. Make sure that no leaves are soaking in the water because they will rot. Change the water every other day. Store in the fridge or on a windowsill. Fresh basil should be kept the same way, but stored at room temperature to prevent the leaves from turning black. The herbs will keep for about a week.

it's not about perfection

Repeat after me: Organization does NOT equal perfection.

Getting organized is about making your life *easier,* not about making it perfect. There's no such thing as perfect, and trying to be perfect will drive you crazy (I'm speaking from experience here). Getting organized is about preventing you from buying four bottles of vanilla extract because the cabinet was so cluttered that you thought you were out of vanilla extract (true story). Getting organized is one of the keys to making life easier. I want your life to be easier, which is why you need to be organized.

Being organized:

*   Prevents you from buying something you already have.

*   Helps you keep track of what you're running low on.

*   Shortens your time spent cooking.

*   Reduces stress.

Bonus: It looks nice, too!

kitchen quick tips

There's more to making kitchen tasks go smoothly than having an organized kitchen equipped with the right tool for each job. Knowing how to melt coconut oil, spiral-slice vegetables, and cook a whole pumpkin, among other essential skills, makes preparing meals so much easier.

how to melt coconut oil

Note: *If you buy coconut oil in bulk like I do, then transfer some to a large mason jar with a lid for daily use.*

1. Place the jar in a small heavy-bottomed pot and fill the pot with enough water to cover about half of the oil in the jar. (If the water level is higher than the oil level, the jar will tip over.)

2. Remove the jar of oil from the pot, then heat the water. (It needs to be hot, but it doesn't need to boil.)

3. Turn off the heat and put the jar back in the water. The oil will liquefy very quickly.

how to melt coconut butter/cream concentrate

Note: *The butter/cream concentrate should be in a glass jar for the purpose of melting it. Buying food in glass containers is always preferable.*

1. Loosen the lid of the jar. Place the jar in a small heavy-bottomed pot and fill the pot with enough water to cover most of the butter/cream in the jar.

2. Remove the jar of butter/cream from the pot, then bring the water to a boil.

3. Turn off the heat and put the jar of butter/cream in the hot water. Leave it to soften for about 20 minutes.

4. Take the jar of butter/cream out of the pot and stir with a butter knife.

how to set up a double boiler

You can create a double boiler with a saucepan and a stainless-steel mixing bowl that is large enough to set on top of the saucepan.

1. Put an inch or two of water in a saucepan and place it over low heat.

2. Set a stainless-steel mixing bowl on top. There should be at least 2 inches of space between the water in the saucepan and the bottom of the bowl.

3. Add the chocolate or whatever it is you're melting to the bowl. As soon as the contents have melted, remove the bowl with an oven mitt.

how to pick and pit an avocado

I like to buy avocados when they're still firm because they're less likely to have bruises if they ripen in my house (where, theoretically, no one is sticking their thumbs in them). I buy Hass avocados when they're still green, and when they start to darken I begin checking them. You can tell that an avocado is ready when the skin is dark, but underneath the stem is still yellow or green. Just pick off the stem "button" and have a look.

To pit an avocado:

1. Holding the avocado in one hand, insert a chef's knife lengthwise into the side of the avocado. Turn the avocado so that the knife goes all the way around.

2. Remove the knife, twist the avocado, and open it.

3. Move one hand away, then gently strike the pit with the chef's knife. Now hold the half with the pit and use the knife to lift the pit out.

how to spiral-slice

Spiral-slicing is easy-peasy. It's also a fantastic way to get more plants into your diet. Here's what you need to know.

- My favorite veggies to spiral-slice (in no particular order) are carrots, beets, zucchini, butternut squash, parsnips, sweet potatoes (regular and white), celeriac (celery root), and parsnips.

- The first step, before spiral-slicing, is to peel vegetables that have hard or inedible skin, such as beets, parsnips, and winter squash. (I wear a cut-resistant glove when I do this, as seen in the top photo, so I don't nick myself accidentally. These gloves are also useful for protecting your hands when grating foods.) It's up to you whether you peel soft-skinned vegetables such as carrots and zucchini first. Personally, I don't.

- Spiral slicers have comb-shaped blades. The wider the comb, the wider the "noodle." Using the flat blade (or removing the comb) creates the widest noodle, which is what I use in my Mediterranean Zucchini Salad (page 226).

- The vegetable should be at least 1½ inches wide in order to get a continuous ribbon of noodles.

- Cut the length of the vegetable to fit your spiral slicer. If a zucchini (for instance) is too long, it won't fit in the spiral slicer, so you will need to cut the zucchini in half.

- Both ends of the vegetable should be cut (flat), and the end that attaches to the handle should be wide enough to ensure an adequate grip. Trim the vegetable if needed for a nice wide grip.

- When spiral-slicing beets, butternut squash, carrots, or sweet potatoes, clean the spiral slicer immediately after use to prevent staining.

- Zucchini shrink like crazy when cooked. Keep this in mind when considering how many you need for zucchini pasta ("zoodles"). I recommend at least two zucchinis per person (or four, if you're like my husband).

- The amount of time that it takes to cook spiral-sliced vegetables varies. I find that white-fleshed sweet potatoes and parsnips cook faster than regular sweet potatoes and celeriac. Feel free to substitute one vegetable for another in any of my pasta recipes, but keep in mind that the cooking time may change.

how to cook a pumpkin

Cooking a pumpkin doesn't have to be hard or dangerous. I've been cooking pumpkin this way for over a decade now, and you can, too!

1. Set the oven to 400°F. Once the oven reaches temperature, place the pumpkin on a rimmed baking sheet and place it in the oven. Do not cut or poke it. The pumpkin will steam inside the skin in about an hour.

2. Remove from the oven and let cool. Once cool, peel off the skin, cut the pumpkin in half, and remove the seeds.

3. Puree the cooked pumpkin in a food processor until completely smooth. Use in recipes, such as Mini Boulder Cream Donuts (page 162), Pumpkin Cinnamon Rolls (page 168), Pumpkin N'Oatmeal (page 181), and No-Bake Pumpkin Pie (page 376). If not using right away, store in the fridge for up to a week or in the freezer for several months.

how to cook a butternut squash

You can cook a butternut squash the same way you cook a pumpkin. However, since most butternut squash will fit inside my slow cooker, I use that instead of the oven. Place the squash in the slow cooker and add 2 cups of water. Cook on high for 4 hours. Once cool, remove the skin, cut the squash in half, and remove the seeds. If the squash is very wet, squeeze it in a clean, dry kitchen towel to remove some of the moisture.

how to remove the insides of a tomato

Slice off the top just below the stem. Similarly to the way you core an apple, use a paring knife to separate the insides from the wall of the tomato, cutting around in a circle until all of the insides are loose. Use a spoon to carefully scoop out the insides.

how to remove the stems from kale and other leafy greens

Fold the leaf to one side. Using your other hand, pull the stem away from the leaf.

Note: *It isn't necessary to remove the stem all the way to the top of the leaf.*

how to make a collard wrap

1. Use a chef's knife to carefully cut out the thickest part of the stem, about halfway up the collard leaf, without tearing the leaf.

2. Prepare the collard leaf as directed on page 232.

3. Lay the prepared collard leaf flat side down and add your fillings to the middle.

4. Lift the bottom of the "wrap" up, overlapping the cut pieces slightly.

5. Fold the outsides in, like wrapping a present.

6. Roll the wrap tightly to resemble a burrito.

chapter 4:
Meal Planning 101

To meal plan or not to meal plan?
Maybe a little of both. Being organized
isn't about perfection, and neither is
meal planning. Meal planning is just
another tool to make your life easier.
But some weeks it's like, "Forget it. I just
can't do it. Let's go to Chipotle!" When
you feel this way, don't beat yourself
up. No one is perfect. I certainly
have weeks when I make nothing but
scrambled eggs or pancakes and go
out to eat. Then, after giving myself
a break, I can get back in the kitchen
again. It's okay.

In this chapter and the next, I'm going
to show you how my family really eats
(spoiler alert: I don't cook every day)
and how using this book can make your
life easier. I like easier, don't you?

For specific weekly meal plans devised
to get you jump-started (I expect
that you will customize your weekly
meal plans once you get on a roll),
jump ahead to chapter 5. To learn
some extremely useful meal-planning
tips that have helped me immensely
and that you can put into practice
immediately, read on.

make a lot for later

- Making large portions, thereby creating leftovers, is one of the simplest strategies for easy meals throughout the week. With this in mind, many of the recipes in this book are designed to yield up to ten servings.

- Another important meal-planning strategy is to double recipes. For instance, if you're making a Burrito Bowl (page 309) on Thursday, you can double the recipe so that you have leftovers for lunch on Friday. This applies to recipes with a standard yield of four to six servings and even to those recipes with larger yields, if you know that you will want lots of leftovers, are serving lots of people, or would like to portion out meals for the freezer. For instance, I always make extra lasagna for the purpose of freezing it; it freezes so well! If you freeze leftovers, remember to label and date those items.

- Sometimes only one part of a meal needs to be doubled. For instance, in the first fall meal plan I suggest a Burrito Bowl one day and Taco Boats (page 306) the next. In this case, only the taco ground beef needs to be doubled.

- As a general rule, I never double any recipe (for leftover purposes) unless I'm sure that my kids will eat it. To discover which recipes are favorites of my kids and their friends, look for the heart-shaped Kids' Favorite icon at the tops of the recipes in Part 3.

finding time

- The most important thing about meal planning is knowing when and what to prepare for. This makes life so much easier. For example, in the second winter meal plan I suggest having yogurt with nuts and berries for breakfast on Thursday and Friday. This means that you need to ferment the yogurt on Tuesday night, then refrigerate it at some point on Wednesday, depending on how sour you like your yogurt. Yogurt is ridiculously easy to make (see my recipe on page 182): It's all about the planning.

- You can reduce the number of times you cook during the week if you and your family don't mind eating the same thing again. For instance, in the second fall meal plan I suggest making bars to have for breakfast on Monday and Tuesday, then pumpkin bread to have on Wednesday and Thursday. If you fall in love with the bars and you don't want to make another breakfast recipe, then plan to make more bars instead, enough to last the entire week.

- Breakfast is the biggest issue for most of my readers. To make time for breakfast, either prepare your breakfasts ahead of time or get breakfast going the moment you wake up so that it has time to cook while you get ready for your day. For example, either make muffins the night before, or crack some eggs into tomatoes and pop them in the oven as soon as your alarm goes off. The same goes for bacon: Make it the night before, or throw it in the oven right when you wake up so that it's ready to go when you are. It's all a matter of planning.

- Work that slow cooker! A slow cooker can be your best friend. It's as simple as putting the ingredients in the slow cooker before you leave for work. For example, I make my barbecue sauce (page 129) in the evening and then add it to my slow cooker with some chicken the next morning. When I get home, I have barbecue chicken waiting for me to use on pizza and salad for the week.

- Choose recipes that don't call for a lot of ingredients. The fewer ingredients, the less time you will need to spend shopping, cleaning, measuring, chopping, and so on, and the faster the recipes will go. The recipes in this book that are made with five ingredients or fewer are listed below.

recipes that use five ingredients or fewer

make-ahead

Make-ahead or "food prep" is just a shorter way of saying "getting your food ready ahead of time." It can be as simple as chopping veggies for salads to eat during the week or preparing your weekly lunches over the weekend. It's really up to you, depending on how much time you have. The less time you have (and the more kids you have!), the more helpful it is to prepare food in advance.

- If you're going to make food ahead, remember to label and date those items.

- Prep your veggies for salad and make your salad dressings (pages 120 to 125; I make one dressing per week) over the weekend. Remember that the dressings will likely solidify in the refrigerator, so consider putting some of the dressing straight into mini packed lunch containers that you can grab in the morning to save time. Stainless-steel LunchBots condiment containers (see page 33) are my favorite.

- Determine which baking mixes you will need during the week and make them over the weekend. This step has seriously changed my life. Now, for example, when I decide one evening that I want to make scones for the following morning, I have only one dry ingredient to measure. It's so fast! Check the index for lists of the recipes that use my baking mixes.

- Determine which spice mixes, condiments, or sauces you will need based on the meal plan you're following and make those items ahead of time.

stretch it

Getting more out of your meals by "stretching" them makes meal planning so much easier. There are two ways to stretch your meals:

- **Use prepared recipe components in multiple recipes during the week.** This simplifies shopping, and it's great for make-ahead. For instance, if you know that you're going to use "cheese" base (pages 110 and 111) or taco ground beef (page 306) in two recipes during the week, then you can make a double batch of each and keep them in the fridge, ready to go.

  The same goes for raw ingredients. For example, I'll buy enough bok choy to use for Brassicas Salad (page 223) and then later in the week for a Burrito Bowl (page 309) and Curried Chicken & Vegetable Soup (page 202). Finding common ingredients like this simplifies shopping. Often the ingredient can be cleaned and prepped all at once so that it is ready to use as needed throughout the week.

- **Make enough of a recipe that you can use it more than once.** For instance, you can have yogurt with nuts and berries one morning, then use the yogurt to make a smoothie the next day, and then use it again to make Greek Pizza (page 290) one evening.

Here are some examples of ingredients or recipes in this book that can be stretched:

Hazelnut Coffee Creamer → Strawberries & Cream N'Oatmeal → Chocolate Hazelnut Cookies
page 114   page 180   page 346

Coconut Yogurt → smoothies → Greek Pizza
page 182   page 290

Pancake & Muffin Mix → Best-Ever Pancakes → pigs in a blanket
page 133   page 158

Pancake & Muffin Mix → Best-Ever Pancakes → pancake sandwiches
page 133   page 158

Magenta Ginger Juice → Ranch Slaw → Rainbow Beet Salad *(all three contain beets)*
page 146   page 218   page 224

Coconut Porridge Mix → Strawberries & Cream N'Oatmeal → Pumpkin N'Oatmeal
page 112   page 180   page 181

cooked pumpkin → Pumpkin Bread → Pumpkin Cinnamon Rolls
page 49   page 274   page 168

Sandwich Bread → sunbutter & jelly sandwiches → grilled turkey sandwiches
page 270

Crispy Potato Boats → Creamy Potato, Sausage → Egg Boats → Hot Dog Boats
page 127   & Kale Soup   page 189   page 304
                     page 205

Brassicas Salad → Burrito Bowl (both contain cabbage and bok choy)
page 223   page 309

Pizza Sauce → One-Pot Pizza Pasta → Tomato Pizza
page 130   page 248   page 286

Slow Cooker Barbecue Chicken → Barbecue Chicken Salad → Barbecue Chicken Pizza
page 298   page 310   page 292

Faux Rotisserie Chicken → Chicken Broth → Curried Chicken & Vegetable Soup, Matzo Ball
page 296   page 131   Soup, Creamy Potato, Sausage & Kale Soup,
                                           Cream of Mushroom Soup, Broccoli Cheese
                                           Soup, or Hot & Sour Soup
                                           page 202, 204, 205, 208, 210, or 214

Individual Pot Pies → Pizza Quiche 2.0 → Portuguese-Inspired (all three use "cheese" base)
page 316   page 192   Skillet Eggs
                                         page 194

taco ground beef → Burrito Bowl → Taco Boats
page 306   page 309   page 306

delegate

I have to work hard at taking my own advice here: DELEGATE. I'm faster (and dare I say better) at cooking and cleaning than my husband and kids are. (Let's keep that just between us, okay?) But it's a vicious cycle: The more I do, the less my family does. And the less my family does, the slower they are when I give them a task, because they're out of practice. They're slow, so I take over again, and . . . as you can see, vicious cycle. So I'm working on breaking this habit of doing everything myself. I assign them a task, and then I have to walk away. Like, far away. Because otherwise I'll just take over whatever it is I've asked them to do.

Also, I kid you not, now that my husband and kids have my baking mixes to use, they sometimes cook without me asking them to!

feeding kids

Let's face it: If you have kids, you know that making them happy at mealtime while feeding them healthy food is one of the greatest challenges of meal preparation. If you can do those two things, your life becomes so much less frustrating. All it takes is a little strategy, a little planning, and making a list of your kids' favorite foods.

- Having trouble feeding your kids? The best solution is to get them involved. Have them make one list of their favorite whole foods (such as pears, yellow bell peppers, olives, and pepperoni) and another list of recipes they like or want to try. (A downloadable PDF of a blank list to fill in can be found on my blog, *The Spunky Coconut*, under Tools.) Give them cookbooks or websites to go through to help them decide. Keep the lists on the fridge as a reminder. Then take them shopping with you for the ingredients and have them help you in the kitchen when it's time to cook. Another way to get kids invested in their meals is to come up with gardening projects for them. Even if your space is limited, you can still do a lot with pots (container gardening) or even grow plants right on the windowsill in your kitchen (see the sidebar on the following page).

- Don't be disappointed if your kids want smoothies instead of what you're eating. It's amazing how much nutrition you can pack into a smoothie: protein, good fat, vitamins, and minerals. When my kids don't want to eat what I've made, I joke, "More for me!" Then I count my blessings and remind myself that there are much worse problems to have. As they say, "I choose to be happy because it is good for my health."

- Keep the kitchen stocked with foods that your kids will eat. For me this means having fresh and frozen fruit, carrots, celery, bell peppers, dip, chips cooked in coconut or avocado oil, and all sorts of olives on hand at all times. (See page 63 for a complete list of my kids' favorites.) It also means making sure that there is always some sort of potatoes ready to eat. Which leads me to my next point . . .

- Whenever you're making something your family likes, double the recipe. I've found that my kids are just as thrilled with my Perfect Crispy Potatoes (page 184) when I make them with white potatoes or sweet potatoes, despite the fact that they're less crispy when made with sweet potatoes. So I use two 12-inch skillets at a time and double the recipe, no matter what color the potatoes are. The leftovers rarely even get reheated; the kids eat them straight from the fridge.

- Try making the Kids' Favorite recipes in this book, marked with the heart icon. These are recipes that not only *my* kids like, but also their friends. You may find that your own kids love these dishes just as much as mine do. You can find a complete list of these recipes on pages 388 and 389.

how to grow celery on your windowsill

Looking for another way to get kids involved in the kitchen? Try this fun project: growing celery!

To do: *Cut an entire bunch of celery about 2 inches above the root end. Place the cut bunch, root end down, in about ½ inch of water and place it on the windowsill. Change the water every other day. In about two weeks, you will have short celery stalks, about 1 to 2 inches in length, at which time you can plant the celery in a pot or straight into the garden to finish growing. The small stalks can be eaten at this stage, but they tend to be more bitter than full-grown stalks and are better for use in cooking, such as soups, than eating raw.*

Fun fact: *You can eat celery leaves, too!*

kids' favorites

Making a list of your kids' favorite foods is one of the best tactics I know of for making meal preparation easy and free of angst. My kids' favorite recipes are indicated throughout Part 3 (look for the Kids' Favorite icon at the tops of the recipes). However, sometimes my kids' meals consist of a smoothie and/or simply whole foods (both raw and cooked).

My kids also love the ice creams in my book *Dairy-Free Ice Cream*. Made with coconut and almond, cashew, or hemp milk, these ice creams are so healthy that my kids eat them as a meal. Most flavors are sweetened with less than two dates per serving, and there are directions in the book for reducing the dates further if you choose.

Another one of my kids' favorite snacks is creamy almond butter or sunflower seed butter mixed with water, cocoa or carob powder, a pinch of salt, and a tiny bit of honey (similar to the donut frosting on page 162). This rich puddinglike butter is a great way to get more good fat, protein, antioxidants, and vitamins into them.

For vegetables that must be cooked, such as potatoes and squash, my kids prefer them roasted, which caramelizes the natural sugars, or fried (as in my Perfect Crispy Potatoes, page 184). Other vegetables, such as carrots, celery, bell peppers, and jicama, they prefer raw, and they often use them like crackers for dips (pages 236 to 238). All three of my kids like beets in smoothies, like Detox Piña Colada (page 144), and juice, like Magenta Ginger Juice (page 146), but only Ashley loves my Rainbow Beet Salad (page 224) as much as I do. They eat peas frozen, right out of the package, or hot with ghee and salt, and they eat parsnips, cabbage, and cauliflower when they're cooked in their favorite recipes.

Following is a sampling of my kids' favorite foods. I buy as many of these foods frozen and in bulk as possible. I use the frozen fruit for smoothies, and I let some thaw in the fridge in a glass container with a lid to be eaten alone or as a topping on my Coconut Porridge (page 178) or Coconut Yogurt (page 182).

I keep this list on the fridge as a reminder. It makes the kids feel good that they can show me all the foods that they like, and it helps me so much with my shopping! Because your kids' favorites may be very different from my kids' favorites, I've made a blank form available for you to fill in and tack to your own fridge. To download this form, go to the Tools section on my blog, *The Spunky Coconut*.

My kids' favorites *

whole foods

apples
apricots
avocados
bananas
blackberries
blueberries
cherries
figs
fresh young coconut
grapefruit
grapes
kiwis
kumquats
mangoes
nectarines
oranges
pears
persimmons
pineapple
raspberries
strawberries
watermelon

beets
bell peppers
broccoli
butternut squash
cabbage
carrots
cauliflower
celery
jicama
mushrooms
parsnips
peas
pumpkin
sweet potatoes
white potatoes

no-cook foods

chips cooked in avocado or coconut oil,
such as Jackson's Honest Potato Chips
dairy-free dark chocolate (80% cacao)
deli meats & hot dogs
dried apricots
fruit spread, without added sugar (for bread)
hard-boiled eggs (made ahead)
naturally fermented sauerkraut, homemade**
or store-bought, such as Bubbies
nuts
olives
pickles
raisins
sardines
smoothies (pages 142 and 144)

top 15 favorite recipes

best-ever pancakes (page 158)
bagels (page 160)
mini boulder cream donuts (page 162)
chocolate chip scones (page 176)
perfect crispy potatoes (page 184)
cheeseburger soup (page 200)
spinach & artichoke dip (page 237)
orange chicken with broccoli (page 254)
meaty tomato lasagna (page 260)
fettuccine alfredo (page 264)
cinnamon raisin bread (page 272)
banana bread (page 276)
faux rotisserie chicken with potatoes (page 296)
chicken nuggets (page 302)
fish-n-chips (page 312)

*To find kid-friendly recipes, look for the Kids' Favorite icon at the tops of the recipes in Part 3 or, for quick reference, see the list on pages 388 and 389.

**I have a recipe for homemade sauerkraut on my blog, The Spunky Coconut.

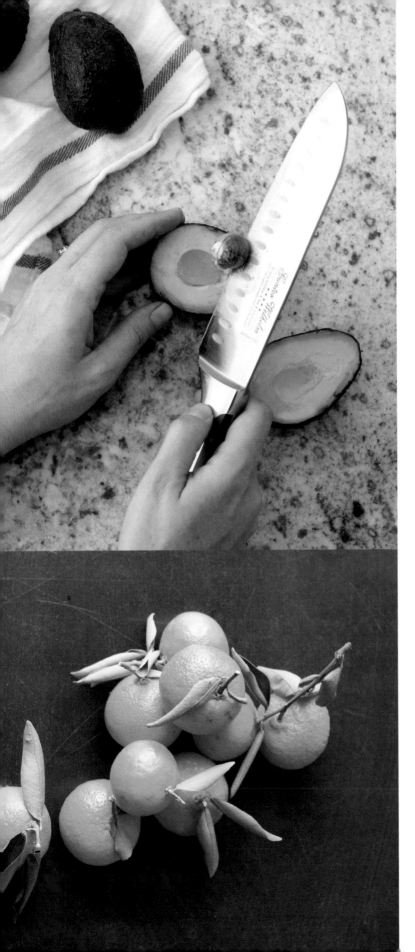

chapter 5

Meal Plans & Menus

When you look at the sample meal plans in this chapter, you will see that the recipes for each week share common ingredients. There is a method to my madness. I created these meal plans around the seasons and also by common ingredients. For instance, when I make a new batch of Scone & Pie Crust Mix over the weekend, it makes sense to make both scones and either pot pies or pizza quiche that week. I also like to buy one food item and use it repeatedly. I'll buy bok choy to use for Brassicas Salad and then later in the week for a Burrito Bowl and Curried Chicken & Vegetable Soup. Finding common ingredients in this way simplifies shopping and meal preparation.

I have also included some menus for the holidays, with make-ahead instructions to help you plan. Finally, there are menu ideas for Friday night dinners. These themed menus are fun when you are having company any time of the year, or even just to celebrate an ordinary Friday night with your family.

tips for using the meal plans

Here are some helpful tips for using the meal plans as well as customizing them for your own family. I hope that you will find them as useful as I do!

- I use as many seasonal foods as possible in my cooking. My favorite foods for each season are listed on the opening page.

- These sample meal plans are based on how my family eats. You will notice that we eat pizza on most Friday nights and pancakes on most Saturday mornings (because it's the law). I left one day off the meal plans to allow for eating out, although I realize it's unlikely that you'll eat out for all three meals on the same day. Feel free to customize the meal plans for however your family eats.

- The meal plans were designed calendar-style at the request of my readers. I have also included corresponding shopping lists to make it even easier for you to pick up the items you need to make these recipes. To download both the weekly meal plans and the shopping lists, go to the Tools section on my blog, *The Spunky Coconut.*

- The recipes in the meal plans and the leftovers they generate are intended to feed an average family of four or five, with two adults and two or three children. Keep in mind that my children are young girls; if you have two teenage boys, you may need more.

- To make cooking and shopping easier, I like to take one ingredient and use it in two meals during the week. For instance, when I make Slow Cooker Barbecue Chicken (page 298), we have it on salad one day and on pizza another day. For more on this strategy, see "Stretch It" on pages 57 and 58.

- To customize a meal plan, first determine how many meals you want to make during the week. You may choose to make more or fewer meals than I have suggested. Then select recipes based on which ingredients are in season. Choose recipes that share common ingredients to simplify shopping. Consider how you might want to stretch your ingredients and recipes throughout the week (refer to the "Stretch It" list on pages 57 and 58). Finally, remember to adjust your shopping list depending on which recipes you need to double, either for the week or to freeze half for later. Remember to label and date leftovers that you store in the freezer.

- To help you customize the meal plans or to allow you to fill out a whole year's worth of meal plans, I've made a blank weekly calendar form available for your use. To download this form, go to the Tools section on my blog, *The Spunky Coconut.*

- If you're looking for more sweet or savory recipes to round out your weekly meal plans, see page 400 for a list of my other cookbooks.

weekly meal plans

Notes on the meal plans and shopping lists:

- I have color-coded the meal plans so that it is easy to see which recipes are enjoyed as leftovers the following day. If a particular recipe is used twice in the same week but doesn't reheat well, the meal plan will direct you to make a new batch on the second day.

- Unless otherwise indicated with "X2," "X4," and so on, each recipe listed is to be made in a single batch.

- Recipes that can be made ahead are marked with a single asterisk (*).

- Other make-ahead tips can be found below each meal plan.

- The shopping lists include salad fixings only for the salads listed in the meal plans. If you wish to have a tossed green salad with dinner, which we usually do, you will need to add extra salad fixings to the shopping list for the week.

- Snacks and desserts are not included in the meal plans, either, so remember to add the ingredients for those to your shopping list if you'd like to include them.

- Salt and black pepper are not included in the shopping lists; I assume you'll always have those on hand.

Spring Favorites

PARSNIPS

RHUBARB

KUMQUATS

ASPARAGUS

MANGO

spring: week 1

	Monday	Tuesday	Wednesday	Thursday	Friday	Saturday
breakfast	Scones (any type)* X2 p. 176		Strawberry Rhubarb Gummies* p. 170		"Coffee" Smoothie X4 p. 142	Best-Ever Pancakes p. 158
lunch	Antipasto Plate p. 311	Cream of Mushroom Soup X2 p. 208		leftover Pizza Quiche 2.0	Antipasto Plate p. 311	Portuguese-Inspired Skillet Eggs p. 194
dinner	Individual Pot Pies X2** p. 316		Pizza Quiche 2.0 p. 192	Southwest Pasta p. 256	Chicken Nuggets X2 p. 302 and Rainbow Beet Salad X2 p. 224	

* *Make ahead.*

** *When doubled, the pot pie recipe makes 12 single-serving pies. The leftover pies can be frozen and enjoyed later.*

X2 = *Make a double batch.*

X4 = *Make 2 double batches.*

Note: *The recipes in this meal plan use a total of 5 batches of "cheese" base. For efficiency, make 2 double batches and 1 single batch in one go and store them in the fridge for use throughout the week. (Note that the quiche and skillet eggs recipes require 1 batch of "Cheese" Base with Cashews; the nut-free version can be used in the pot pies and soup, if desired.)*

shopping list

Produce:

assortment of veggies for Antipasto Plate (see p. 311 for ideas), 4 pounds

basil or cilantro, fresh, 1 small bunch

carrots, 8 large (two of them fat, ideally 2 inches wide)

celery, 2 bunches

golden beets, 2 large or 4 small

green onions, 2

mushrooms, sliced, 32 ounces

red beets, 2 large or 4 small

red bell peppers, 2

red onion, 1 small

rhubarb, fresh or frozen, 10 ounces

tomatoes, 2 large

vegetable and/or meat pizza toppings, 1½ cups prepped

white-fleshed sweet potatoes, 1¼ pounds (about 3 large)

yellow onions, 4

apples, 2

blood oranges, 2

lemons, 2

Meat & Broth:

assortment of nitrate-free deli meat for Antipasto Plate (see p. 311 for ideas), 2 pounds

chicken breast, boneless and skinless, 7 pounds

ground beef, 1 pound

chicken broth (p. 131), 15½ cups

Eggs & Milk:

eggs, 2 dozen large

almond milk, unsweetened, 3 cups

coconut milk, full-fat, 3½ (13½-ounce) cans, plus 4 cans if making Nut-Free "Cheese" Base for Individual Pot Pies and Cream of Mushroom Soup

Nuts & Seeds:

cashews, raw, 1½ cups, plus 6 cups if making "Cheese" Base with Cashews for Individual Pot Pies and Cream of Mushroom Soup

golden flax seeds, ¼ cup

walnut pieces, raw or roasted, ½ to ¾ cup (optional)

Fats & Oils:

avocado oil, ¼ cup

ghee or avocado oil, ½ cup plus 2 tablespoons

ghee or bacon fat, 1 tablespoon

ghee or coconut oil, 1 cup (8 ounces)

ghee or palm shortening or coconut oil, 1 cup (8 ounces)

Frozen Foods:

strawberries, frozen, 10 ounces

Sweeteners:

honey, about ¾ cup

liquid vanilla stevia, 10 drops

maple syrup (for serving with pancakes)

Medjool dates, 4

Flours & Baking Mixes:

almond flour, 4 cups

arrowroot or tapioca flour, 1 tablespoon, plus ½ cup if making Nut-Free "Cheese" Base for Individual Pot Pies and Cream of Mushroom Soup

Pancake & Muffin Mix (p. 133), 1⅔ cups

Note: *If you do not have premade mix on hand, you will need 3¼ cups (410 g) coconut flour, 3¼ cups (406 g) arrowroot or tapioca flour, 2¾ cups (306 g) almond or cashew flour, and 2 tablespoons (36 g) baking soda.*

Scone & Pie Crust Mix (p. 133), 9½ cups

Note: *If you do not have premade mix on hand, you will need 3¼ cups (410 g) coconut flour, 3¼ cups (406 g) arrowroot or tapioca flour, 2¾ cups (306 g) almond or cashew flour, 1¼ cups (145 g) ground golden flax seeds, 2 tablespoons (36 g) baking soda, and ½ teaspoon (6 g) fine sea salt.*

Spices:

chili powder, 2 teaspoons

chipotle powder, ¼ teaspoon

ground cumin, 1½ teaspoons

garlic powder, ¼ teaspoon

Italian seasoning, 1 teaspoon

onion powder, ¼ teaspoon

smoked paprika, ½ teaspoon

Everyday Seasoning (p. 117), about 1½ tablespoons

> Note: *If you do not have premade seasoning on hand, you will need 2 tablespoons onion powder, 2 tablespoons garlic powder, 2 tablespoons fine sea salt, 1 tablespoon smoked paprika, and 1 teaspoon chili powder.*

Salt Blend (p. 117), 1½ tablespoons

> Note: *If you do not have premade seasoning on hand, you will need ¼ cup leek flakes or 2¾ teaspoons celery seeds, 2½ tablespoons fine sea salt, 1 tablespoon herbes de Provence, 1 teaspoon onion powder, and ½ teaspoon garlic powder. (Herbamare salt blend is a good store-bought alternative.)*

Condiments, Dressings & Sauces:

Apple Cider Vinaigrette (p. 121), ½ cup

> Note: *If you do not have premade dressing on hand, you will need ¾ cup extra-virgin olive oil, ¼ cup apple cider vinegar, 2 teaspoons honey, ½ teaspoon fine sea salt, and ⅛ teaspoon ground black pepper.*

Creamy Honey Dijon Dressing (p. 121), 1 cup

> Note: *If you do not have premade dressing on hand, you will need ½ cup raw cashews, ½ cup extra-virgin olive oil, 1 tablespoon apple cider vinegar, 1 teaspoon honey, 1 teaspoon gluten-free Dijon mustard, ½ teaspoon fine sea salt, and ⅛ teaspoon onion powder.*

Miscellaneous Items:

marinated artichoke hearts, 2 (6½-ounce) jars

For the scones: ½ cup dairy-free chocolate chips (70% cacao), or 1 heaping cup freeze-dried strawberries, or 1 cup sliced almonds and ¼ teaspoon almond extract

powdered collagen (also called collagen hydrolysate or collagen peptides), ½ cup

cooking sherry, ¼ cup

dandelion tea, 8 bags

gelatin, grass-fed, ⅓ cup

garlic-stuffed green olives, 16 ounces

Kalamata olives, pitted, 16 ounces

pickles, naturally fermented, 8

sun-dried tomatoes, about ½ cup

roasted red peppers, 16-ounce jar

spring: week 2

	Monday ^	Tuesday	Wednesday	Thursday	Friday	Saturday
breakfast	Strawberries & Cream N'Oatmeal X4 p. 180	Crepes p. 157	Strawberries & Cream N'Oatmeal< X4 p. 180	Cherry Muffins* p. 172		Yellow Pepper Baked Eggs X2 with bacon p. 191
lunch	BLT on Sandwich Bread* p. 270	Apple & Jicama Sandwiches X2 p. 300 and Ranch Slaw X2 p. 218	Apple & Jicama Sandwiches X2 p. 300 and leftover Ranch Slaw	deli turkey on Sandwich Bread p. 270	leftover Orange Chicken with Broccoli	Antipasto Plate p. 311
dinner	Veggie Burritos** X2 p. 232	One-Pot Pizza Pasta X2 p. 248		Orange Chicken with Broccoli X2 p. 254	Cracker Pizzas p. 284	Faux Rotisserie Chicken with Potatoes*** p. 296

* Make ahead. (Make 2 loaves of Sandwich Bread for the week.)

** On Monday morning, soak the sunflower seeds for the Veggie Burritos.

*** Put the chicken in the slow cooker on Saturday morning.

^Optional: On Monday morning, put 2 cans of coconut milk in the fridge to chill for making Whipped Coconut Cream for the crepes on Tuesday morning.

< Though the N'Oatmeal is eaten twice in the week, it doesn't reheat well, so it should be made in 2 quadruple batches.

X2 = Make a double batch.

X4 = Make a quadruple batch.

shopping list

Produce:

assortment of veggies for Antipasto Plate (see p. 311 for ideas), 2 pounds

basil, fresh, 16 large leaves

broccoli, 2 heads (about 3 pounds total)

butternut squash, 2 large

carrots, ½ pound (about 1 bunch)

cherry tomatoes, 8

collard greens, 4 large leaves

garlic, 4 cloves

ginger, fresh, 2-inch piece

golden beets, 2 large or 4 small

green onions, 4

jicama, 4 fist-sized or larger

lettuce, 1 small head

red cabbage, 2 heads

red onion, 1

romaine lettuce, 8 leaves

russet potatoes, 2½ pounds (about 6 large)

tomatoes, 2 large

watercress, 2 bunches

white-fleshed sweet potatoes, 2½ pounds (about 6 large)

yellow bell peppers, 2

apples, 4

berries of choice, 1 pint, for crepes (optional)

cherries, fresh or frozen, 1½ cups

oranges (for juicing), 7

lemon, 1 small

Meat & Broth:

assortment of nitrate-free deli meat for Antipasto Plate (see p. 311 for ideas), 1 pound

deli meat of choice, nitrate-free, for Jicama Sandwiches, 1 pound

deli turkey for sandwiches, 1 pound

bacon, 3 (8-ounce) packages

chicken breast, boneless and skinless, 2 pounds

chicken, whole, 3 to 4 pounds

Italian sausage, mild, 18 ounces

pepperoni, 5 ounces

chicken broth (p. 131), 3½ cups

Eggs & Milk:

eggs, 2 dozen large

almond milk, unsweetened, 6½ cups

> Note: *For nut-free Strawberries & Cream N'Oatmeal, replace 6 cups of the almond milk with 3½ [13½-ounce] cans of full-fat coconut milk.*

coconut milk, full-fat, 13½-ounce can, plus 2 cans (if making Whipped Coconut Cream for crepes), plus 1 can (if making Nut-Free "Cheese" Base for One-Pot Pizza Pasta), plus ½ cup (if making nut-free mashed potatoes)

Hazelnut Coffee Creamer (p. 114; optional), ¼ cup

> Note: *To make, you will need 8 ounces (1¾ cups) blanched hazelnuts and 2 soft pitted Medjool dates.*

Nuts & Seeds:

cashews, raw, 1½ cups (if making "Cheese" Base with Cashews for One-Pot Pizza Pasta) plus 1 cup (if making cashew milk for mashed potatoes)

sesame seeds, for garnish (optional)

sunflower seeds, raw, 1 cup

Fats & Oils:

avocado oil, ½ cup plus 2 tablespoons

coconut oil, ¼ cup, plus more for cooking

ghee, 1 tablespoon

ghee or avocado oil, ¼ cup plus 2 tablespoons

ghee or bacon fat, 2 tablespoons

ghee or palm shortening, ¼ cup

Sweeteners:

honey, up to ⅓ cup

liquid vanilla stevia, about ¼ teaspoon

maple syrup, ¼ cup

Flours & Baking Mixes:

arrowroot or tapioca flour, 2 teaspoons, plus 2 tablespoons if making Nut-Free "Cheese" Base for One-Pot Pizza Pasta

Coconut Porridge Mix (p. 112), 6 cups

Note: *If you do not have premade mix on hand, you will need ½ cup plus 2 tablespoons golden flax seeds, 10 cups unsweetened shredded coconut, 1 teaspoon ground cinnamon, and ½ teaspoon fine sea salt.*

Pancake & Muffin Mix (p. 133), 2 cups

Note: *If you do not have premade mix on hand, you will need 3¼ cups (410 g) coconut flour, 3¼ cups (406 g) arrowroot or tapioca flour, 2¾ cups (306 g) almond or cashew flour, and 2 tablespoons (36 g) baking soda.*

Pizza & Bread Mix (p. 133), 4½ cups

Note: *If you do not have premade mix on hand, you will need 3¼ cups (410 g) coconut flour, 3¼ cups (406 g) arrowroot or tapioca flour, just under 2 tablespoons (30 g) baking soda, 1 tablespoon plus 2 teaspoons (14 g) psyllium husk powder, and 1 tablespoon plus 1½ teaspoons (30 g) fine sea salt.*

Scone & Pie Crust Mix (p. 133), 1 scant cup

Note: *If you do not have premade mix on hand, you will need 3¼ cups (410 g) coconut flour, 3¼ cups (406 g) arrowroot or tapioca flour, 2¾ cups (306 g) almond or cashew flour, 1¼ cups (145 g) ground golden flax seeds, 2 tablespoons (36 g) baking soda, and ½ teaspoon (6 g) fine sea salt.*

Spices:

ground cinnamon (optional substitute for lemon juice in Apple Sandwiches)

garlic powder, ¼ teaspoon

Italian seasoning, 1 teaspoon

red pepper flakes (for garnish; optional)

Everyday Seasoning (p. 117), 1 tablespoon, plus more if using to season Easy Chicken

Note: *If you do not have premade seasoning on hand, you will need 2 tablespoons onion powder, 2 tablespoons garlic powder, 2 tablespoons fine sea salt, 1 tablespoon smoked paprika, and 1 teaspoon chili powder.*

Salt Blend (p. 117), 1 tablespoon plus 1¼ teaspoons, plus more if using to season Easy Chicken

Note: *If you do not have premade seasoning on hand, you will need ¼ cup leek flakes or 2¾ teaspoons celery seeds, 2½ tablespoons fine sea salt, 1 tablespoon herbes de Provence, 1 teaspoon onion powder, and ½ teaspoon garlic powder. (Herbamare salt blend is a good store-bought alternative.)*

Condiments, Dressings & Sauces:

mustard, gluten-free, or Paleo-friendly mayonnaise (optional; for sandwiches)

Ranch Dressing (p. 120), 1 to 2 cups

Note: *To make 1 batch (about 1½ cups), you will need ½ cup raw cashews, ½ cup extra-virgin olive oil, ½ lemon, 1 tablespoon apple cider vinegar, ½ teaspoon dried dill weed, ½ teaspoon onion powder, and 1 small clove garlic.*

Pizza Sauce (p. 130), 2½ cups

Note: *To make a double batch, you will need two 7-ounce jars tomato paste, 14 ounces strained tomatoes (from one 24-ounce jar), 2 teaspoons apple cider vinegar, 1 tablespoon plus 1 teaspoon Italian seasoning, 1 teaspoon onion powder, and ½ teaspoon garlic powder.*

Miscellaneous Items:

apple cider vinegar, ¼ cup plus 1 tablespoon

coconut aminos (for dipping burritos)

active dry yeast, about 1½ tablespoons

freeze-dried strawberries, ½ cup

garlic-stuffed green olives, 8 ounces

gelatin, grass-fed, 1 teaspoon (optional; for Whipped Coconut Cream)

Kalamata olives, pitted, 8 ounces

marinated artichoke hearts, 6½-ounce jar

pickles, naturally fermented, 4

powdered collagen (also called collagen hydrolysate or collagen peptides), about 1½ tablespoons

roasted red peppers, 8 ounces

strained tomatoes, 2 cups

sunflower seed butter, without added sugar, ½ cup

vanilla extract, 1 teaspoon (optional; for Whipped Coconut Cream)

white rice, 2 cups cooked, for Veggie Burritos, or 1 small head cauliflower (enough to make 2 cups cooked cauli-rice)

Summer Favorites

TOMATOES

ZUCCHINI

PLUMS

PEACHES

SWISS CHARD

summer: week 1

	Monday	Tuesday	Wednesday^	Thursday	Friday	Saturday
breakfast	Banana Bread* p. 276		Blueberry Muffins p. 174		Detox Piña Colada X4 p. 144	Best-Ever Pancakes p. 158
lunch	Curry Chicken Salad Wraps* X2 p. 307		Barbecue Chicken Salad p. 310	Egg Boats X2 p. 189	leftover Creamy Roasted Tomato Soup and Focaccia	Hot Dog Boats p. 304
dinner	Zucchini Lime Cilantro Pie p. 196	Barbecue Chicken Salad p. 310	Fettuccine Alfredo p. 264	Creamy Roasted Tomato Soup X2 p. 206 and Focaccia X2 p. 278	Barbecue Chicken Pizza p. 292	Mediterranean Zucchini Salad p. 226

* Make ahead.

<On Tuesday morning, put the ingredients for Slow Cooker Barbecue Chicken (p. 298) in the slow cooker for Barbecue Chicken Salad and Barbecue Chicken Pizza.

^On Wednesday, make 1 batch of Slow Cooker Baked Potatoes (p. 126) for Egg Boats and Hot Dog Boats.

X2 = Make a double batch.

X4 = Make two double batches.

Note: The recipes in this meal plan use a total of 2½ or 3 batches of "cheese" base. For efficiency, make the batches in one go and store them in the fridge for use throughout the week.

shopping list

Produce:

basil, fresh, 1 small bunch

broccoli, 1 head (about 1½ pounds)

celery, 8 stalks

cherry tomatoes, 1 pint

cilantro, fresh, 1 bunch

garlic, 2 cloves

ginger, fresh, 2-inch piece, or 2 teaspoons ginger powder

golden beets, 4

green onion, 1

lettuce, 2 heads

lettuce or collard leaves, 8 to 10 (for chicken salad wraps)

mint, fresh, 1 handful (optional)

parsley, fresh, 1 bunch

red onion, 1

russet potatoes or sweet potatoes, 6 large

tomatoes, 6 pounds

turmeric, fresh, 2-inch piece, or 2 teaspoons turmeric powder

white-fleshed sweet potatoes, 1¼ pounds, or 2 (9-ounce) packages Cappello's fettuccine

yellow onions, 2

yellow zucchini, 8

zucchini, 2

bananas, 4

blueberries, fresh or frozen, 2 cups

lemon, 1 small

lime, 1

pineapple, 4 cups chunked fresh, or 1 pineapple (about 2½ pounds)

Meat & Broth:

chicken breast, boneless and skinless, 6 pounds

hot dogs, nitrate-free, 8

sardines, 2 (3.75-ounce) cans

chicken broth (p. 131), 4 to 6 cups (quantity depends on type of noodle used for Fettuccine Alfredo)

Eggs & Milk:

eggs, 2½ dozen large

almond milk, unsweetened, 1 cup

coconut milk, full-fat, 2 (13½-ounce) cans, plus 2½ or 3 cans if making Nut-Free "Cheese" Base (quantity depends on type of noodle used for Fettuccine Alfredo)

Nuts & Seeds:

almonds, sliced, 1 cup

cashews, raw, 3¾ or 4½ cups, if making "Cheese" Base with Cashews (quantity depends on type of noodle used for Fettuccine Alfredo)

walnuts, raw, ½ cup (optional; for Banana Bread)

Fats & Oils:

avocado oil, ½ cup, plus more for cooking

coconut oil, ½ cup

coconut oil or ghee, ½ cup

extra-virgin olive oil (for serving with focaccia)

ghee or avocado oil, ¾ cup

ghee or coconut oil, 2 tablespoons, plus more for cooking

Sweeteners:

coconut sugar, ½ cup

honey, about ⅓ cup

liquid vanilla stevia, about 1 teaspoon

maple syrup (for serving with pancakes)

Flours & Baking Mixes:

almond flour, 2¾ cups

arrowroot or tapioca flour, 1¼ cups, plus 3 or 4 tablespoons if making Nut-Free "Cheese" Base (quantity depends on type of noodle used for Fettuccine Alfredo)

coconut flour, 1 cup

Pancake & Muffin Mix (p. 133), 1⅔ cups

Note: *If you do not have premade mix on hand, you will need 3¼ cups (410 g) coconut flour, 3¼ cups (406 g) arrowroot or tapioca flour, 2¾ cups (306 g) almond or cashew flour, and 2 tablespoons (36 g) baking soda.*

Pizza & Bread Mix (p. 133),
2½ cups

> Note: *If you do not have premade mix on hand, you will need 3¼ cups (410 g) coconut flour, 3¼ cups (406 g) arrowroot or tapioca flour, just under 2 tablespoons (30 g) baking soda, 1 tablespoon plus 2 teaspoons (14 g) psyllium husk powder, and 1 tablespoon plus 1½ teaspoons (30 g) fine sea salt.*

Spices:

ground cinnamon, 2 teaspoons

ground cumin, ½ teaspoon

curry powder, 2 teaspoons

garlic powder, ½ teaspoon

Italian seasoning, 2 teaspoons

Salt Blend (p. 117), up to
2½ teaspoons

> Note: *If you do not have premade seasoning on hand, you will need ¼ cup leek flakes or 2¾ teaspoons celery seeds, 2½ tablespoons fine sea salt, 1 tablespoon herbes de Provence, 1 teaspoon onion powder, and ½ teaspoon garlic powder. (Herbamare salt blend is a good store-bought alternative.)*

Condiments, Dressings &
Sauces:

Barbecue Sauce (p. 129),
2½ cups

> Note: *To make, you will need 2 (7-ounce) jars tomato paste, ½ cup honey, ⅓ cup apple cider vinegar, 1 ounce dairy-free dark chocolate (70% cacao or higher), 1 to 3 teaspoons chili powder, 1 teaspoon tamarind paste (optional), 1 teaspoon Red Boat fish sauce, ¾ teaspoon fine sea salt, ½ teaspoon garlic powder, and ¼ teaspoon ground celery seed.*

Caesar Dressing (p. 125) or
Creamy Italian Dressing (p.
124), about 1 cup

> Note: *If making Caesar Dressing, you will need ½ cup raw cashews, ½ cup extra-virgin olive oil, 1 tablespoon fresh-squeezed lemon juice or apple cider vinegar, 1 teaspoon honey, ⅛ teaspoon onion powder, and 1 small clove garlic.*
>
> *If making Creamy Italian Dressing, you will need ½ cup raw cashews, ½ cup extra-virgin olive oil, ¼ cup apple cider vinegar, ½ teaspoon Italian seasoning, and ¼ teaspoon garlic powder.*

hot sauce of choice

mayonnaise, Paleo-friendly,
1 cup

Ranch Dressing (p. 120), about
1 cup

> Note: *To make, you will need ½ cup raw cashews, ½ cup extra-virgin olive oil, ½ lemon, 1 tablespoon apple cider vinegar, ½ teaspoon dried dill weed, ½ teaspoon onion powder, and 1 small clove garlic.*

Miscellaneous Items:

active dry yeast, 2 teaspoons

apple cider vinegar, 1 tablespoon

applesauce, unsweetened, ¼ cup

baking soda, 1½ teaspoons

Cappello's fettuccine, 2
(9-ounce) packages, or 1¼
pounds white-fleshed sweet
potatoes

chocolate, dark (80% cacao),
3 ounces (optional; for Banana
Bread)

Kalamata olives, pitted, ½ cup

pickle relish, naturally
fermented, ¼ cup

powdered collagen (also
called collagen hydrolysate or
collagen peptides), ¼ cup

raisins, 1 cup

sauerkraut, naturally
fermented, ½ cup

sun-dried tomatoes, 4 (optional)

tomato paste, ½ cup

summer: week 2

	Monday	Tuesday	Wednesday	Thursday	Friday	Saturday
breakfast	Cinnamon Raisin Bread* with eggs p. 272		Eggs Baked in Tomatoes X2 p. 190	Coconut Yogurt*@ X2 with nuts and berries p. 182		Best-Ever Pancakes p. 158
lunch	mixed green salad tossed with dressing of choice, with deli meat and chips	Funa Salad Wraps** p. 228		Antipasto Plate p. 311	Apple &Jicama Sandwiches X2 with your favorite no-cook foods (chips, olives, pickles, nuts, etc.) p. 300	mixed green salad tossed with dressing of choice, with leftover Easy Chicken@ and chips
dinner	burgers or brats and Faux Grilled Vegetables p. 222	Matzo Ball Soup p. 204	Baja Drumsticks X2 p. 314 and Slow Cooker Baked Potatoes*** X1½ p. 126		Greek Pizza@ p. 290	Fish-n-Chips p. 312

* *Make ahead.*

** *On Monday night, soak the sunflower seeds for the Funa Salad.*

*** *Put the potatoes in the slow cooker on Wednesday morning.*

@ *Use yogurt for breakfast and Greek Pizza. Use Easy Chicken for Greek Pizza and to top salad for Saturday lunch.*

X1½ = *Make one and a half batches.*

X2 = *Make a double batch.*

shopping list

Produce:

assortment of veggies for Antipasto Plate (see p. 311 for ideas), 2 pounds

assortment of veggies for Faux Grilled Vegetables (see p. 222 for ideas), 3 pounds

arugula or spinach, 1 handful (optional)

basil, fresh, 1 handful

celery, 3 stalks

cherry tomatoes, 1 cup

collard greens, 8 large leaves

garlic, 1 clove

green bell pepper, 1 small

jicama, 2 fist-sized or larger

parsley, fresh, 1 small bunch

red onion, 1 large or 2 medium

romaine lettuce, 4 leaves

russet or sweet potatoes, 9 large

salad fixings for lunch salads on 2 days: 2 heads lettuce plus additional fixings of choice, such as cucumber, cherry tomatoes, and mushrooms

tomatoes, 4 large

apples, 2

berries of choice, 2 cups

lemons, 2

Meat & Broth:

assortment of nitrate-free deli meat for salads and sandwiches, 2½ pounds

chicken breast, boneless and skinless, 2 pounds

chicken drumsticks, 16

ground beef (for burgers) or brats, about 1½ pounds

chicken broth (p. 131), 11 cups

Eggs & Milk:

eggs, 2 dozen large

almond milk, unsweetened, 1 cup

coconut milk, full-fat, 6 (13½-ounce) cans

Nuts & Seeds:

nuts of choice, raw, about 1 cup (for topping yogurt)

sunflower seeds, raw, 1½ cups

Fats & Oils:

avocado oil, 1¼ cups, plus more for cooking

2 tablespoons ghee

ghee or avocado oil, ¼ cup

ghee or coconut oil, ¼ cup, plus more for cooking

Sweeteners:

coconut sugar, 1 tablespoon

honey, about ½ cup

liquid vanilla stevia, ¼ teaspoon

maple syrup, 2 tablespoons, plus more for serving with pancakes

Flours & Baking Mixes:

almond flour, ¼ cup

arrowroot or tapioca flour, ½ cup

coconut flour, ¼ cup

Pancake & Muffin Mix (p. 133), 1⅔ cups

> Note: *If you do not have premade mix on hand, you will need 3¼ cups (410 g) coconut flour, 3¼ cups (406 g) arrowroot or tapioca flour, 2¾ cups (306 g) almond or cashew flour, and 2 tablespoons (36 g) baking soda.*

Pizza & Bread Mix (p. 133), 3¾ cups

> Note: *If you do not have premade mix on hand, you will need 3¼ cups (410 g) coconut flour, 3¼ cups (406 g) arrowroot or tapioca flour, just under 2 tablespoons (30 g) baking soda, 1 tablespoon plus 2 teaspoons (14 g) psyllium husk powder, and 1 tablespoon plus 1½ teaspoons (30 g) fine sea salt.*

Scone & Pie Crust Mix (p. 133), ½ cup

> Note: *If you do not have premade mix on hand, you will need 3¼ cups (410 g) coconut flour, 3¼ cups (406 g) arrowroot or tapioca flour, 2¾ cups (306 g) almond or cashew flour, 1¼ cups (145 g) ground golden flax seeds, 2 tablespoons (36 g) baking soda, and ½ teaspoon (6 g) fine sea salt.*

Spices:

ground cinnamon, 1 tablespoon

dill weed, dried, about 1 tablespoon

garlic powder, ¼ teaspoon

herbes de Provence, ½ teaspoon

Easy Taco Seasoning (p. 116), 2 teaspoons

Note: *If you do not have premade seasoning on hand, you will need 2 tablespoons chili powder, 2 tablespoons ground cumin, 2 teaspoons onion powder, 2 teaspoons garlic powder, 2 teaspoons fine sea salt, and ½ teaspoon ground chipotle powder.*

Everyday Seasoning (p. 117), about 2 teaspoons, plus more if using to season Easy Chicken

Note: *If you do not have premade seasoning on hand, you will need 2 tablespoons onion powder, 2 tablespoons garlic powder, 2 tablespoons fine sea salt, 1 tablespoon smoked paprika, and 1 teaspoon chili powder.*

Salt Blend (p. 117), to season Easy Chicken (or use Everyday Seasoning)

Note: *If you do not have premade seasoning on hand, you will need ¼ cup leek flakes or 2¾ teaspoons celery seeds, 2½ tablespoons fine sea salt, 1 tablespoon herbes de Provence, 1 teaspoon onion powder, and ½ teaspoon garlic powder. (Herbamare salt blend is a good store-bought alternative.)*

Condiments, Dressings & Sauces:

Dijon mustard, gluten-free, 1 teaspoon, plus more if desired for sandwiches

mayonnaise, Paleo-friendly, ⅓ cup, plus more if desired for sandwiches

salad dressing of choice, enough for lunch salads on 2 days and to accompany Faux Grilled Vegetables (see pp. 120 to 125 for ingredients)

Miscellaneous Items:

active dry yeast, about 1½ tablespoons

almond or lemon extract (optional; for yogurt)

apple cider vinegar, 3 tablespoons

chips cooked in coconut or avocado oil, 4 (5-ounce) bags

garlic-stuffed green olives, 8 ounces

gelatin, grass-fed, about 3 tablespoons, or 1 tablespoon agar powder

Kalamata olives, pitted, 10 ounces

marinated artichokes, 6½-ounce jar

pickle relish, naturally fermented, ⅓ cup

pickles, naturally fermented, 4

powdered collagen (also called collagen hydrolysate or collagen peptides), 2 teaspoons

probiotic capsules, dairy-free, equal to about 70 billion active cultures

raisins, ¾ cup

roasted red peppers, 8 ounces

salmon, canned wild Alaskan, 12 ounces

seaweed, dried, ½ teaspoon ground (optional)

sunflower seed butter, without added sugar, ¼ cup

vanilla beans, 2

Fall Favorites

APPLES

PERSIMMONS

CRANBERRIES

PUMPKINS

BUTTERNUT SQUASH

fall: week 1

	Monday	Tuesday	Wednesday	Thursday	Friday	Saturday
breakfast	Mini Boulder Cream Donuts* X2 p. 162		Portobello & Ham Baked Eggs X2 p. 188	Crepes p. 157	Coconut Porridge X4 p. 178	Best-Ever Pancakes p. 158
lunch	Brassicas Salad@ X2 p. 223 and Poached Eggs with bacon p. 188	leftover Brassicas Salad and Poached Eggs with bacon p. 188	mixed green salad tossed with dressing of choice@, with deli meat and chips	leftover Curried Chicken & Vegetable Soup and Nacho Cheese Cauliflower Poppers	Taco Boats p. 306	Hot Dog Boats p. 304
dinner	Fettuccine Alfredo p. 264	Sausage & Egg Pizza p. 288	Curried Chicken & Vegetable Soup X2 and p. 202 Nacho Cheese Cauliflower Poppers X2 p. 234	Burrito Bowl** p. 309	Taco Rice Skillet X2 p. 315	

* Make ahead.

< Optional: On Wednesday morning, put 2 cans of coconut milk in the fridge to chill for making Whipped Coconut Cream for the crepes on Thursday morning.

@ Use Ranch Dressing for Brassicas Salad and salad with deli meat.

^ On Thursday, make 1 batch of Slow Cooker Baked Potatoes (p. 126) for Taco Boats and Hot Dog Boats.

** When making the Burrito Bowl, make a double batch of taco ground beef and reserve half for Taco Boats.

X2 = Make a double batch.

X4 = Make a quadruple batch.

shopping list

Produce:

avocados, 9

bell peppers, any color, 4

bok choy, 4 to 5 bunches (about 3½ pounds)

broccoli, 1 head (about 1½ pounds)

butternut squash, 1½ pounds, or 1½ pounds pumpkin, or 1 pound sweet potato (for 1 cup homemade puree) or 1 cup prepared pumpkin puree (from one 15-ounce can)

cabbage, 3 heads

carrots, 4 large

cauliflower, 2 large heads

cilantro, fresh, 1 bunch

garlic, 2 cloves

onions or leeks, 2

parsnips, 7 large

portobello mushroom caps, 4

rainbow chard, 1 small bunch or 8 large leaves

red onion, 1

russet or sweet potatoes, 8 large

salad fixings for lunch salads on 1 day: 1 head lettuce plus additional fixings of choice, such as cucumber, cherry tomatoes, and mushrooms

white-fleshed sweet potatoes, 1¼ pounds, or 2 (9-ounce) packages Cappello's fettuccine

yellow onions, 2

berries of choice, 1 to 2 pints, for topping crepes and/or porridge (optional)

lemon, 1

limes, 3

Meat & Broth:

bacon, 3 (8-ounce) packages

breakfast sausage, 8 ounces precooked or 12 ounces raw

chicken breast, boneless and skinless, 2 pounds

deli meat of choice, nitrate-free, for salads, 1 pound

ground beef, 4 pounds

ham, 4 thin slices

hot dogs, nitrate-free, 8

chicken broth (p. 131), 8 to 9 cups (quantity depends on type of noodle used for Fettuccine Alfredo)

Eggs & Milk:

eggs, 2½ dozen large

almond milk, unsweetened, 1 cup

almond milk, unsweetened, or cashew milk, 1½ cups (if using cashew milk, purchase 1 cup raw cashews to make cashew milk recipe on p. 143)

almond milk, unsweetened, or full-fat coconut milk, 3 cups (or 2 cans coconut milk)

coconut milk, full-fat, 2½ (13½-ounce) cans, plus ½ or 1 can if making Nut-Free "Cheese" Base for Fettuccine Alfredo (quantity depends on type of noodle used), plus 2 cans if making Whipped Coconut Cream for serving with crepes

Hazelnut Coffee Creamer (p. 114), 2 tablespoons (optional)

Note: *To make, you will need 8 ounces (1¾ cups) blanched hazelnuts and 2 soft pitted Medjool dates.*

Nuts & Seeds:

almonds, sliced, ¼ cup (optional)

cashews, raw, 2 cups, plus ¾ cup or 1½ cups if making "Cheese" Base with Cashews for Fettuccine Alfredo (quantity depends on type of noodle used)

Fats & Oils:

avocado oil, 2 tablespoons, plus more for cooking

bacon fat, 3 tablespoons, plus more for cooking

coconut butter/cream concentrate, 2 cups

coconut oil, ¼ cup, plus more for cooking

ghee, about ¾ cup

ghee or avocado oil, ¼ cup, plus 3 tablespoons if using sweet potato noodles for Fettuccine Alfredo

ghee or bacon fat, 2 tablespoons

ghee or coconut oil, 2 tablespoons, plus more for cooking

Sweeteners:

coconut sugar, for topping porridge (optional)

honey, about 1¼ cups

liquid vanilla stevia, about ½ teaspoon

maple syrup (for serving with pancakes)

Flours & Baking Mixes:

arrowroot or tapioca flour, 1 or 2 tablespoons, if making Nut-Free "Cheese" Base for Fettuccine Alfredo (quantity depends on type of noodle used)

coconut flour, 1 cup plus 2 tablespoons

Coconut Porridge Mix (p. 112), 3 cups

Note: *If you do not have premade mix on hand, you will need ¼ cup plus 1 tablespoon golden flax seeds, 5 cups unsweetened shredded coconut, ½ teaspoon ground cinnamon, and ¼ teaspoon fine sea salt.*

Pancake & Muffin Mix (p. 133), 2⅓ cups

Note: *If you do not have premade mix on hand, you will need 3¼ cups (410 g) coconut flour, 3¼ cups (406 g) arrowroot or tapioca flour, 2¾ cups (306 g) almond or cashew flour, and 2 tablespoons (36 g) baking soda.*

Pizza & Bread Mix (p. 133), 1½ cups

Note: *If you do not have premade mix on hand, you will need 3¼ cups (410 g) coconut flour, 3¼ cups (406 g) arrowroot or tapioca flour, just under 2 tablespoons (30 g) baking soda, 1 tablespoon plus 2 teaspoons (14 g) psyllium husk powder, and 1 tablespoon plus 1½ teaspoons (30 g) fine sea salt.*

Spices:

ground cinnamon, for topping porridge (optional)

ground cumin, ½ teaspoon

curry powder, 2 tablespoons

garlic powder, 1 teaspoon

onion powder, 1 teaspoon

Easy Taco Seasoning (p. 116), ½ cup plus 2 tablespoons

Note: *If you do not have premade seasoning on hand, you will need 2 tablespoons chili powder, 2 tablespoons ground cumin, 2 teaspoons onion powder, 2 teaspoons garlic powder, 2 teaspoons fine sea salt, and ½ teaspoon ground chipotle powder.*

Salt Blend (p. 117), about 1 teaspoon

Note: *If you do not have premade seasoning on hand, you will need ¼ cup leek flakes or 2¾ teaspoons celery seeds, 2½ tablespoons fine sea salt, 1 tablespoon herbes de Provence, 1 teaspoon onion powder, and ½ teaspoon garlic powder. (Herbamare salt blend is a good store-bought alternative.)*

Condiments, Dressings & Sauces:

Dijon mustard, gluten-free, 1 tablespoon plus 1 teaspoon

Ranch Dressing (p. 120), ½ to 1 cup

Note: *If you do not have premade dressing on hand, you will need ½ cup raw cashews, ½ cup extra-virgin olive oil, ½ lemon, 1 tablespoon apple cider vinegar, ½ teaspoon dried dill weed, ½ teaspoon onion powder, ½ teaspoon fine sea salt, and 1 small clove garlic.*

salad dressing of choice, enough for lunch salads on 1 day (see pp. 120 to 125 for ingredients)

Miscellaneous Items:

active dry yeast, 2 teaspoons

apple cider vinegar, ¼ cup plus 1 tablespoon

baking soda, ½ teaspoon

Cappello's fettuccine, 2 (9-ounce) packages, or 1¼ pounds white-fleshed sweet potatoes

chips cooked in coconut or avocado oil, 5-ounce bag

cocoa powder, ¼ cup

gelatin, grass-fed, 1 teaspoon

pickle relish, naturally fermented, ¼ cup

psyllium husk powder, ¼ cup

raisins, about ½ cup (optional; for topping porridge)

salsa of choice, 1¼ cups, plus more for serving with Burrito Bowl

sauerkraut, naturally fermented, ½ cup

tomato paste, ½ cup

vanilla extract, 3 tablespoons

fall: week 2

	Monday	Tuesday ^	Wednesday `	Thursday `	Friday	Saturday
breakfast	Cherry Almond Bars* X2 p. 165		Pumpkin Bread with Cream Cheese Swirl*@ p. 274		Pumpkin N'Oatmeal X4 p. 181	Pumpkin N'Oatmeal X4 p. 181
lunch	sunflower seed butter & jelly on Sandwich Bread* p. 270	mixed green salad tossed with dressing of choice, with deli meat and chips	leftover Cider Cabbage & Kielbasa and Mashed Potatoes	Poached Eggs p. 188 and Perfect Crispy Potatoes* p. 184	mixed green salad tossed with dressing of choice and leftover Holiday Turkey	Portobello & Ham Baked Eggs X2 p. 188 and Perfect Crispy Potatoes p. 184
dinner	One-Pot Pizza Pasta@ p. 248	Cider Cabbage & Kielbasa p. 308 and Mashed Potatoes p. 242	Pho* p. 212	turkey sandwiches on Sandwich Bread* p. 270 with Holiday Turkey and fixings p. 320	Tomato Pizza p. 286	Cheeseburger Soup p. 200

* Make ahead. (Make 2 loaves of Sandwich Bread for the week. If you have time on Thursday, you can make 2 batches of Perfect Crispy Potatoes to save yourself time later and to have a more leisurely Saturday lunch.)

^ On Tuesday morning, place the ingredients for the Cider Cabbage & Kielbasa in the slow cooker, but add an additional 14-ounce kielbasa (for 2 sausages total). Reserve one of the sausages and half of the cabbage and apple mixture for Wednesday lunch.

< On Wednesday morning, place the ingredients for the Pho in the slow cooker.

@ Use pumpkin puree for Pumpkin Bread and Pumpkin N'Oatmeal. Use Pizza Sauce for One-Pot Pizza Pasta and Tomato Pizza.

X2 = Make a double batch.

X4 = Make a quadruple batch.

Note: The recipes in this meal plan use a total of 1½ batches of "cheese" base. For efficiency, make the batches in one go and store them in the fridge for use throughout the week.

shopping list

Produce:

basil, fresh, 1 handful

bean sprouts, 2 handfuls (optional)

butternut squash, 1 large

cilantro, fresh, 1 handful

garlic, 1 head

ginger, fresh, 3-inch piece

Granny Smith apples, 2

green onions, 4

kale, 1 bunch

lettuce, ½ head (to garnish Cheeseburger Soup)

portobello mushroom caps, 4

pumpkin, 7 pounds (to make homemade puree), or 3 (15-ounce) cans pumpkin puree

red cabbage, 1 head

rosemary, fresh, 4 sprigs

russet potatoes, 8 to 9 pounds

salad fixings for lunch salads on 2 days: 2 heads lettuce plus additional fixings of choice, such as cucumber, cherry tomatoes, and mushrooms

thyme, fresh, 4 sprigs

vegetable and/or meat pizza toppings, about 1½ cups prepped (total)

yellow onions, 3

Meat & Broth:

beef shin bones, 3 (about 3 pounds)

breakfast sausage, 8 ounces precooked or 12 ounces raw (optional; for serving with Saturday lunch)

deli meat of choice, nitrate-free, for salads, 1 pound

ground beef, 2 pounds

ham, 4 thin slices

Italian sausage, mild, 9 ounces

kielbasa, 28 ounces

meat and/or vegetable pizza toppings, about 1½ cups prepped (total)

pepperoni, 2½ ounces

sirloin, 1 pound

turkey parts, 12 to 14 pounds

chicken broth (p. 131), 4 cups

Eggs & Milk:

eggs, 2½ dozen large

almond milk, unsweetened, ¼ cup

cashew milk (p. 143), 1 cup

coconut milk, full-fat, 1½ (13½-ounce) cans, plus 1½ cans if making Nut-Free "Cheese" Base

Nuts & Seeds:

almonds, slivered, 3 cups

cashews, raw, ½ cup, plus 2¼ cups if making "Cheese" Base with Cashews

walnuts, raw, about ½ cup (optional; for topping N'Oatmeal)

Fats & Oils:

avocado oil, ½ cup, plus more for cooking

bacon fat, ¼ cup plus 2 tablespoons

bacon fat or avocado oil, 1 tablespoon

coconut oil or ghee, ¼ cup plus 3 tablespoons

ghee or avocado oil, ¼ cup

ghee or bacon fat, 1 tablespoon

Sweeteners:

coconut sugar, ¾ cup

honey, 2 tablespoons (or more if using as a substitute for stevia)

liquid vanilla stevia, up to ½ teaspoon

maple syrup (optional; for topping N'Oatmeal)

Flours & Baking Mixes:

arrowroot or tapioca flour, ½ cup, plus 3 tablespoons if making Nut-Free "Cheese" Base

coconut flour, 1 cup

Coconut Porridge Mix (p. 112), 6 cups

Note: *If you do not have premade mix on hand, you will need ½ cup plus 2 tablespoons golden flax seeds, 10 cups unsweetened shredded coconut, 1 teaspoon ground cinnamon, and ½ teaspoon fine sea salt.*

Pizza & Bread Mix (p. 133), 6 cups

Note: *If you do not have premade mix on hand, you will need 3¼ cups (410 g) coconut flour, 3¼ cups (406 g) arrowroot or tapioca flour, just under 2 tablespoons (30 g) baking soda, 1 tablespoon plus 2 teaspoons (14 g) psyllium husk powder, and 1 tablespoon plus 1½ teaspoons (30 g) fine sea salt.*

Spices:

black peppercorns, 1 teaspoon

ground cinnamon, 2 teaspoons

coarse pink salt, ½ cup

garlic powder, ¼ teaspoon

Italian seasoning, for garnish

pho spice (found at Asian markets), 1 packet, or 6 star anise, 3 cinnamon sticks, 2 teaspoons coriander seeds, 2 teaspoons fennel seeds, and 3 whole cloves

red pepper flakes, for garnish (optional; for One-Pot Pizza Pasta)

Everyday Seasoning (p. 117), 1 tablespoon

Note: *If you do not have premade seasoning on hand, you will need 2 tablespoons onion powder, 2 tablespoons garlic powder, 2 tablespoons fine sea salt, 1 tablespoon smoked paprika, and 1 teaspoon chili powder.*

Pumpkin Spice Blend (p. 118), about 2 tablespoons

Note: *If you do not have premade seasoning on hand, you will need ¼ cup ground cinnamon, 2 tablespoons ginger powder, 2 teaspoons ground cloves or allspice, and 2 teaspoons ground nutmeg.*

Salt Blend (p. 117), about 1½ tablespoons

Note: *If you do not have premade seasoning on hand, you will need ¼ cup leek flakes or 2¾ teaspoons celery seeds, 2½ tablespoons fine sea salt, 1 tablespoon herbes de Provence, 1 teaspoon onion powder, and ½ teaspoon garlic powder. (Herbamare salt blend is a good store-bought alternative.)*

Condiments, Dressings & Sauces:

mayonnaise, Paleo-friendly, for turkey sandwiches (optional)

Pizza Sauce (p. 130), 1½ cups

Note: *To make, you will need one 7-ounce jar tomato paste, 7 ounces strained tomatoes (from a 24-ounce jar), 2 teaspoons Italian seasoning, 1 teaspoon apple cider vinegar, ½ teaspoon onion powder, ½ teaspoon fine sea salt, and ¼ teaspoon garlic powder.*

fish sauce, 1 tablespoon

salad dressing of choice, enough for lunch salads on 2 days (see pp. 120 to 125 for ingredients)

Tart Cranberry Sauce (p. 137), for turkey sandwiches (optional)

Note: *To make, you will need 16 ounces fresh cranberries, 2 tablespoons finely grated orange zest, 2 cinnamon sticks, 1 cup fresh-squeezed orange juice, ½ cup coconut sugar, ¼ teaspoon ginger powder (optional), and ⅛ teaspoon fine sea salt. This makes more than you will need for the sandwiches, but it keeps well.*

Miscellaneous Items:

active dry yeast, 1 tablespoon plus 1 teaspoon

apple cider, ½ cup

apple cider vinegar, about ½ cup

baking soda, 1 teaspoon

chips cooked in coconut or avocado oil, 5-ounce bag

fruit spread, without added sugar, about ¼ cup

pumpkin puree, 3 (15-ounce) cans, or 1 (7-pound) pumpkin (to make homemade puree)

sour cherries, dried, 2 cups

strained tomatoes, 1 cup

sunflower seed butter, without added sugar, about ¼ cup

Thai white rice noodles, 8.8-ounce package, 9-ounce package Cappello's fettuccine, or 12-ounce package kelp noodles

tomato paste, ¼ cup

tomato puree, 2 cups

vanilla extract, 1 teaspoon

Winter Favorites

CABBAGE

CELERIAC

BROCCOLI

CAULIFLOWER

SWEET POTATO

winter: week 1

	Monday	Tuesday	Wednesday	Thursday	Friday ^	Saturday
breakfast	Bagels* X2 p. 160		Pumpkin N'Oatmeal X4 p. 181	Pumpkin Spice Latte X4 with bacon and eggs p. 153	Pumpkin N'Oatmeal< X4 p. 181	Poached Eggs p. 188 and Perfect Crispy Potatoes p. 184
lunch	mixed green salad tossed with dressing of choice, with deli meat and chips	leftover Curried Turkey Meatloaf and Creamed Kale	leftover Orange Chicken with Broccoli	mixed green salad tossed with dressing of choice, with deli meat and chips	Sun-Dried Tomato & Roasted Red Pepper Dip** X2 with deli meat and chips p. 236	Veggie Burritos*** X2 p. 232
dinner	Curried Turkey Meatloaf p. 318 and Creamed Kale X2 p. 219	Orange Chicken with Broccoli X2 p. 254	Meaty Tomato Lasagna p. 260		Bacon & Ranch Twice-Baked Potatoes* X2 p. 299 and Broccoli Cheese Soup p. 210	Beef Stroganoff p. 252

*Make ahead.

** On Thursday evening, soak the cashews for the Sun-Dried Tomato & Roasted Red Pepper Dip.

*** On Saturday morning, soak the sunflower seeds for the Veggie Burritos.

< Though the N'Oatmeal is eaten twice in the week, it doesn't reheat well, so it should be made in 2 quadruple batches.

^ On Friday morning, put 4 large russet potatoes in the slow cooker to make the Slow Cooker Baked Potatoes needed for a double batch of Twice-Baked Potatoes.

X2 = Make a double batch.

X4 = Make a quadruple batch.

Note: The recipes in this meal plan use a total of 3½ batches of "cheese" base. For efficiency, make the batches in one go and store them in the fridge for use throughout the week.

shopping list

Produce:

basil, fresh, 1 small bunch

broccoli, 3 heads (about 1½ pounds each)

carrots, 4 large

celery, 2 stalks

cherry tomatoes, 1 pint

collard greens, 4 large leaves

garlic, 1 head

ginger, fresh, 2½-inch piece

jicama, 2 fist-sized

kale, 4 large bunches

mushrooms, 8 ounces

pumpkin, about 4 pounds (to make homemade puree) or 2 (15-ounce) cans pumpkin puree

red onion, 1

russet potatoes, 3½ to 4 pounds

salad fixings for lunch salads on 2 days: 2 heads lettuce plus additional fixings of choice, such as cucumber, cherry tomatoes, and mushrooms

white-fleshed sweet potatoes, 3¾ pounds

yellow onions, 2

lemons, 2

oranges, 6

Meat & Broth:

bacon, 3 (8-ounce) packages

breakfast sausage, 12 ounces precooked or 1 pound raw (optional; for serving with Saturday breakfast)

chicken breast, boneless and skinless, 2 pounds

deli meat of choice, nitrate-free, 3 pounds

ground beef, 3 pounds

ground turkey, 2 pounds

chicken broth (p. 131), 10 cups

Eggs & Milk:

eggs, 1½ dozen large

coconut milk, full-fat, 5 (13½-ounce) cans, plus 3½ cans if making Nut-Free "Cheese" Base

Nuts & Seeds:

almonds, sliced, ¼ cup (optional)

cashews, raw, 2½ cups, plus 5¼ cups if making "Cheese" Base with Cashews

golden flax seeds, 1 cup

macadamia nuts, raw, ¼ cup (optional)

sesame seeds, about 2 teaspoons (optional)

sunflower seeds, raw, 1 cup

walnuts, raw, about 1 cup (optional; for topping N'Oatmeal)

Fats & Oils:

avocado oil, 1 tablespoon

bacon fat, about ¼ cup

bacon fat or ghee, ¼ cup

bacon fat or ghee or avocado oil, ¼ cup

coconut oil, ½ cup

ghee, about ⅓ cup

ghee or avocado oil, ¾ cup

Sweeteners:

honey, 2 tablespoons

liquid vanilla stevia, about ¼ teaspoon

maple syrup, about 3 tablespoons, plus more for topping N'Oatmeal (optional)

Flours & Baking Mixes:

arrowroot or tapioca flour, 3 tablespoons, plus ½ cup if making Nut-Free "Cheese" Base

coconut flour, ⅓ cup

Coconut Porridge Mix (p. 112), 6 cups

Note: *If you do not have premade mix on hand, you will need ½ cup plus 2 tablespoons golden flax seeds, 10 cups unsweetened shredded coconut, 1 teaspoon ground cinnamon, and ½ teaspoon fine sea salt.*

Pizza & Bread Mix (p. 133), 2 cups

Note: *If you do not have premade mix on hand, you will need 3¾ cups (410 g) coconut flour, 3¾ cups (406 g) arrowroot or tapioca flour, just under 2 tablespoons (30 g) baking soda, 1 tablespoon plus 2 teaspoons (14 g) psyllium husk powder, and 1 tablespoon plus 1½ teaspoons (30 g) fine sea salt.*

Spices:

ground cinnamon, 2 to 4 teaspoons (if making cinnamon raisin bagels)

curry powder, 1½ teaspoons

dill weed, dried, 1 teaspoon

garlic powder, 1¼ teaspoons

Italian seasoning, 1 tablespoon plus 1 teaspoon

onion powder, 1 teaspoon, plus 1 to 2 teaspoons if making onion bagels

smoked paprika, 2 teaspoons

turmeric powder, 1½ teaspoons

Everyday Seasoning (p. 117), up to 1 tablespoon

Note: *If you do not have premade seasoning on hand, you will need 2 tablespoons onion powder, 2 tablespoons garlic powder, 2 tablespoons fine sea salt, 1 tablespoon smoked paprika, and 1 teaspoon chili powder.*

Pumpkin Spice Blend (p. 118), 1 tablespoons plus 2 teaspoons

Note: *If you do not have premade seasoning on hand, you will need ¼ cup ground cinnamon, 2 tablespoons ginger powder, 2 teaspoons ground cloves or allspice, and 2 teaspoons ground nutmeg.*

Salt Blend (p. 117), about ¼ cup

Note: *If you do not have premade seasoning on hand, you will need ¼ cup leek flakes or 2¾ teaspoons celery seeds, 2½ tablespoons fine sea salt, 1 tablespoon herbes de Provence, 1 teaspoon onion powder, and ½ teaspoon garlic powder. (Herbamare salt blend is a good store-bought alternative.)*

Condiments, Dressings & Sauces:

Dijon mustard, gluten-free, 1 teaspoon

Ranch Dressing (p. 120), ½ cup

Note: *If you do not have premade dressing on hand, you will need ½ cup raw cashews, ½ cup extra-virgin olive oil, ½ lemon, 1 tablespoon apple cider vinegar, ½ teaspoon dried dill weed, ½ teaspoon onion powder, ½ teaspoon fine sea salt, and 1 small clove garlic.*

salad dressing of choice, enough for lunch salads on 2 days (see pp. 120 to 125 for ingredients)

Miscellaneous Items:

apple cider vinegar, about ½ cup

Cappello's grain-free lasagna noodles, 12-ounce package, or 12 ounces butternut squash noodles (from 1 large butternut squash)

chips cooked in coconut or avocado oil, 3 (5-ounce) bags

coconut aminos, 1 tablespoon, plus more for dipping

coffee, enough to make 4 cups brewed, or 4 dandelion tea bags

cooking sherry, 2 tablespoons

pumpkin puree, 2 (15-ounce) cans, or 1 (4-pound) pumpkin (to make homemade puree)

raisins, ½ cup (optional; for bagels)

roasted red peppers, 1 cup

strained tomatoes, 4 cups

sun-dried tomatoes, ½ cup

white rice, 2 cups cooked, for Veggie Burritos, or 1 small head cauliflower (enough to make 2 cups cooked cauli-rice)

winter: week 2

	Monday	Tuesday	Wednesday	Thursday	Friday	Saturday
breakfast	Pumpkin Cinnamon Rolls* p. 168		Coconut Porridge X4 p. 178	Coconut Yogurt* with nuts and berries p. 182		Best-Ever Pancakes p. 158
lunch	mixed green salad tossed with dressing of choice and Crepes** p. 157	Funa Salad Wraps**** with chips p. 228		Spinach & Artichoke Dip**** X2 p. 237 with Crackers X2 and deli meat p. 282		Yellow Pepper Baked Eggs X2 p. 191 and Perfect Crispy Potatoes p. 184
dinner	Faux Rotisserie Chicken with Potatoes*** p. 296	Chicken & Mushroom Alfredo p. 250	Spaghetti with Turkey Meatballs@ p. 266		Swedish Meatballs p. 324 and Green Bean Casserole p. 244	

* Make ahead.

** Optional: On Sunday morning, put 2 cans of coconut milk in the fridge to chill for making Whipped Coconut Cream for the crepes.

*** On Monday morning, put the ingredients for the Faux Rotisserie Chicken with Potatoes in the slow cooker.

**** On Monday evening, soak the sunflower seeds for the Funa Salad. On Wednesday evening, Soak the cashews for the Spinach & Artichoke Dip.

@ Double the noodles and sauce for the Spaghetti with Turkey Meatballs.

X2 = Make a double batch.

X4 = Make a quadruple batch.

shopping list

Produce:

carrots, 2 large

celery roots (celeriac), 2

celery stalks, 6

collard greens, 8 large leaves

mushrooms, 24 ounces

parsley, fresh, 1 bunch

red onion, 1

rosemary, fresh, 3 sprigs

russet potatoes, 4 to 4½ pounds

salad fixings for lunch salads on 1 day: 1 head lettuce plus additional fixings of choice, such as cucumber, cherry tomatoes, and mushrooms

yellow bell peppers, 2 large

yellow onions, 4

zucchini, 2½ pounds, or 4 (9-ounce) packages Cappello's fettuccine

berries of choice, 1 pint, for topping yogurt, plus more for topping porridge and/or crepes (optional)

lemons, 2

Frozen Produce:

green beans, frozen, 2½ pounds (40 ounces)

spinach, frozen, 2 (10-ounce) packages

Meat & Broth:

bacon, 4 slices

breakfast sausage, 8 ounces precooked or 12 ounces raw (optional; for serving with Saturday lunch)

chicken, whole, 3 to 4 pounds

chicken breast, boneless and skinless, 1 pound

deli meat of choice, nitrate-free, for Thursday and Friday lunch, 2 pounds

ground beef, 1 pound

ground pork, 1 pound

ground turkey, 2 pounds

chicken broth (p. 131), 2½ cups

Eggs & Milk:

eggs, 1½ dozen large

almond milk, unsweetened, 1 cup

almond milk, unsweetened, or full-fat coconut milk, 3 cups

cashew milk (p. 143) or full-fat coconut milk, 3½ cups

coconut milk, full-fat, 3½ (13½-ounce) cans, plus ½ cup (if making frosting for cinnamon rolls), plus 1 can (if making Nut-Free "Cheese" Base for Chicken & Mushroom Alfredo), plus 2 cans (if making Whipped Coconut Cream to serve with crepes)

Hazelnut Coffee Creamer (p. 114), 2 tablespoons (optional)

> Note: *To make, you will need 8 ounces (1¾ cups) blanched hazelnuts and 2 soft pitted Medjool dates.*

Nuts & Seeds:

cashews, raw, 1 cup, plus 1½ cups if making "Cheese" Base with Cashews for Chicken & Mushroom Alfredo

macadamia nuts, raw, up to ¾ cup (if making frosting for cinnamon rolls)

nuts of choice, raw, about 2 cups (for topping yogurt)

sunflower seeds, raw, 1½ cups

Fats & Oils:

avocado oil, 1½ teaspoons

bacon fat, 3 tablespoons

coconut oil, about ¾ cup, plus more for cooking

ghee, about ½ cup, plus more for cooking and topping porridge

ghee or avocado oil, ¼ cup

ghee or coconut oil, 2 tablespoons, plus more for cooking

Sweeteners:

coconut sugar, ½ cup, plus more for topping porridge (optional)

honey, ¼ cup, plus 2 tablespoons if making frosting for cinnamon rolls, plus 2 tablespoons if making Whipped Coconut Cream to serve with crepes

liquid vanilla stevia, up to ½ teaspoon

maple syrup, 1 tablespoon, plus more for serving with pancakes

Flours & Baking Mixes:

almond flour, ¾ cup, or ⅓ cup coconut flour

almond or cashew flour, 2 cups

arrowroot or tapioca flour, 2 tablespoons, plus 2 tablespoons if making Nut-Free "Cheese" Base for Chicken & Mushroom Alfredo

Coconut Porridge Mix (p. 112), 3 cups

Note: *If you do not have premade mix on hand, you will need ¼ cup plus 1 tablespoon golden flax seeds, 5 cups unsweetened shredded coconut, ½ teaspoon ground cinnamon, and ¼ teaspoon fine sea salt.*

Pancake & Muffin Mix (p. 133), about 2⅓ cups

Note: *If you do not have premade mix on hand, you will need 3¼ cups (410 g) coconut flour, 3¼ cups (406 g) arrowroot or tapioca flour, 2¾ cups (306 g) almond or cashew flour, and 2 tablespoons (36 g) baking soda.*

Pizza & Bread Mix (p. 133), 2 cups

Note: *If you do not have premade mix on hand, you will need 3¼ cups (410 g) coconut flour, 3¼ cups (406 g) arrowroot or tapioca flour, just under 2 tablespoons (30 g) baking soda, 1 tablespoon plus 2 teaspoons (14 g) psyllium husk powder, and 1 tablespoon plus 1½ teaspoons (30 g) fine sea salt.*

Spices:

ground allspice, 1 teaspoon

ground cinnamon, 1½ teaspoons, plus more for topping porridge (optional)

dill weed, dried, 2 teaspoons

garlic powder, 1½ tablespoons

Italian seasoning, about ⅓ cup

onion powder, 1 tablespoon

Everyday Seasoning (p. 117), about 2 tablespoons

Note: *If you do not have premade seasoning on hand, you will need 2 tablespoons onion powder, 2 tablespoons garlic powder, 2 tablespoons fine sea salt, 1 tablespoon smoked paprika, and 1 teaspoon chili powder.*

Pumpkin Spice Blend (p. 118), 1½ teaspoons

Note: *If you do not have premade seasoning on hand, you will need ¼ cup ground cinnamon, 2 tablespoons ginger powder, 2 teaspoons ground cloves or allspice, and 2 teaspoons ground nutmeg.*

Salt Blend (p. 117), about 1½ tablespoons

Note: *If you do not have premade seasoning on hand, you will need ¼ cup leek flakes or 2¾ teaspoons celery seeds, 2½ tablespoons fine sea salt, 1 tablespoon herbes de Provence, 1 teaspoon onion powder, and ½ teaspoon garlic powder. (Herbamare salt blend is a good store-bought alternative.)*

Condiments, Dressings & Sauces:

mayonnaise, Paleo-friendly, about ⅔ cup

salad dressing of choice, enough for lunch salads on 1 day (see pp. 120 to 125 for ingredients)

Miscellaneous Items:

almond or lemon extract (optional; for yogurt)

apple cider vinegar, about ⅓ cup

baking soda, 1 teaspoon

Cappello's fettuccine, 4 (9-ounce) packages, or 2½ pounds zucchini

chips cooked in coconut or avocado oil, 2 (5-ounce) bags

Crackers (p. 282), double batch (for serving with Spinach & Artichoke Dip)

Note: *To make, you will need just under 2 cups (276 g) Scone & Pie Crust Mix (p. 133), ½ cup ghee or palm shortening, 2 tablespoons apple cider vinegar, and 2 teaspoons Italian seasoning.*

gelatin, grass-fed, 1 tablespoon plus 1 teaspoon, or 1½ teaspoons agar powder

marinated artichokes, 2 (6½-ounce) jars

pickle relish, naturally fermented, ⅓ cup

probiotic capsules, dairy-free, equal to about 35 million active cultures

psyllium husk powder, 1 tablespoon plus 1 teaspoon

pumpkin puree, 1¼ cups (from one 15-ounce can)

raisins, for topping porridge (optional)

dried seaweed, ground, ½ teaspoon (optional)

strained tomatoes, 8 cups (from three 24-ounce jars)

vanilla bean, 1

vanilla extract, 1 teaspoon (optional; for Whipped Coconut Cream)

menus

The following is a sampling of my family's favorite menus for the holidays and for Friday night dinners throughout the year.

holiday menus

Thanksgiving Menu

Poultry Brine (page 128)
Holiday Turkey (page 320)
Tart Cranberry Sauce (page 137)
Holiday Stuffing (page 322)
Orange & Almond Salad (page 220)
Mashed Potatoes & Gravy (page 242)
No-Bake Pumpkin Pie (page 376)
Harvest Cupcakes (page 330)

2 days ahead:
Make the brine.
Put the turkey in the brine as directed.
Make the cranberry sauce and stuffing.

1 day ahead:
Make the pumpkin pie and cupcakes.

The morning of:
Take the turkey out of the brine and follow the instructions for cooking it.
Make the mashed potatoes, gravy, and salad.

Just before serving:
Reheat the stuffing and warm the mashed potatoes and gravy while the turkey rests.

Christmas Menu

Swedish Meatballs (page 324)
Sweet Potatoes au Gratin (page 240)
Green Bean Casserole (page 244)
Eggnog (page 149)
Salted Caramel Pecan Pie (page 372)
Mint Chocolate Christmas Cake (page 336)

2 days ahead:
Make the Swedish Meatballs and Sweet Potatoes au Gratin.

1 day ahead:
Make the pecan pie and chocolate cake.

The morning of:
Make the Green Bean Casserole and eggnog.

Just before serving:
Reheat the meatballs and sweet potatoes.
Warm the Green Bean Casserole and eggnog if needed.

Breakfast for Dinner

Choose something light or fluffy:
Crepes (page 157)
Best-Ever Pancakes (page 158)

Or maybe something baked:
Cherry Muffins (page 172)
Bagels (page 160)

And have it with an egg:
Portobello & Ham Baked Eggs (page 188)
Eggs Baked in Tomatoes (page 190)
Yellow Pepper Baked Eggs (page 191)

Mexican Night

Choose one or two vegetable dishes:
Zucchini Lime Cilantro Pie (page 196)
Nacho Cheese Cauliflower Poppers (page 234)

And one or more main dishes:
Southwest Pasta (page 256)
Taco Boats (page 306)
Burrito Bowl (page 309)
Taco Rice Skillet (page 315)

Game Night

Pick two of the following:
Sun-Dried Tomato & Roasted Red Pepper Dip
(page 236)
Spinach & Artichoke Dip (page 237)
Roasted Garlic Bean Dip (page 238)
Guacamole (page 130)
Nacho Cheese Cauliflower Poppers (page 234)

Plus all of these:
Baja Drumsticks (page 314)
Cheeseburger Soup (page 200)
Mini Boulder Cream Donuts (page 162)

Asian Faux Takeout

First, have some tea:
Jasmine Green Tea or Hibiscus Tea (page 150)

Begin with salad:
Mixed green salad tossed with Asian Dressing
(page 121)

Then choose a main dish:
Orange Chicken with Broccoli (page 254)
Pho (page 212)
Hot & Sour Soup (page 214)

And for dessert:
Crunchy Arrowroot Cookies (page 344)

Picnic Dinner

Have some slaw:
Ranch Slaw (page 218)

Then choose a main dish:
Chicken & Mushroom Alfredo (page 250)
Pizza Quiche 2.0 (page 192)
Chicken Nuggets (page 302)
Curry Chicken Salad Wraps (page 307)
Faux Rotisserie Chicken (page 296)

Plus one of these:
Bacon & Ranch Twice-Baked Potatoes
(page 299)
Curry Twice-Baked Potatoes (page 241)

And one of these for dessert:
No-Bake Coconut Fig Bites (page 343)
Black-Bottom Cupcakes (page 328)

Italian Dinner

Begin with salad and bread:
Mixed green salad tossed with
Creamy Italian Dressing (page 124)
Kalamata Focaccia Quick Bread (page 278)

Then choose a main dish:
One-Pot Pizza Pasta (page 248)
Meaty Tomato Lasagna (page 260)
Chicken Amatriciana (page 258)
Fettuccine Alfredo (page 264)
Spaghetti with Turkey Meatballs (page 266)
Cracker Pizzas (page 284)
Tomato Pizza (page 286)

And for dessert:
Chocolate Hazelnut Cookies (page 346)

Fall Celebration

Mixed green salad tossed with
Apple Cider Vinaigrette (page 121)
Pumpkin Lasagna (page 262)
Pumpkin Spice Cheesecake (page 360)

part 3:

the recipes

I pushed my jumbo shopping cart up to the register at Costco. As the checkout lady scanned my bags of organic frozen fruits, vegetables, and meats, she commented to her coworker, "Wow, look at all this real food. Nothing bad in here." The coworker loading the boxes into my cart grumbled, "Yeah, well, I can't do that. I'm too tired. I have to eat junk food." I was afraid to tell her, "If you ate this food, then you wouldn't be so tired."

A study done at the University of California, Los Angeles, in 2014 set out to answer the question: Does eating junk food make you lazy, or does laziness make you eat junk food? What researchers found was that diet is the cause of fatigue. Eating highly processed food, grains, refined oils, and sugars makes you tired. Continuing down this path of poor food choices leads to obesity, diabetes, heart disease, and more. Celebrity chef Jamie Oliver said, "Homicide is 0.8 percent of deaths. Diet-related disease is over 60 percent. But no one f***ing talks about it."

Restaurants use a ton of sugar, not only in their desserts but also in their dressings, sauces, and main dishes. By dining out much less frequently and choosing higher-quality restaurants when you do eat out, you are choosing health.

Eating whole foods is easy. If you're just transitioning to a Paleo lifestyle, start with my slow-cooked recipes (pages 126, 212, 296, 298, and 308), soups (see chapter 10), Antipasto Plate (page 311), and recipes made with five ingredients or fewer (see the list on page 55). When you're ready to take it up a notch, I've got all kinds of easy recipes that are full of flavor, from simple pastas made with spiral-sliced vegetables to pizzas to baked goods and desserts.

The recipes in this book are made entirely of real food. They are completely devoid of refined sugars, vegetable oils, grains, and dairy. When you use this book, you can feel good knowing that you and your loved ones are eating nutrient-dense, healthy food. After all, this book illustrates exactly how I feed my own family, and I wouldn't have it any other way.

chapter 6:

Staples

bacon fat

Makes about ½ cup | Prep Time: 5 minutes | Cook Time: 25 minutes

Bacon fat is dee-licious in so many recipes, but my favorite way to use it is for frying Perfect Crispy Potatoes (page 184). New to Paleo and concerned that bacon fat is bad for you? Not so! Check out the book Beyond Bacon: Paleo Recipes that Respect the Whole Hog, *by Stacy Toth and Matthew McCarry, to get the scoop. Have the cooked bacon for breakfast during the week or use it on soups, salads, and baked potatoes.*

2 (8-ounce) packages bacon

1. Set the oven to 350°F. Place the bacon in a single layer on two rimmed baking sheets. Place the bacon in the oven and cook until almost crispy, about 25 minutes.

2. Remove the bacon from the baking sheets and enjoy immediately or reserve for later use. Place a fine-mesh sieve over a wide-mouth glass jar. (I reuse empty ghee jars for bacon fat.) Pour the bacon fat through the sieve into the jar and let cool.

3. Seal the jar with the lid and refrigerate for up to a month. Bacon fat also freezes well.

Bacon
Fat

"cheese" base with cashews

Makes 3½ cups | Prep Time: 5 minutes

Make my "cheese" base (either with cashews or nut-free) over the weekend to save time during the week. This cashew base is amazing for thickening soups and sauces. For a complete list of the recipes that use these bases, see the index.

2 cups chicken broth (page 131)

1½ cups raw cashews

½ teaspoon Salt Blend (page 117)

Place all of the ingredients in a high-powered blender and puree until completely smooth. Use right away or refrigerate in a glass container for up to a week.

Note: *If you're making multiple recipes during the week that call for "cheese" base, it will be more efficient to double or even quadruple the recipe. Some of the weekly meal plans (see pages 70, 78, and 94), for example, use two to four batches of "cheese" base. Based on the capacity of most blender jars, it is best to make no more than a double batch at a time. To make a double batch, you will need the following quantities: 4 cups chicken broth, 3 cups raw cashews, and 1 teaspoon Salt Blend.*

nut-free "cheese" base

Makes about 3½ cups | Prep Time: 5 minutes

This base isn't as thick as the version made with cashews (opposite), but sometimes I'm in the mood for a lighter base, and this one is perfect for those times.

2 cups chicken broth (page 131)

1 (13½-ounce) can full-fat coconut milk

2 tablespoons arrowroot or tapioca flour

½ teaspoon Salt Blend (page 117)

Place all of the ingredients in a blender (standard or high-powered) and puree until completely smooth. Use right away or refrigerate in a glass container for up to a week.

Note: *If you're making multiple recipes during the week that call for "cheese" base, it will be more efficient to double or even quadruple the recipe. Based on the capacity of most blender jars, it is best to make no more than a double batch at a time. To make a double batch, you will need the following quantities: 4 cups chicken broth, 2 (13½-ounce) cans full-fat coconut milk, ¼ cup arrowroot or tapioca flour, and 1 teaspoon Salt Blend.*

coconut porridge mix

Makes 3¾ cups or ¾ cup | Prep Time: 10 minutes

I prefer to grind my own flax seeds for this recipe, but you can substitute packaged flax meal if you want. Use ½ cup plus 2 tablespoons of flax meal to make five servings of mix, or use 2 tablespoons of flax meal to make one serving. Always store flax seeds and flax meal in an airtight container in the refrigerator; otherwise they will go rancid.

For 5 servings of porridge (3¾ cups of mix):

¼ cup plus 1 tablespoon golden flax seeds

5 cups unsweetened shredded coconut

½ teaspoon ground cinnamon

¼ teaspoon fine sea salt

For 1 serving of porridge (¾ cup of mix):

1 tablespoon golden flax seeds

1 cup unsweetened shredded coconut

2 pinches of ground cinnamon

Pinch of fine sea salt

1. Make sure that all of your equipment is completely dry or the mix will form clumps in the fridge.

2. Grind the flax seeds in a Magic Bullet blender or coffee grinder. (They will not be fully ground if you throw them in whole with the shredded coconut.)

3. Place the shredded coconut in a food processor fitted with the S-blade. Pulse 15 times. Remove the lid and stir the coconut, then pulse until the mixture is finely ground, about 1 minute, stopping twice to scrape the sides.

4. Add the ground flax seeds, cinnamon, and salt. Continue to pulse, scraping the sides as needed, until the mixture is well combined.

5. Store in a glass container in the refrigerator for up to 2 weeks.

Notes: *A professional blender (like a Blendtec or Vitamix) will work instead of a food processor, but will grind your coconut so well that it will be on its way to becoming coconut butter. This is fine if you'll be eating the porridge immediately, but not good if you want to store it in the refrigerator for later use, because it will solidify once cold.*

My kids love their porridge really fine-textured, so I make the mix ahead of time in my food processor (as directed above), and then, right before making their breakfast, I throw a couple of servings of the mix (1½ cups total) into my Blendtec and puree it until it sticks together. Then I use it to make a double recipe of Coconut Porridge (page 178), Strawberries & Cream N'Oatmeal (page 180), or Pumpkin N'Oatmeal (page 181).

hazelnut coffee creamer

Makes 2½ cups | Wait Time: overnight | Prep Time: 10 minutes

Did you ever buy packaged hazelnut coffee creamer? I used to buy it in college, so it's been a while for me. I decided to make the real deal—not like the artificially flavored, refined sugar version for sale in stores, but literally hazelnut cream made with . . . hazelnuts. Call me crazy! Add a splash to coffee or to dandelion tea for a caffeine-free "coffee." And make sure to save the pulp for making my Chocolate Hazelnut Cookies (page 346)! The pulp will last for a week in the fridge or can be frozen for at least a month. You can find blanched hazelnuts online.

8 ounces (1¾ cups) blanched hazelnuts

2½ cups water, plus more for soaking the nuts

2 soft Medjool dates, pitted

Pinch of fine sea salt

1. Soak the hazelnuts in the refrigerator overnight in enough water to cover, plus 2 inches.

2. Drain the nuts and rinse thoroughly. Place the nuts, 2½ cups of water, dates, and salt in a high-powered blender and puree until completely smooth.

3. Place a large piece of cheesecloth or a nut milk bag in a 4-cup glass measuring cup with a spout. Pour the puree through the cheesecloth or into the bag, then lift the cloth or bag, twist, and squeeze the creamer into the cup.

4. Transfer the creamer to a glass container and store in the refrigerator for up to a week.

Note: *Since this creamer lasts for only about a week in the fridge, I like to freeze half in an 8-ounce glass jar in case I don't use it fast enough. If you freeze some, make sure to leave a couple of inches at the top of the jar for expansion.*

my go-to seasonings 🚫 🚫

These spice blends are my favorite seasonings, the ones I reach for constantly. The method and storage are the same for all three. To make, place all of the ingredients in a small jar with a lid. Tightly secure the lid, then shake to combine. Let the blend settle before opening the jar. Store in a cool, dark place, such as a cabinet. The blends are good as long as they're still aromatic.

easy taco seasoning

Makes about ⅓ cup | Prep Time: 5 minutes

2 tablespoons chili powder
2 tablespoons ground cumin
2 teaspoons onion powder
2 teaspoons garlic powder
2 teaspoons fine sea salt
½ teaspoon ground chipotle powder

salt blend

Makes about ¼ cup | Prep Time: 5 minutes

I've used Herbamare seasoning for many years. It's awesome stuff, but many of my readers have asked how to make it at home. This is my copycat recipe. You may use Herbamare (found in most health food stores and online) in any of my recipes that call for Salt Blend.

¼ cup leek flakes or 2¾ teaspoons celery seeds, ground to a powder

2½ tablespoons fine sea salt, ground to a powder

1 tablespoon herbes de Provence, ground to a powder

1 teaspoon onion powder

½ teaspoon garlic powder

everyday seasoning

Makes about ⅓ cup | Prep Time: 5 minutes

2 tablespoons onion powder

2 tablespoons garlic powder

2 tablespoons fine sea salt

1 tablespoon smoked paprika

1 teaspoon chili powder

pumpkin spice blend

Makes a scant ½ cup | Prep Time: 5 minutes

This blend can be used for Pumpkin Spice Latte (page 153), Pumpkin Cinnamon Rolls (page 168), Pumpkin N'Oatmeal (page 181), Pumpkin Bread with Cream Cheese Swirl (page 274), Pumpkin Spice Cheesecake (page 360), and No-Bake Pumpkin Pie (page 376). So much pumpkin-y goodness!

¼ cup ground cinnamon

2 tablespoons ginger powder

2 teaspoons ground cloves or allspice

2 teaspoons ground nutmeg

1. Place all of the ingredients in a small jar with a lid. Tightly secure the lid, then shake to combine. Let the blend settle before opening the jar.

2. Store in a cool, dark place, such as a cabinet. The blend is good as long as it is still aromatic.

ranch dressing

Makes about 1½ cups | Prep Time: 5 minutes

½ cup raw cashews

½ cup extra-virgin olive oil

¼ cup water, plus more if needed

1 tablespoon fresh-squeezed lemon juice

1 tablespoon apple cider vinegar

½ teaspoon dried dill weed

½ teaspoon onion powder

½ teaspoon fine sea salt

1 small clove garlic

A few cranks of black pepper

russian dressing

Makes just over 1 cup | Prep Time: 5 minutes

½ cup extra-virgin olive oil

¼ cup water, plus more if needed

2 tablespoons raw cashews

2 tablespoons apple cider vinegar

2 tablespoons packed sun-dried tomatoes

1 teaspoon honey

1 green onion, roughly chopped

½ teaspoon fine sea salt

⅛ teaspoon garlic powder

A few cranks of black pepper

orange & almond dressing

Makes just under 1 cup | Prep Time: 5 minutes

¼ cup fresh-squeezed orange juice

¼ cup extra-virgin olive oil

¼ cup raw almond butter

1 tablespoon honey

1 teaspoon apple cider vinegar

1 teaspoon gluten-free tamari or coconut aminos

Instructions for all three dressings:

1. Place all of the ingredients in a blender and puree until smooth. Thin the dressing with water as needed to reach the desired consistency.

2. Store in a glass container in the refrigerator and use within a month.

asian dressing

Makes just under 1 cup | Prep Time: 5 minutes

¼ cup extra-virgin olive oil

¼ cup raw cashews

¼ cup coconut aminos

2 tablespoons cooking sherry

1 teaspoon honey

1 small clove garlic

½ teaspoon minced fresh ginger

1. Place all of the ingredients in a blender and puree until smooth.

2. Store in a glass container in the refrigerator and use within a month.

Note: *I use cooking sherry instead of sake because it's what I have on hand. You may substitute sake if you prefer.*

apple cider vinaigrette

Makes just over 1 cup | Prep Time: 5 minutes

¾ cup extra-virgin olive oil

¼ cup apple cider vinegar

2 teaspoons honey

½ teaspoon fine sea salt

⅛ teaspoon ground black pepper

1. Place all of the ingredients in a blender and puree until smooth.

2. Store in a glass container in the refrigerator and use within a month.

creamy honey dijon dressing

Makes about 1½ cups | Prep Time: 5 minutes

½ cup raw cashews

½ cup extra-virgin olive oil

¼ cup water, plus more if needed

1 tablespoon apple cider vinegar

1 teaspoon honey

1 teaspoon gluten-free Dijon mustard

½ teaspoon fine sea salt

⅛ teaspoon onion powder

1. Place all of the ingredients in a blender and puree until smooth. Thin the dressing with water as needed to reach the desired consistency.

2. Store in a glass container in the refrigerator and use within a month.

ranch

orange
& almond

russian

asian

creamy
honey
dijon

apple cider
vinaigrette

creamy italian dressing

Makes about 1½ cups | Prep Time: 5 minutes

½ cup raw cashews
½ cup extra-virgin olive oil
¼ cup water, plus more if needed
¼ cup apple cider vinegar
½ teaspoon Italian seasoning
½ teaspoon fine sea salt
¼ teaspoon garlic powder
A few cranks of black pepper

1. Place all of the ingredients in a blender and puree until smooth. Thin the dressing with water as needed to reach the desired consistency.

2. Store in a glass container in the refrigerator and use within a month.

caesar dressing

Makes about 1½ cups | Prep Time: 5 minutes

½ cup raw cashews

½ cup extra-virgin olive oil

¼ cup water, plus more if needed

1 tablespoon fresh-squeezed
lemon juice or apple cider vinegar

1 teaspoon honey

1 small clove garlic

½ teaspoon fine sea salt

⅛ teaspoon onion powder

A few cranks of black pepper

1. Place all of the ingredients in a blender and puree until
smooth. Thin the dressing with water as needed to reach
the desired consistency.

2. Store in a glass container in the refrigerator and use
within a month.

easy chicken

Makes about 1½ pounds, 5 cups chopped | Prep Time: 5 minutes | Cook Time: 20 minutes

I've been cooking chicken this way for as long as I can remember. I use this chicken for Chicken & Mushroom Alfredo (page 250), Greek Pizza (page 290), Curry Chicken Salad Wraps (page 307), Individual Pot Pies (page 316), and more.

1 tablespoon avocado oil

2 pounds boneless, skinless chicken breast (about 4 breast halves)

Everyday Seasoning or Salt Blend (page 117), to season

¼ cup water

1. Place a tablespoon of avocado oil in a 12-inch skillet over medium heat. Sprinkle the chicken on both sides with Everyday Seasoning or Salt Blend. Place the chicken in the skillet and cook for about 1 minute. Flip the chicken over, add the water, and cover, with the lid slightly cracked. Reduce the heat to low and cook until the chicken is done, about 20 minutes.

2. Store in a glass container in the refrigerator for up to a week.

slow cooker baked potatoes

Makes 6 | Prep Time: 10 minutes | Cook Time: 3 to 4 hours

You can pretty much always find Slow Cooker Baked Potatoes in my fridge. They're as easy as can be to make and can be eaten in so many ways. You can use them for Curry Twice-Baked Potatoes (page 241) or Bacon & Ranch Twice-Baked Potatoes (page 299) or to make Crispy Potato Boats (recipe follows).

6 large russet potatoes or sweet potatoes (about 2½ pounds)

For serving:

Ghee or bacon fat (page 108)

Fine sea salt

1. Scrub the potatoes, then poke them once with a fork. Put the potatoes in a dry slow cooker and cook on high until fork-tender, about 4 hours for russets or 3 hours for faster-cooking sweet potatoes. The exact cooking time depends on the size of the potatoes.

2. Enjoy the baked potatoes hot with ghee or bacon fat, seasoned with salt.

crispy potato boats

Makes 12 | Prep Time: 15 minutes | Cook Time: 15 minutes

These potato boats are a great alternative to bread, as an "open-faced sandwich" option. I use them as a vessel for baked eggs (page 189) and as a base for barbecue chicken (page 298), hot dogs (page 304), and taco filling (page 306), but you can fill them with just about anything you like, as you would fill a sandwich. These boats can be made with either russet potatoes or sweet potatoes, but I prefer the flavor of russets for this recipe.

1 batch Slow Cooker Baked Potatoes (opposite), preferably made with russets, chilled in the fridge overnight

Avocado oil

Fine sea salt

1. Set the oven to 450°F. Cut each potato in half lengthwise and scrape out the middle to create two boats. (Save the scooped-out potato flesh for Creamy Potato, Sausage & Kale Soup, page 205.)

2. Use a silicone basting brush to brush the skin of each potato boat with avocado oil, then sprinkle the oiled skins with salt. Grease a rimmed baking sheet with more avocado oil, then lay the potato boats skin side up on the sheet.

3. Bake for about 15 minutes, until crispy.

poultry brine

Makes 6¾ cups or 3 cups | Prep Time: 5 minutes | Wait Time: 30 minutes, plus time to cool

This brine is a must for your Thanksgiving turkey (see my Holiday Turkey recipe on page 320), but I have to tell you: I use it for chicken throughout the year, when turkey isn't as readily available. (Try my Brined Chicken Thighs with Potatoes on page 296.) It's so good that you'll never want to eat turkey or chicken that hasn't been brined again!

To make 6¾ cups (enough for 12 to 14 pounds of turkey parts):

6 cups water

½ cup coarse pink salt

¼ cup coconut sugar

4 sprigs fresh rosemary

4 sprigs fresh thyme

4 cloves garlic, smashed with the side of a knife

1 teaspoon black peppercorns

To make 3 cups (enough for 3 pounds of bone-in chicken parts):

3 cups water

¼ cup coarse pink salt

2 tablespoons coconut sugar

2 sprigs fresh rosemary

2 sprigs fresh thyme

2 cloves garlic, smashed with the side of a knife

½ teaspoon black peppercorns

1. Bring the water to a boil. Turn off the heat, add the rest of the brine ingredients, cover, and let sit for 30 minutes.

2. Remove the lid and let the brine come to room temperature before using.

barbecue sauce

Makes 3 cups | Prep Time: 10 minutes

2 (7-ounce) jars tomato paste

½ cup honey

⅓ cup apple cider vinegar

1 ounce dairy-free dark chocolate (70% cacao or higher), melted in a double boiler (see page 46)

1 to 3 teaspoons chili powder, to taste

1 teaspoon tamarind paste (optional)

1 teaspoon gluten-free fish sauce

¾ teaspoon fine sea salt

½ teaspoon garlic powder

¼ teaspoon ground celery seed

⅛ teaspoon ground black pepper

This sauce is from my book The Paleo Chocolate Lovers' Cookbook, *which includes eleven dinner recipes.*

1. Place all of the ingredients in a blender and puree until smooth.

2. Store the sauce in a glass container in the refrigerator for up to 2 weeks. If you freeze it, leave an inch of space at the top of the jar for expansion.

guacamole

Makes about 2 cups | Prep Time: 10 minutes

Like my homemade chicken broth (opposite), you can add more ingredients to this recipe (such as cumin, cayenne, jalapeño pepper, or diced onion) if you want to boost the flavor even further. This book is all about keeping it real, and this recipe, as written, is how I really make it. Just these four fresh ingredients make excellent guacamole. We put guac on salad, eggs, and sliced jicama, in addition to Taco Boats (page 306) and Burrito Bowls (page 309).

2 cups mashed avocado (about 4 avocados)

2 teaspoons packed chopped fresh cilantro, plus more for garnish, if desired

2 tablespoons fresh-squeezed lime juice

½ teaspoon fine sea salt

Combine all of the ingredients in a bowl. Serve garnished with cilantro, if desired.

pizza sauce

Makes about 1¾ cups | Prep Time: 5 minutes

1 (7-ounce) jar tomato paste

7 ounces strained tomatoes (from a 24-ounce jar)

2 teaspoons Italian seasoning

1 teaspoon apple cider vinegar

½ teaspoon onion powder

½ teaspoon fine sea salt

¼ teaspoon garlic powder

1. Place the tomato paste in a small mixing bowl. Use the empty tomato paste jar to measure the same amount of strained tomatoes and add them to the mixing bowl. Add the rest of the ingredients and stir well to combine.

2. Store the sauce in a glass container in the refrigerator for up to 2 weeks.

chicken broth

Makes about 2 quarts | Prep Time: 5 minutes | Cook Time: 10 hours

I make my slow-cooked Faux Rotisserie Chicken (page 296) almost every week, and I use the leftover bones and juices to make broth. However, you can make broth with any bones that you have on hand. If you're making Brined Chicken Thighs (page 296) or Baja Drumsticks (page 314), then you can use those bones instead.

The ingredients listed below are the bare minimum you need to make great broth. To make your broth even more amazing, add two whole carrots, two stalks of celery, and a handful of fresh parsley. Discard them after cooking as you do the onion, garlic, and bones.

My kids love this broth just as it is. Ashley and I often drink a hot mug of it first thing in the morning. But the kids' favorite way to enjoy this broth is in soups; look for those that are have the Kids' Favorite icon.

Bones left over from Faux Rotisserie Chicken (page 296)

Juices reserved from Faux Rotisserie Chicken (page 296)

1 onion, cut in half

3 cloves garlic, smashed with the side of a knife

1 tablespoon apple cider vinegar

1 teaspoon fine sea salt

1. Place all of the ingredients in a 7-quart slow cooker. Fill the slow cooker with water, leaving about 2 inches of space at the top. Cover and cook on low for 10 hours.

2. Allow the broth to cool, then strain through a fine-mesh sieve. Discard the solids.

3. Store the broth in a glass container in the refrigerator for up to a week, or freeze for later use. If you freeze it, leave an inch of space at the top of the jar for expansion.

baking mixes

After a decade of baking without using mixes, I became fairly quick at measuring out multiple flours, baking soda, salt, and so on. However, every time I use my mixes, I continue to be amazed at how much faster and easier it is. My husband and kids, who never used to cook before, now bake with my mixes constantly.

For complete lists of the recipes that use each of these mixes, see the index. To ensure perfection in every one of those recipes, and to make the mixes more quickly, use a scale and weigh your ingredients. You can also purchase my baking mixes premade from my website, The Spunky Coconut.

Tips for Using My Mixes

· *Make sure to combine your mixes REALLY well. I use 1-gallon cracker jars (shown below) to hold my mixes, so I shake, shake, and shake some more. Then, when I think they're well combined, I shake again. You get the point.*

· *Store nut-free mixes tightly sealed in a cabinet or pantry for up to a month. Mixes containing nut flour can be stored tightly sealed in the refrigerator for a month or more.*

· *When you are making a recipe with a mix and using a scale to measure the ingredients, do NOT dump the mix straight into the bowl, or you will end up with a mess. Instead, use a scoop or serving spoon to add the mix to the bowl until the weight is correct.*

pizza & bread mix

Makes about 6¾ cups | Prep Time: 10 minutes

This mix can be used to make Bagels (page 160), Pumpkin Cinnamon Rolls (page 168), Sandwich Bread (page 270), and Barbecue Chicken Pizza (page 292). This amount of mix is enough for four pizzas, two loaves of bread plus two batches of bagels, or three batches of cinnamon rolls.

3¼ cups (410 g) coconut flour

3¼ cups (406 g) arrowroot or tapioca flour

Just under 2 tablespoons (30 g) baking soda

1 tablespoon plus 2 teaspoons (14 g) psyllium husk powder

1 tablespoon plus 1½ teaspoons (30 g) fine sea salt

scone & pie crust mix

Makes about 10 cups | Prep Time: 10 minutes

This amount of mix makes seven batches of Chocolate Chip Scones (page 176), four batches of Pizza Quiche 2.0 (page 192), or six Sweet Pie Crusts (page 135) plus two batches of Crackers (page 282).

3¼ cups (410 g) coconut flour

3¼ cups (406 g) arrowroot or tapioca flour

2¾ cups (306 g) almond or cashew flour

1¼ cups (145 g) ground golden flax seeds

2 tablespoons (36 g) baking soda

½ teaspoon (6 g) fine sea salt

pancake & muffin mix

Makes almost 9 cups | Prep Time: 10 minutes

This amount of mix makes four batches of Best-Ever Pancakes (page 158) plus two batches of Crepes (page 157), or five batches of Cherry Muffins (page 172).

3¼ cups (410 g) coconut flour

3¼ cups (406 g) arrowroot or tapioca flour

2¾ cups (306 g) almond or cashew flour

2 tablespoons (36 g) baking soda

Instructions for all three mixes:

Mix the ingredients together very well. See "Tips for Using My Mixes," opposite, for directions on storing and using the mixes.

savory pie crust

Makes one 10-inch, deep-dish pie crust or two 7-inch pie crusts | Prep Time: 5 to 10 minutes

You can use this crust for any quiche recipe you like. I use it mainly for making Pizza Quiche 2.0 (page 192), because it's our favorite.

2⅓ cups (322 g) Scone & Pie Crust Mix (page 133)

½ cup softened ghee, palm shortening, or melted coconut oil

½ cup water

Place all of the ingredients in a large mixing bowl. Combine with a handheld mixer until the mixture begins to clump together. Press into the bottom and up the sides of one 10-inch pie pan (as shown opposite) or two 7-inch pie pans.

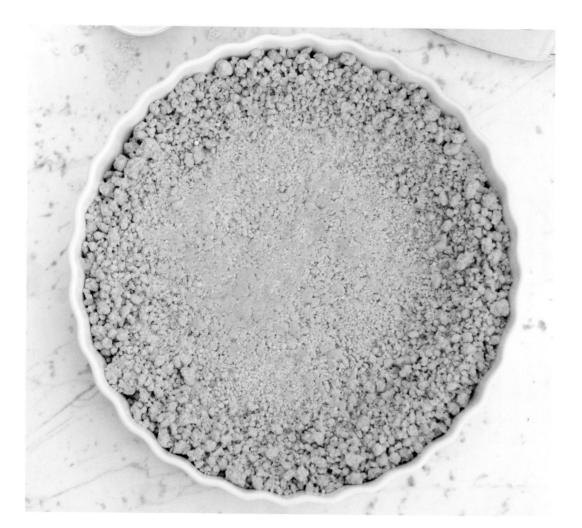

sweet pie crust

Makes one 9-inch pie crust | Prep Time: 5 to 10 minutes

My family adores pie, as you might have guessed given the number of pie recipes I have included in this book (see chapter 16). My pies are lightly sweetened, easy to make, and real crowd-pleasers. The Blueberry Pie (page 368) is probably my favorite, but I love them all.

1 cup plus 3 tablespoons (160 g) Scone & Pie Crust Mix (page 133)

¼ cup softened ghee, palm shortening, or melted coconut oil

¼ cup water

⅛ teaspoon liquid vanilla stevia

Place all of the ingredients in a large mixing bowl. Combine with a handheld mixer until the mixture begins to clump together (as shown opposite). Press into the bottom and up the sides of a 9-inch pie pan.

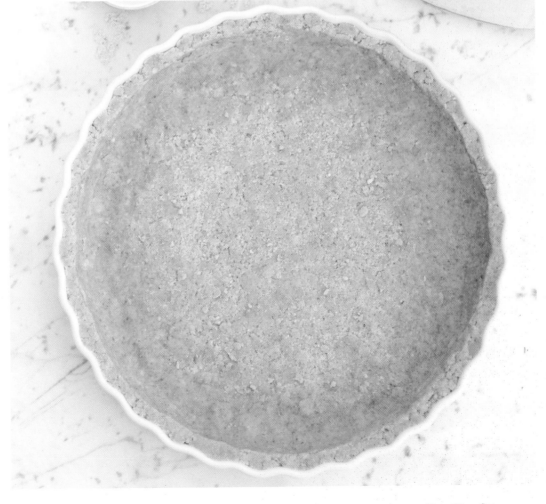

orange chutney

Makes 1 cup | Prep Time: 10 minutes | Cook Time: 30 minutes

I am crazy about this chutney. I first had it at my friend Marlene's house, and I was instantly hooked. I make it the same way she does, then use all the self-control I can muster not to eat the whole batch in one day. Spread it on bread or just eat it with a spoon!

1 packed cup finely chopped navel orange peel

1 cup water

¼ cup honey

Big pinch of fine sea salt

1. Place all of the ingredients in a small heavy-bottomed pot and bring to a simmer. Cover and continue simmering for about 30 minutes, until the orange peel is tender. Let cool.

2. Store in a glass container in the refrigerator for up to a week.

tart cranberry sauce

Serves 8 | Prep Time: 10 minutes | Cook Time: 20 minutes

This recipe is from my book Dairy-Free Ice Cream. *It's a Thanksgiving favorite, of course, but I love to use it on ice cream throughout the fall season!*

16 ounces fresh cranberries

2 tablespoons finely grated orange zest

1 cup fresh-squeezed orange juice

½ cup coconut sugar

2 cinnamon sticks

¼ teaspoon ginger powder (optional)

⅛ teaspoon fine sea salt

1. Discard any crushed or bad cranberries, then place the cranberries in a medium-sized heavy-bottomed pot. Add the orange zest, orange juice, coconut sugar, cinnamon sticks, ginger (if using), and salt. Simmer, uncovered, until the cranberries are tender, about 20 minutes. Remove and discard the cinnamon sticks and let the sauce cool.

2. Store in a glass container in the refrigerator for up to 2 weeks. Cranberry sauce also freezes well.

strawberry rose hip jam

Makes 1 scant cup | Prep Time: 10 minutes | Wait Time: 30 minutes | Cook Time: 5 to 10 minutes

Rose hips are known for being high in vitamin C, B-complex vitamins, and more, making them a powerful tool for fighting colds and flu. My family really enjoys this rose hip jam and the tea that results from the steeping process. My dear friend Amanda, who is an herbalist, tells me that soaking rose hips in juice is another common way to make rose hip jam. I buy organic rose hips online.

⅓ cup plus 2 tablespoons rose hips

1 quart plus ¼ cup water

10 ounces fresh or frozen strawberries

1 tablespoon fresh-squeezed lemon juice

1 tablespoon coconut sugar

Big pinch of fine sea salt

1. Pick out any stems or seeds from the rose hips, then place the rose hips in a 2-liter glass jug. Bring the water almost to a boil, then pour it into the jug with the rose hips. Let the rose hips steep in the water for about 30 minutes, until softened. (Alternatively, use the overnight, cold brew method found on page 150.)

2. Strain the liquid into another jug and serve it as rose hip tea, sweetened with a little honey. Place the rose hips in a blender or a food processor fitted with the S-blade. Add the strawberries, lemon juice, coconut sugar, and salt and puree until almost smooth.

3. Transfer the puree to a small heavy-bottomed pot and bring to a simmer. Reduce the heat to low, cover, and simmer for 5 to 10 minutes, until thickened slightly. Let cool.

4. Store in a glass container in the refrigerator for up to a week.

chapter 7:
Drinks

"coffee" smoothie

Serves 1 | Prep Time: 5 minutes

Dandelion tea is a great herbal alternative to coffee. It also helps with regularity and reduces inflammation.

½ cup chilled dandelion tea (brewed with 2 bags)

½ cup unsweetened almond milk

1 soft Medjool date, pitted

1 tablespoon golden flax seeds

2 tablespoons powdered collagen (see page 26)

6 cubes frozen full-fat coconut milk

Place all of the ingredients in a blender and puree until completely smooth.

Note: *To make enough for the meal plan (see page 70), you will need to quadruple this recipe. Based on the capacity of most blender jars, this is best done in two double batches, each consisting of the following quantities: 1 cup chilled dandelion tea (brewed with 4 bags), 1 cup unsweetened almond milk, 2 Medjool dates, 2 tablespoons golden flax seeds, ¼ cup powdered collagen, and 12 cubes frozen full-fat coconut milk.*

salted caramel shake

Serves 1 | Prep Time: 5 minutes

1 cup unsweetened almond milk

2 tablespoons powdered collagen (see page 26)

1 tablespoon golden flax seeds

1 soft Medjool date, pitted

1½ teaspoons cocoa powder

⅛ teaspoon fine sea salt

6 cubes frozen full-fat coconut milk

Place all of the ingredients in a blender and puree until completely smooth.

cashew milk

Makes about 4 cups | Wait Time: overnight | Prep Time: 5 minutes

I use cashew milk to make some of the ice cream in my book Dairy-Free Ice Cream *and in this book to make Mashed Potatoes & Gravy (page 242) and Green Bean Casserole (page 244). You can substitute coconut milk for a nut-free option, but I don't recommend substituting almond milk in recipes that call for cashew milk. If you use a high-powered blender, you do not need to strain the cashew milk as you do milks made with other kinds of nuts, such as almonds or hazelnuts.*

1 cup (132 g) raw cashews

4 cups water, plus more for soaking

1. Soak the cashews in the refrigerator overnight in enough water to cover, plus 2 inches. In the morning, drain and rinse the cashews and discard the soaking water, which contains enzyme inhibitors.

2. Puree the nuts with the 4 cups of water in a high-powered blender until completely smooth.

3. Store in a glass container in the refrigerator for up to 5 days.

Note: *To make cashew milk without a high-powered blender, use as little water as possible to puree, then slowly add the rest of the water while blending. The milk will be more likely to separate, so stir before using.*

Variation: Almond Milk.
Almond milk is made exactly the same way. The only difference is that after pureeing the soaked nuts with the water, you need to strain almond milk using either a nut milk bag or cheesecloth to remove the pulp. I stopped making my own almond milk, though, except on those rare occasions when I want to use the wet pulp to make cookies or biscuits. For convenience, I buy store-bought almond milk that is non-GMO and free of carrageenan.

detox piña colada

Makes 1 large or 2 small smoothies | Prep Time: 10 minutes

Mason jar straw lids are popping up everywhere, and my family loves them! These lids have a hole and come with a reusable straw. You can find them in craft stores and home goods stores and online. They are perfect for sipping this yummy and refreshing drink, which contains several ingredients that are good for detox, including turmeric and beets.

¼ to ½ cup water, as needed to puree

1 cup coarsely chopped or chunked fresh pineapple

1 golden beet, scrubbed, trimmed, and chopped

1 (½-inch) piece fresh peeled turmeric or ½ teaspoon turmeric powder

1 (½-inch) piece fresh peeled ginger or ½ teaspoon ginger powder

1 tablespoon powdered collagen (see page 26)

6 cubes frozen full-fat coconut milk

A few fresh mint leaves (optional)

10 drops liquid vanilla stevia (optional)

Place all of the ingredients in the order listed in a high-powered blender, beginning with ¼ cup water. Puree until completely smooth, adding up to ¼ cup more water as needed.

Note: *To make enough for the meal plan (see page 78), you will need to quadruple this recipe. Based on the capacity of most blender jars, this is best done in two double batches, each consisting of the following quantities: ½ to 1 cup water, as needed, 2 cups chopped pineapple, 2 golden beets, 1 (1-inch) piece fresh peeled turmeric or 1 teaspoon turmeric powder, 1 (1-inch) piece fresh peeled ginger or 1 teaspoon ginger powder, 2 tablespoons powdered collagen, 12 cubes frozen full-fat coconut milk, 5 or 6 fresh mint leaves (optional), and ⅛ scant teaspoon liquid vanilla stevia (optional).*

magenta ginger juice

Serves 2 | Prep Time: 10 minutes

1 large or 2 small beets, scrubbed, trimmed, and cut in half

2 Granny Smith apples, cored and quartered

1 lemon, peeled and seeded

1 (½-inch) piece fresh ginger

1 (½-inch) piece turmeric root or ½ teaspoon turmeric powder

1 bunch chard or kale

Big pinch of fine sea salt

Naturally sparkling water (optional)

Liquid vanilla stevia (optional)

1. In a juicer, juice all of the ingredients, except for the sparkling water and stevia. I find that it works best to sandwich the chard or kale, ginger, turmeric, and salt between pieces of apple or beet in the juicer.

2. Pour the juice into two glasses. Add a splash of sparkling water and stevia to taste, if desired.

Note: *This drink is great for liver detox, and Ashley and I can't get enough of it. My husband and youngest daughter enjoy it, too.*

chilled dandelion mocha

Serves 2 | Prep Time: 5 minutes | Wait Time: overnight

My kids are crazy for carob, which is naturally sweet, and they love how this drink looks in a clear glass with a straw. After all, you eat first with your eyes! I love that they're getting dandelion, which is good for detoxification.

2½ cups water, just off the boil

6 tea bags dandelion tea

1 (13½-ounce) can full-fat coconut milk

3 tablespoons carob powder

1 tablespoon honey

Splash of Hazelnut Coffee Creamer (page 114) (optional; omit for nut-free)

Pinch of fine sea salt

1. Place the water and bags of dandelion tea in a large glass measuring cup with a spout. Steep the tea for 5 minutes, then remove the bags.

2. Add the steeped tea and the rest of the ingredients to a blender and puree. Divide the mocha evenly between two glasses and refrigerate overnight to chill completely and create the lovely ombré effect shown in the photo.

eggnog

Makes about 2 quarts | Prep Time: 10 minutes | Cook Time: 5 minutes

8 large egg yolks

2 (13½-ounce) cans full-fat coconut milk, divided

3 cups unsweetened almond milk (or more coconut milk for nut-free)

¾ cup coconut sugar

1 tablespoon vanilla extract

2 teaspoons ground cinnamon

½ teaspoon ground nutmeg

⅛ teaspoon ground allspice

For serving (optional):

Whipped Coconut Cream (page 366)

Ground nutmeg

1. In a blender, puree the egg yolks with the contents of one can of coconut milk. Pour into a large mixing bowl. Set aside.

2. Place a large heavy-bottomed pot over medium heat. Add the almond milk, the second can of coconut milk, coconut sugar, vanilla, cinnamon, nutmeg, and allspice to the pot and bring to a simmer.

3. Very slowly ladle a little of the hot liquid into the egg yolk mixture, whisking constantly. Continue this process until you have whisked in about 2 cups of the hot liquid, then transfer the tempered egg yolk mixture to the pot. Simmer, while whisking, for about 3 minutes to thicken and cook the eggs.

4. Remove from the heat and serve hot, or refrigerate for later if you prefer it chilled. Garnish each serving with a dollop of Whipped Coconut Cream and a sprinkle of ground nutmeg, if desired.

tea

Many people find that cold-brewed coffee and tea are less bitter and therefore need less sweetener. Both methods are presented below, and either can be used to make the four flavors of tea that follow.

Cold Brew Method: *Soak the tea (or flowers or rose hips) in 1 quart of water overnight. Pour the tea-infused water through a fine-mesh sieve into a 2-quart glass pitcher. Heat 1 cup of fresh water and use it to dissolve the honey, adding the remaining 3 cups of water to the tea. Add the honey water to the pitcher and stir.*

Hot Brew Method: *Heat 1 quart of water until it's hot. (It doesn't have to boil.) Place the hot water and tea in a heatproof glass pitcher and steep for 5 minutes. Pour the tea through a fine-mesh sieve into a 2-quart glass pitcher. Add the honey to the warm tea and stir to dissolve. Add the remaining quart of water to the tea as well.*

jasmine green tea

Makes 2 quarts | Steep Time: 5 minutes or overnight, depending on method used

3 tablespoons loose-leaf jasmine green tea

2 quarts water, divided

1 tablespoon honey

hibiscus tea

Makes 2 quarts | Steep Time: 5 minutes or overnight, depending on method used

3 to 6 tablespoons dried hibiscus flowers

2 quarts water, divided

1 tablespoon honey

chamomile tea

Makes 2 quarts | Steep Time: 5 minutes or overnight, depending on method used

⅓ cup plus 2 tablespoons dried chamomile flowers

2 quarts water, divided

1 tablespoon honey

Note: *Chamomile is great for anxiety, upset stomach, and insomnia, but we enjoy it even when we aren't treating one of those issues.*

rose hip tea

Makes 2 quarts | Steep Time: 5 minutes or overnight, depending on method used

⅓ cup plus 2 tablespoons dried rose hips

2 quarts water, divided

1 tablespoon honey

Note: *Rose hips have more vitamin C than oranges or any other citrus fruit and are excellent at preventing and fighting colds and flu. Rose hip tea, brewed in a slightly different manner, is also the basis of my recipe for Strawberry Rose Hip Jam (page 138).*

molten chocolate

Serves 2 to 4 | Prep Time: 5 minutes | Cook Time: 5 minutes

This recipe comes from my healthy chocolate book The Paleo Chocolate Lovers' Cookbook. *Make it once, and you will see that there is no better way to enjoy hot chocolate.*

1 cup full-fat coconut milk

3 ounces dairy-free dark chocolate, melted

4 soft Medjool dates, pitted

1 vanilla bean, split lengthwise and scraped

1¼ cups unsweetened almond milk (or more coconut milk for nut-free)

1. In a blender, puree the coconut milk, melted chocolate, dates, and vanilla bean seeds until completely smooth.

2. Add the almond milk to the chocolate puree in the blender. Puree again until smooth.

3. Pour the chocolate mixture into a saucepan and heat gently until molten.

4. Serve hot.

pumpkin spice latte

Serves 1 | Prep Time: 5 minutes | Cook Time: 5 minutes

1 cup brewed coffee or dandelion tea (for decaf)

1 cup full-fat coconut milk

2 teaspoons maple syrup

¼ teaspoon Pumpkin Spice Blend (page 118)

1. Place all of the ingredients in a small saucepan and bring almost to a simmer, watching carefully so that it doesn't boil over.

2. Pour the hot liquid into a blender with a vented lid (it must have a vent or it could explode). Puree on low speed for 30 seconds.

3. Serve hot.

Note: *To make enough latte for the meal plan (see page 94), you will need to quadruple this recipe. Based on the capacity of most blender jars, this is best done in two double batches, each consisting of the following quantities: 2 cups brewed coffee or dandelion tea, 2 cups full-fat coconut milk, 1 tablespoon plus 1 teaspoon maple syrup, and ½ teaspoon Pumpkin Spice Blend.*

chapter 8:
Breakfast Anytime

crepes

Makes seven 6-inch crepes | Prep Time: 5 minutes | Cook Time: 20 minutes

Unlike the crepe recipes in my earlier book The Paleo Chocolate Lovers' Cookbook, *these crepes use whole eggs to make life easier.*

Batter:

4 large eggs

½ cup full-fat coconut milk

½ cup (70 g) Pancake & Muffin Mix (page 133)

1 tablespoon ghee

6 drops liquid vanilla stevia

3½ teaspoons coconut oil, divided

For serving (optional):

Fresh berries of choice

1 batch Whipped Coconut Cream (page 366)

1. Place the batter ingredients in a blender and puree until smooth.

2. Heat an 8-inch stainless-steel skillet over medium-low heat. After the skillet has heated for 1 to 2 minutes, add ½ teaspoon of coconut oil and swirl it around.

3. When the coconut oil has melted, measure ¼ cup of the batter and pour it into the skillet. Lift the skillet and swirl the batter outward, making the crepe slightly larger in diameter. When it's golden on the bottom, flip the crepe and cook for only a few seconds on the other side.

4. Repeat with the rest of the batter, melting ½ teaspoon of coconut oil in the skillet before making each crepe.

5. Serve the crepes topped with fresh berries and Whipped Coconut Cream, if desired.

best-ever pancakes

Makes about fifteen 4-inch pancakes | Prep Time: 5 minutes | Cook Time: 20 minutes

These pancakes are extremely popular with my readers, who began sharing them on Instagram with the hashtag #besteverpaleopancakes. With my Pancake & Muffin Mix in your pantry, they are easier than ever to make!

Batter:

5 large eggs

1⅔ cups (233 g) Pancake & Muffin Mix (page 133)

1 cup unsweetened almond milk

2 tablespoons melted ghee or coconut oil, plus more for greasing the pan

2 tablespoons honey

For serving:

Maple syrup, warmed

1. Place the batter ingredients in a blender and puree until smooth.

2. Heat a 12-inch skillet over low to medium heat. (Note that these pancakes need to cook over lower heat than traditional pancakes, so make sure not to let the burner get too hot.) Grease the pan with coconut oil, then pour four small pancakes, each about 3 inches in diameter. Quickly spread each pancake with the back of a spoon so that they are about 4 inches wide. Cook until browned on the first side, about 90 seconds, then flip and cook until nicely browned on the other side.

3. Repeat with the remaining batter, greasing the pan again before making each batch.

4. Serve the pancakes with warm maple syrup.

Note: *You may need to adjust the mix-to-milk ratio slightly, depending on the brands of flour that you use in your mix. If your batter is too thick, add another ½ cup of milk. The next time you make the pancakes, you can use 1 cup of milk but decrease the amount of mix by ⅓ cup.*

bagels

Makes 4 bagels | Prep Time: 20 minutes | Cook Time: 25 minutes

The traditional way to make bagels is to boil them before baking them, but I don't have time for that. These bagels are super easy, and I promise you're going to love them. I've included optional add-ins for making cinnamon raisin bagels and onion bagels because those are my family's favorites, but feel free to make yours garlic, sesame, or any other flavor you like. This dough also makes great rolls for burgers and sandwiches.

½ cup (80 g) golden flax seeds

¾ cup hot water

1 tablespoon apple cider vinegar

1 tablespoon honey

¼ cup melted coconut oil

1 cup (136 g) Pizza & Bread Mix (page 133)

Add-ins for cinnamon raisin bagels (optional):

2 teaspoons ground cinnamon

¼ cup raisins

Add-in for onion bagels (optional):

1 teaspoon onion powder

1. Set the oven to 350°F and line a baking sheet with unbleached parchment paper.

2. Grind the flax seeds in a Magic Bullet blender or coffee grinder, then transfer them to a mixing bowl. Pour the hot water on top and gently stir to combine. Add the vinegar, honey, and coconut oil and stir again.

3. Add the Pizza & Bread Mix and the add-ins of your choice. Combine with a handheld mixer for about 20 seconds. Use a flexible spatula to press the dough into one solid mass, then divide it into four equal-sized pieces. Roll each ball of dough in your hands, then push your thumb through the middle and shape the dough into a ring around your thumb. Smooth the bagels as best you can with your fingers, then lay them on the prepared baking sheet. Bake for about 25 minutes, until golden.

4. Store in an airtight container at room temperature for up to 2 days or in the refrigerator for up to a week. If they have been refrigerated, toast the bagels to soften them before serving.

mini boulder cream donuts

Makes 8 mini donuts | Prep Time: 30 minutes | Cook Time: 35 minutes

This dough can be fussy because not all squash is the same. The drier the squash, the less coconut flour you need. But have no fear: Even if the donuts deflate and the insides are chewy, these donuts are crazy good. Also, they become drier the next day, so donuts that seemed too doughy will become less doughy. For more reliable results, measure the flour by weight (grams) rather than volume (cups).

Dough:

¾ cup unsweetened almond or cashew milk (page 143)

½ cup cooked and pureed butternut squash, sweet potato, or pumpkin* (or use canned pumpkin puree)

¼ cup honey

2 tablespoons melted ghee

1 tablespoon vanilla extract

½ teaspoon fine sea salt

¼ teaspoon baking soda

⅛ teaspoon liquid vanilla stevia

2 tablespoons psyllium husk powder

½ cup lightly packed (80 g) coconut flour, sifted

Cream filling:

½ cup melted coconut butter/cream concentrate

2 tablespoons honey

1 teaspoon vanilla extract

1 tablespoon coconut flour, sifted, if needed

4 to 6 tablespoons water, as needed

Chocolate coconut butter frosting:

½ cup melted coconut butter/cream concentrate

2 tablespoons cocoa powder (sift if lumpy)

2 tablespoons honey

1 teaspoon vanilla extract

4 to 6 tablespoons water, as needed

1. Set the oven to 375°F and line a baking sheet with unbleached parchment paper.

2. Place the almond milk, squash, honey, melted ghee, vanilla, salt, baking soda, and stevia in a blender. Add the psyllium husk powder last, right before blending. Puree for about 20 seconds, then immediately pour the mixture into a mixing bowl. Add the coconut flour and combine with a handheld mixer.

3. Pack the dough firmly into a large ice cream scoop with a lever and level it off. Use the lever to transfer the dough to the prepared baking sheet. Repeat with the remaining dough, making 8 donuts total. Bake the donuts for about 35 minutes, until golden brown. Let cool completely before filling and frosting.

4. Make the filling: Place the melted coconut butter/cream concentrate, honey, and vanilla in a small bowl and stir. If the mixture is very runny, like maple syrup, add a tablespoon of coconut flour. Add a tablespoon of water at a time until the filling is smooth. (See step-by-step photos, opposite.)

5. Make the frosting: Place the melted coconut butter/cream concentrate, cocoa powder, honey, and vanilla in another small bowl and stir. Add a tablespoon of water at a time until the frosting is smooth. (See step-by-step photos, opposite.)

6. Insert a paring knife into the side of each donut, being careful not to go all the way through.

*See page 49 for how to cook a butternut squash or pumpkin.

Move the knife from left to right inside the donut to make the space for the filling. Add the cream filling to a plastic food storage bag and cut ⅛ inch off a corner of the bag. Insert the tip of the bag into each donut and slowly fill the space you created with the cream filling. Frost the top of each donut with the chocolate frosting.

7. Store in an airtight container at room temperature for up to 2 days. These donuts are even better as leftovers.

Ingredients for the chocolate coconut butter frosting (left) and the cream filling (right) before being stirred.

The chocolate coconut butter frosting and cream filling after being stirred, but before being thinned to the proper consistency with water.

The chocolate coconut butter frosting and cream filling thinned to a smooth consistency.

Note: *Boston cream was my favorite donut flavor before I was diagnosed with celiac disease. I call this healthier version Boulder Cream Donuts because I created it when we lived near Boulder, Colorado.*

MINI BOULDER
CREAM DONUTS

cherry almond bars

Makes 6 bars | Prep Time: 10 minutes | Wait Time: overnight

1½ cups slivered almonds

1 cup dried sour cherries

⅛ teaspoon fine sea salt

1 to 3 teaspoons water, as needed

1. Line an 8-inch square baking dish with unbleached parchment paper and pinch the corners to help the paper stay in place. Set aside.

2. Place the almonds, cherries, and salt in a food processor fitted with the S-blade. Puree for about 30 seconds, until finely ground. Slowly add the water, a teaspoon at a time, stopping when a ball begins to form.

3. Press the mass into the prepared dish and refrigerate overnight. Slice into 6 bars and serve for breakfast or as a snack.

4. Store in the refrigerator for up to a week.

cheese danish

Makes 4 | Prep Time: 20 minutes | Cook Time: 10 minutes | Wait Time: 20 minutes

The most popular recipe in my book The Paleo Chocolate Lovers' Cookbook *is the Chocolate Swirl Cheese Danish Cake. I combined the "cream cheese" component of that recipe with my Pizza & Bread Mix for a more breadlike cheese Danish. Top these with fresh fruit or jam, if you like.*

Cream cheese:

½ cup raw cashews

¼ cup unsweetened almond milk

2 tablespoons melted coconut oil or ghee

1 large egg white

1 tablespoon honey

1 teaspoon vanilla extract

⅛ teaspoon fine sea salt

Dough:

¾ cup (102 g) Pizza & Bread Mix (page 133)

¼ cup water

¼ cup ghee or palm shortening

1 large egg

1 tablespoon honey

1. Set the oven to 350°F and line a baking sheet with unbleached parchment paper.

2. In a mini blender, puree the cream cheese ingredients until completely smooth. Set aside.

3. In a mixing bowl, combine the dough ingredients with a handheld mixer. Press the dough into one solid mass, then divide it into four equal-sized pieces. Roll each piece into a ball, then flatten it on the baking sheet. Press it into a 4-inch circle with your fingers and create a ¼-inch "wall" around the edge of the dough.

4. Add the cream cheese to each well that you created so that it is level with the top of the wall.

5. Bake the Danish for about 10 minutes, until the edges are golden. Let cool on the baking sheet, then put the baking sheet in the refrigerator for 20 minutes to set the Danish completely.

6. Enjoy the Danish at room temperature.

7. Store in the refrigerator for up to a week.

pumpkin cinnamon rolls

Makes 8 | Prep Time: 25 minutes | Cook Time: 35 minutes

Like my bagels (page 160), these rolls are going to blow your mind. They're fluffy, chewy, and light, with just the right amount of sweetness. Don't omit the psyllium husk powder—it's the key ingredient for all of the qualities I just mentioned. I buy it on iHerb.com.

Dough:

2 cups (272 g) Pizza & Bread Mix (page 133)

1 tablespoon plus 1 teaspoon psyllium husk powder

1 teaspoon baking soda

¾ cup pumpkin puree

2 tablespoons apple cider vinegar

2 tablespoons honey

¼ teaspoon liquid vanilla stevia

½ cup melted coconut oil, plus more for greasing the baking dish

Filling:

½ cup pumpkin puree

½ cup coconut sugar

1½ teaspoons Pumpkin Spice Blend (page 118)

1½ teaspoons ground cinnamon

Frosting (optional; omit for nut-free):

½ cup full-fat coconut milk

½ cup raw macadamia nuts, plus more as needed

2 tablespoons honey

1. In a mixing bowl, whisk together the Pizza & Bread Mix, psyllium husk powder, and baking soda until very well combined.

2. To the bowl with the dry ingredients, add the pumpkin puree, vinegar, honey, and stevia. Add the melted coconut oil last, just before mixing. Combine with a handheld mixer for about 20 seconds to form the dough.

3. Press the dough into one solid mass and lay it on a piece of unbleached parchment paper. Place another piece of parchment on top and roll the dough into a rectangle about ¼ inch thick. As you roll, occasionally remove the top piece of parchment and use your hands to press the edges in for a nice rectangle shape.

4. Set the oven to 350°F and grease a 1½- to 2-quart baking dish with coconut oil. Set aside.

5. Place the filling ingredients in a clean mixing bowl and stir to combine. Pour the filling over the dough, then use a flexible spatula to spread it evenly. Leave a 1-inch border without filling along one long side of the dough.

6. Begin tightly rolling the long side that has the filling. Continue rolling until you get to the edge without filling. To keep the filling from spilling out, use the parchment to help you lift the dough as you roll it up.

7. Cut the dough crosswise into 8 rolls using a chef's knife, slicing slowly and using a back-and-forth motion to avoid flattening the rolls. Lay the rolls cut side up in the pan and bake for about 35 minutes, until the edges are slightly brown.

8. While the rolls are baking, puree the frosting ingredients in a blender (a mini blender works best for this amount). Add more nuts until the preferred thickness is reached.

9. Serve the rolls warm, right after you remove them from the oven, drizzled with the frosting.

10. Store unfrosted rolls in an airtight container at room temperature for up to 2 days or refrigerate for up to a week. The frosting must be refrigerated.

strawberry rhubarb gummies

Makes about 12 | Prep Time: 10 minutes | Cook Time: 20 minutes | Wait Time: 3 hours

Gummies for breakfast may seem a little unorthodox, but gelatin's many health benefits make it a surefire winner. My littlest adores dinosaurs, so I got her a dinosaur cookie cutter for these gummies, which we all love.

10 ounces frozen strawberries

10 ounces fresh rhubarb (about 3 stalks), cut into 1-inch lengths, or 10 ounces precut frozen rhubarb

½ cup water

⅓ cup fresh-squeezed lemon juice

¼ cup honey

⅓ cup grass-fed gelatin

Pinch of fine sea salt

10 drops liquid vanilla stevia, or to taste

1. Place the strawberries and rhubarb in a medium-sized pot and bring to a simmer. Continue to simmer until the rhubarb is tender, about 15 minutes. Let cool while you make the gelatin mixture.

2. Place the water, lemon juice, and honey in a small saucepan and bring to a simmer. Gradually whisk in the gelatin. Continue to simmer, whisking constantly, until the gelatin has fully dissolved.

3. Combine the strawberries and rhubarb and the gelatin mixture in a blender with a vented lid and puree until smooth. (Or use a stick blender to puree.) Add the salt and stevia and blend once more to combine.

4. Pour the puree into a 13 by 9-inch baking dish lined with unbleached parchment paper and refrigerate for at least 3 hours, until set.

5. Use cookie cutters to cut out about 12 gummies, or slice into 12 squares.

6. Store in the refrigerator for up to a week.

cherry muffins

Makes 12 | Prep Time: 15 minutes | Cook Time: 24 minutes

I always keep frozen cherries handy for making muffins. To quickly thaw the cherries, spread them evenly in a baking dish and pop them in a 350°F oven for about 5 minutes, until just thawed. These muffins are great to grab and go on busy mornings.

¼ cup melted coconut oil

1½ cups (223 g) Pancake & Muffin Mix (page 133)

½ cup unsweetened almond milk

¼ cup maple syrup*

5 large eggs, room temperature (see Note)

1½ cups pitted fresh or frozen cherries

*You may substitute honey, but the bottoms will be drier. These muffins are better when made with maple syrup.

1. Set the oven to 350°F and line a 12-well muffin pan with unbleached paper liners.

2. Place all of the ingredients, except for the cherries, in a large mixing bowl. Mix with a handheld mixer until just combined. Immediately fold in the cherries. (The batter will thicken as it sits, so if you wait to add the cherries, it will be harder to fold them in.)

3. Divide the batter evenly among the muffin cups, filling them nearly full. Bake for about 24 minutes, until the tops are slightly golden. Remove from the pan and allow to cool.

4. Store in an airtight container at room temperature for up to 2 days or refrigerate for up to a week.

Note: *If you've forgotten to take the eggs out of the fridge to come to room temperature, you can hurry up the process by setting them in a bowl of hot tap water for about 10 minutes.*

blueberry muffins

Makes 12 | Prep Time: 15 minutes | Cook Time: 24 minutes

In a word, these muffins are buttery. Sometimes a really buttery muffin is what I want, and these are just that, even without being buttered.

2 cups (224 g) almond flour

½ cup (68 g) arrowroot or tapioca flour

½ teaspoon baking soda

½ teaspoon fine sea salt

¼ cup honey

¼ cup unsweetened applesauce

3 large eggs, room temperature (see Note, page 172)

½ cup melted coconut oil

2 cups fresh or frozen blueberries

1. Set the oven to 350°F and line a 12-well muffin pan with unbleached paper liners.

2. In a mixing bowl, combine the flours, baking soda, and salt with a whisk. Add the honey, applesauce, eggs, and coconut oil and mix with a handheld mixer. Immediately fold in the blueberries. (The batter will thicken as it sits, so if you wait to add the blueberries, it will be harder to fold them in.)

3. Divide the batter evenly among the muffin cups, filling them nearly full. Bake for about 24 minutes, until the tops are slightly golden. Remove from the pan and allow to cool.

4. Store in an airtight container at room temperature for up to 2 days or refrigerate for up to a week.

chocolate chip scones

Makes 4 | Prep Time: 10 minutes | Cook Time: 15 minutes | Wait Time: 1 hour

These have been my favorite scones since I went gluten-free over a decade ago. They're buttery and crumbly, and I've yet to serve them to anyone who doesn't love them. You can also use the dough (minus the chocolate chips) as a crumble topping for Peach Cobbler (page 358), or make plain scones and top them with strawberries and Whipped Coconut Cream (page 366) for delicious strawberry shortcake!

1¼ cups (170 g) Scone & Pie Crust Mix (page 133)

¼ cup dairy-free chocolate chips (70% cacao)

¼ cup plus 3 tablespoons softened ghee or coconut oil

2 tablespoons honey

1. Set the oven to 350°F. In a large mixing bowl, combine all of the ingredients with a handheld mixer for about 30 seconds. Use a flexible spatula to press the dough into one mass.

2. Line a baking sheet with unbleached parchment paper. Lay the dough on top of the parchment and use your hands to shape it into a square about ¾ inch thick. Slice all the way through the square to make four triangles, but do not pull the triangles apart yet.

3. Bake the scones for about 15 minutes, until slightly golden. Let cool to room temperature on the baking sheet (do not attempt to move them), then refrigerate until cold before serving. They crumble less after being refrigerated.

4. Separate the scones and enjoy.

5. Store in the refrigerator for up to a week. The scones are best eaten later.

Variations:
Strawberry Scones. *Replace the chocolate chips with ½ heaping cup (14 g) whole freeze-dried strawberries, crushed slightly in your hand.*

Almond Scones (my favorite). *Replace the chocolate chips with ½ cup sliced almonds and add ⅛ teaspoon almond extract.*

coconut porridge

Serves 1 | Prep Time: 5 minutes | Cook Time: less than 5 minutes

Top this porridge with ghee, a few pinches of coconut sugar, raisins, and cinnamon, or use fresh seasonal berries. It's best made with almond milk or another dairy-free milk, not water.

¾ cup unsweetened almond milk or full-fat coconut milk (use coconut milk for nut-free)

Splash of Hazelnut Coffee Creamer (page 114; optional, omit for nut-free)

¾ cup Coconut Porridge Mix (page 112)

Toppings (as desired):

Ghee

Coconut sugar

Raisins

A pinch or two of ground cinnamon or a handful of fresh berries

1. Place the almond milk and coffee creamer (if using) in a small heavy-bottomed pot. Bring the mixture to a simmer, then add the Coconut Porridge Mix and whisk to combine. Continue whisking for about 20 seconds, then turn off the heat. The porridge will thicken slightly as it cools.

2. Serve the porridge topped with a spoonful each of ghee and coconut sugar, some raisins, and a pinch or two of cinnamon (according to your taste) or a handful of fresh berries.

Note: *To make enough porridge for the meal plans (see pages 86 and 97), you will need to quadruple the recipe, as follows: 3 cups unsweetened almond milk or full-fat coconut milk, 2 tablespoons Hazelnut Coffee Creamer (optional), and 3 cups Coconut Porridge Mix.*

strawberries & cream n'oatmeal

Serves 1 | Prep Time: 5 minutes | Cook Time: 5 minutes

When I was in high school, I loved those flavored instant oatmeal packets, which are full of refined sugar, artificial flavors, and hydrogenated soybean oil. I still eat "oatmeal" all the time, but my recipes are so much healthier.

¾ cup unsweetened almond milk or full-fat coconut milk (use coconut milk for nut-free)

Splash of Hazelnut Coffee Creamer (page 114; optional, omit for nut-free)

A few drops of liquid vanilla stevia or 2 teaspoons honey

¾ cup Coconut Porridge Mix (page 112)

1 tablespoon finely ground freeze-dried strawberries, plus more for garnish, if desired

Place the almond milk, coffee creamer (if using), and stevia in a small heavy-bottomed pot. Bring to a simmer, then add the Coconut Porridge Mix and ground freeze-dried strawberries and whisk to combine. Continue whisking for about 20 seconds, then turn off the heat. The mixture will thicken slightly as it cools.

Note: *To make enough N'Oatmeal for the meal plan (see page 73), you will need to quadruple the recipe, as follows: 3 cups unsweetened almond milk or full-fat coconut milk, 2 tablespoons Hazelnut Coffee Creamer (optional), 12 drops liquid vanilla stevia or 1 tablespoon plus 1 teaspoon honey, 3 cups Coconut Porridge Mix, and ¼ cup finely ground freeze-dried strawberries.*

pumpkin n'oatmeal

Serves 1 | Prep Time: 5 minutes | Cook Time: 5 minutes

⅓ cup pumpkin puree

⅓ cup water

⅓ cup full-fat coconut milk

A few drops of liquid vanilla stevia or 2 teaspoons honey

¾ cup Coconut Porridge Mix (page 112)

½ teaspoon Pumpkin Spice Blend (page 118)

Big pinch of fine sea salt

Toppings (optional):

Handful of chopped raw walnuts (omit for nut-free)

Maple syrup, for drizzling

1. Place the pumpkin puree, water, coconut milk, and stevia in a small heavy-bottomed pot. Bring to a simmer, then add the Coconut Porridge Mix, Pumpkin Spice Blend, and salt and whisk to combine. Continue whisking for about 20 seconds, then turn off the heat. The mixture will thicken slightly as it cools.

2. Serve topped with a handful of chopped walnuts and a drizzle of maple syrup, if desired.

Note: *To make enough N'Oatmeal for the meal plan (see pages 89 and 94), you will need to quadruple the recipe, as follows: 1⅓ cups pumpkin puree, 1⅓ cups water, 1⅓ cups full-fat coconut milk, 12 drops liquid vanilla stevia or 2 tablespoons plus 2 teaspoons honey, 3 cups Coconut Porridge Mix, 2 teaspoons Pumpkin Spice Blend, and ¼ teaspoon fine sea salt.*

coconut yogurt

Makes about 6 cups | Prep Time: 20 minutes | Wait Time: 20 to 32 hours

If you miss dairy yogurt or you want to get off of store-bought dairy-free yogurt, which is not only expensive but also full of sugar, then this recipe is your answer. Make it once and you will see how easy it is! Real-deal yogurt like this, without all the added sugar, is essential to the health of your gut. You can use this to make frozen yogurt (as directed in my book Dairy-Free Ice Cream*) and smoothies, or simply enjoy a bowl of it with some fresh fruit.*

3 (13½-ounce) cans full-fat coconut milk

1 tablespoon maple syrup

⅛ teaspoon liquid vanilla stevia, or to taste

Seeds scraped from 1 vanilla bean

½ cup boiling water

1 tablespoon plus 1 teaspoon grass-fed gelatin or 1½ teaspoons agar powder

Contents of enough dairy-free probiotic capsules to equal about 35 billion active cultures (see Note)

Add-in (optional):

A few drops of almond or lemon extract

Special equipment:

Candy thermometer

1. Before you begin, sterilize all of your equipment in the dishwasher or in boiling water. In a large heavy-bottomed pot, bring the coconut milk, maple syrup, stevia, and vanilla bean seeds to a simmer. Simmer for 30 seconds, then turn off the heat.

2. Place the water, just off the boil, in a mug. Immediately stir in the gelatin or agar powder and continue stirring until completely dissolved. Add the mixture to the coconut milk in the pot.

3. Pour the liquids into a bowl and, if you used gelatin, put the bowl in a larger one of cold (but not iced) water. If you used agar powder, let it cool down on its own so it doesn't get lumpy. Whisking will help it cool down faster.

4. When the mixture has reached about 92°F, add the contents of enough probiotic capsules to equal about 35 billion active cultures. Ladle into jars and keep warm for 12 to 24 hours, until the taste is to your liking. I put my jars on top of a heating pad with no automatic shutoff, sandwiched between two cloth napkins. A yogurt maker also works. If you used gelatin, a clear pool will form at the bottom while it sits. Make sure that the lids are secure, then shake the jars to mix in the liquid before refrigerating.

5. Refrigerate the yogurt for 8 hours before eating. It will keep in the fridge for up to a week.

Notes: *The brand of probiotics that I add to my homemade yogurt is Ther-biotic Complete, by Klaire Labs.*

If you are doubling this recipe for the meal plans on pages 81 and 97, transfer the yogurt to one large glass pitcher with a lid (3 quarts or larger) rather than several smaller jars.

perfect crispy potatoes

Serves 4 | Prep Time: 20 minutes | Cook Time: 15 minutes

Crispy breakfast potatoes are an easy thing to perfect, or so I thought. Many seasoning blends later, I finally got it: the perfect crispy potatoes. By cooking them in healthy bacon fat and resisting the urge to stir, you are really going to wow your whole family with these. My kids also love it when I use sweet potatoes instead of white potatoes, despite the fact that sweet potatoes don't get as crispy. They even love the leftovers cold, straight from the fridge.

1½ to 2 pounds russet potatoes (enough to cover the bottom of a 12-inch skillet when diced)

2 to 3 tablespoons bacon fat (page 108), plus more for topping

1½ teaspoons Everyday Seasoning (page 117)

½ teaspoon Salt Blend (page 117)

For serving (optional):

1 batch Poached Eggs (page 188)

Fresh spinach, wilted

1. Set a 12-inch skillet over medium heat.

2. While the pan is heating, scrub the potatoes well, then cut them into ¾-inch dice. Place the bacon fat in the hot skillet and swirl the pan to coat it evenly. Add the potatoes, Everyday Seasoning, and Salt Blend. Stir well, then spread the potatoes evenly so that they don't overlap.

3. Set a timer for 5 minutes and resist the urge to stir the potatoes during that time. When the 5 minutes are up, stir the potatoes, spread them evenly, and set the timer for another 5 minutes. Repeat the process a third time, for a total of 15 minutes, at which point the potatoes should be browned and fork-tender.

4. If desired, serve with poached eggs and wilted spinach.

chapter 9:

Eggs

poached eggs

Makes 4 | Prep Time: 10 minutes | Cook Time: 5 minutes

I first heard of this technique for making poached eggs from my friends Bill and Hayley of the blog Primal Palate. *After doing further research, I discovered that you can also use silicone egg rings, but most of us already own mason jars, so why buy another gadget?*

2 tablespoons apple cider vinegar

Big pinch of fine sea salt

Bacon fat (page 108), for greasing the rings

4 large eggs, or more as desired

Special equipment:

4 mason jar rings or silicone egg rings

1. Pour enough water into a 12-inch skillet to just cover the ring of a mason jar lid. Add the vinegar and salt and bring to a gentle simmer (not a boil). Generously grease the insides of the mason jar rings with bacon fat, but don't put them in the water yet.

2. Crack one egg into a small dish. Lay one of the greased rings upside down in the water, then gently pour the egg into the ring. Repeat the process until all of the eggs are in the water.

3. Poach the eggs until the whites are just set, about 4 minutes, then use a spatula to remove the eggs in the rings from the water. Flip them over onto a plate and the rings will come off easily.

4. Serve right away.

portobello & ham baked eggs

Makes 2 | Prep Time: 10 minutes | Cook Time: 20 minutes

2 portobello mushroom caps

Fine sea salt and black pepper

2 thin slices ham

2 large eggs

1. Set the oven to 375°F and line a rimmed baking sheet with unbleached parchment paper. Carefully cut out the stem and scrape out the gills of each mushroom cap and lay the caps on the prepared baking sheet.

2. Set the mushroom caps on the prepared baking sheet and sprinkle the insides with salt and pepper. Press a thin slice of ham into each cap, then crack an egg on top. Bake for about 20 minutes, until the eggs are cooked to your preference. (At 20 minutes, the yolks will be soft-set and the whites will be set.) The eggs will continue cooking slightly after coming out of the oven.

3. Enjoy right away.

egg boats

Makes 2 | Prep Time: 5 minutes | Cook Time: 18 minutes

2 Crispy Potato Boats (page 127), preferably made with russets

Fine sea salt and black pepper

2 large eggs

For garnish:

Hot sauce of choice

Chopped fresh parsley or cilantro

Sliced green onions

1. Set the oven to 375°F and line a rimmed baking sheet with unbleached parchment paper.

2. Set the potato boats on the prepared baking sheet and sprinkle the insides with salt and pepper, then crack an egg into each potato. Bake for about 18 minutes, until the eggs are cooked to your preference. (At 18 minutes, the yolks will be soft-set and the whites will be set.) The eggs will continue cooking slightly after coming out of the oven.

3. Garnish with hot sauce, parsley or cilantro, and green onions and enjoy right away.

eggs baked in tomatoes

Makes 2 | Prep Time: 10 minutes | Cook Time: 25 minutes

Do you watch Portlandia? *My husband loves it. Remember the "Put a bird on it" skit? These recipes featuring eggs baked in tomatoes, bell peppers, portobello mushroom caps, and potato boats make me want to say, "Put an egg in it!"*

2 large tomatoes

Fine sea salt and black pepper

2 large eggs

Sliced fresh basil leaves, for garnish

1. Set the oven to 375°F and line a rimmed baking sheet with unbleached parchment paper. Level the bottoms of the tomatoes very slightly to keep them upright. Slice off the tops just below the stems and carefully remove the insides (see the technique on page 50).

2. Set the tomatoes on the prepared baking sheet and sprinkle the insides with salt and pepper, then crack an egg into each tomato. Bake for about 25 minutes, until the eggs are cooked to your preference. (At 25 minutes, the yolks will be soft-set and the whites will be set.) The eggs will continue cooking slightly after coming out of the oven.

3. Garnish with basil and enjoy right away.

yellow pepper baked eggs

Makes 2 | Prep Time: 10 minutes | Cook Time: 25 minutes

1 large yellow bell pepper

Fine sea salt and black pepper

2 large eggs

Snipped or crumbled cooked bacon, for garnish

1. Set the oven to 375°F and line a rimmed baking sheet with unbleached parchment paper. Slice the pepper lengthwise, through the stem, and carefully remove the insides.

2. Set the pepper halves on the prepared baking sheet and sprinkle the insides with salt and pepper, then crack an egg into each pepper half. Using the sides of the baking sheet to keep them upright, bake for about 25 minutes, until the eggs are cooked to your preference. (At 25 minutes, the yolks will be soft-set and the whites will be set.) The eggs will continue cooking slightly after coming out of the oven.

3. Garnish with bacon and enjoy right away.

pizza quiche 2.0

Serves 8 | Prep Time: 20 minutes | Cook Time: 30 minutes

This quiche is based on a popular recipe on my blog, The Spunky Coconut. *It's perfect for eating at any time of day. The real time-saver here is the pie crust mix. I love how much faster I can whip up a quiche when I don't have to measure out a bunch of flours for the crust first!*

1 batch Savory Pie Crust dough (page 134)

1½ cups diced or sliced pizza toppings of choice (see Note)

½ batch "Cheese" Base with Cashews (page 110)

2 teaspoons arrowroot or tapioca flour

¼ teaspoon garlic powder

¼ teaspoon onion powder

4 large eggs

½ (13½-ounce) can full-fat coconut milk

3 or 4 sun-dried tomatoes

1 teaspoon Italian seasoning, plus more for garnish

¼ teaspoon fine sea salt

1. Set the oven to 350°F. Make the pie crust dough according to the directions and press it into a 10-inch pie pan. Add the pizza toppings to the crust.

2. Make the "cheese" base according to the directions, but add the arrowroot flour, onion powder, and garlic powder to the blender with the other ingredients. Pour the "cheese" base over the pizza toppings.

3. In the blender, puree the eggs, coconut milk, sun-dried tomatoes, Italian seasoning, and salt. Pour the egg puree over the "cheese" base and garnish with more Italian seasoning.

4. Bake for about 30 minutes, until the top doesn't jiggle. Let cool.

5. Serve the quiche at room temperature.

6. Store leftovers covered in the refrigerator for up to a week.

Note: *For toppings, try chopped cooked Italian sausage, sliced pepperoni, bell peppers, and onions.*

portuguese-inspired skillet eggs

Serves 6 | Prep Time: 15 minutes | Cook Time: 22 minutes

1 tablespoon ghee or bacon fat (page 108)

2 red bell peppers, sliced

2 large tomatoes, chopped

1 small red onion, sliced

¼ teaspoon fine sea salt

½ batch "Cheese" Base with Cashews (page 110)

½ teaspoon chili powder

½ teaspoon smoked paprika

¼ teaspoon chipotle powder

7 large eggs, divided in use

Chopped fresh basil or cilantro, for garnish

1. Set the oven to 375°F. Place the ghee in a 10-inch ovenproof skillet over low to medium heat. Add the bell peppers, tomatoes, onion, and salt. Cook for about 10 minutes, until the peppers have softened.

2. Meanwhile, make the "cheese" base as directed, but add the chili powder, smoked paprika, chipotle powder, and one of the eggs.

3. Pour the "cheese" base over the peppers, tomatoes, and onion in the skillet. Crack the six remaining eggs on top.

4. Cover the skillet with an oven-safe lid and place it in the oven. Bake for about 12 minutes, until the egg whites are almost set. The eggs will quickly go from runny to hard, so keep a close eye on them. They will continue cooking slightly after coming out of the oven.

5. Remove the lid and let cool for 5 minutes. Slice and serve garnished with fresh basil.

zucchini lime cilantro pie

Serves 4 | Prep Time: 15 minutes | Cook Time: 25 minutes

Yellow zucchini are less common than green zucchini. While either color will work, I love to use yellow zucchini because it makes such a stunning pie.

8 cups spiral-sliced unpeeled yellow zucchini (about 6 whole zucchini)

¾ cup (90 g) almond flour

¼ cup (34 g) arrowroot or tapioca flour

¼ cup roughly chopped fresh cilantro, plus more for garnish

½ teaspoon fine sea salt

½ teaspoon ground cumin

¼ teaspoon garlic powder

1 tablespoon plus 1 teaspoon fresh-squeezed lime juice, plus more for serving

5 large eggs, divided in use

1 tablespoon ghee or avocado oil

1. Steam the zucchini noodles in a steamer pot until wilted and tender, about 10 minutes. Turn the hot noodles over onto a plate covered with a clean, dry kitchen towel and place it in the freezer to cool the noodles.

2. Set the oven to 350°F. In a mixing bowl, combine the flours, cilantro, salt, cumin, and garlic powder with a whisk. Add the lime juice and one of the eggs to the dry ingredients and stir to combine.

3. When the noodles are cool enough to handle, remove them from the freezer and squeeze them in the towel to remove as much moisture as possible. Add the noodles to the mixing bowl and gently work everything together with your hands.

4. Place a 10-inch cast-iron skillet over medium heat. Add the ghee to the skillet and swirl it around to coat the pan. Place the zucchini mixture in the pan and use a fork to spread it evenly. It won't spread out on its own.

5. Cook the pie on the stovetop for about 10 minutes, until the bottom is starting to brown, then remove it from the heat. Crack the four remaining eggs on top, cover the skillet with an oven-safe lid, and place the pie in the oven. Bake for about 5 minutes, until the egg whites are almost set. The eggs will continue cooking slightly after the pie comes out of the oven.

6. Serve at room temperature, sprinkled with chopped cilantro and a squeeze of fresh lime juice.

chapter 10:
Soups

cheeseburger soup

Serves 4 | Prep Time: 15 minutes | Cook Time: 20 minutes

Like the rest of the soups in this chapter, this Cheeseburger Soup is easy to make. Plus, my whole family loves soup, so it's a win-win.

1 tablespoon bacon fat (page 108) or avocado oil

1 yellow onion, chopped

3 cloves garlic, minced

2 pounds ground beef

1 batch "cheese" base (with cashews or nut-free; pages 110 and 111)

¼ cup tomato paste

2 cups tomato puree

1 teaspoon fine sea salt

Toppings:

Chopped lettuce

Sliced green onions

1. Set a large heavy-bottomed pot over low to medium heat. Melt the bacon fat in the pot, then add the onion, garlic, and ground beef. Break up the beef with a spatula and cook until no longer pink.

2. Make the "cheese" base according to the directions, but add the tomato paste to the blender with the other ingredients. Pour the "cheese" mixture and tomato puree into the pot and increase the heat to medium-high.

3. Bring the soup to a simmer, then turn off the heat.

4. Serve hot, topped with lettuce and green onions.

curried chicken & vegetable soup

Serves 4 | Prep Time: 15 minutes | Cook Time: 20 minutes

Bok choy is packed with vitamins A and C and numerous antioxidants. Substitute more cabbage for the bok choy if bok choy is not in season.

2 tablespoons coconut oil

2 to 3 cups chopped bok choy

2 to 3 cups chopped cabbage

1 cup chopped yellow onion

1 clove garlic, minced

2 large carrots, peeled into ribbons or finely sliced

½ batch Easy Chicken (page 126), chopped

3 cups chicken broth (page 131)

1 (13½-ounce) can full-fat coconut milk

1 tablespoon curry powder, or to taste

½ teaspoon fine sea salt, or to taste

1. Set a large heavy-bottomed pot over low to medium heat. Melt the coconut oil in the pot, then add the bok choy, cabbage, onion, and garlic. Cook until the cabbage is almost tender, about 10 minutes. Add the carrot ribbons and cook for about 5 minutes more.

2. Add the cooked chicken, broth, coconut milk, curry powder, and salt. Bring the soup to a simmer, then turn off the heat.

3. Serve hot.

matzo ball soup

Serves 4 | Prep Time: 15 minutes | Cook Time: 15 minutes

I grew up near Baltimore, Maryland, and my parents' best friends were Jewish. Jewish food, like this soup, is comfort food to me. It takes me back.

8 cups chicken broth (page 131)

¼ cup (34 g) coconut flour, sifted

¼ cup (30 g) almond flour

½ cup (68 g) arrowroot or tapioca flour

½ teaspoon fine sea salt

½ teaspoon herbes de Provence

¼ teaspoon garlic powder

2 tablespoons softened ghee

3 large eggs

Handful of arugula or spinach (optional)

1. Bring the broth to a simmer in a large heavy-bottomed pot.

2. Whisk the flours, salt, herbes de Provence, and garlic powder in a mixing bowl. Add the ghee and eggs and mix with a handheld mixer for 30 seconds, until well combined.

3. Use a large spoon to drop balls of the dough into the simmering broth (you should have about 8 balls). Reduce the heat to low and cover, with the lid slightly cracked. The matzo balls will be ready in about 10 minutes.

4. To serve: Place a pinch of arugula, if using, in the bottom of each bowl. Place the matzo balls on top of the greens, two per bowl, then ladle the broth over the top. Serve hot.

creamy potato, sausage & kale soup

Serves 4 | Prep Time: 20 minutes | Cook Time: 25 minutes

This soup is really creamy and rich. For a lighter version, omit the "cheese" base and add an additional 3½ cups of chicken broth (page 131). It is delicious both ways!

2 tablespoons ghee or avocado oil

1 yellow onion, chopped

2 cloves garlic, minced

1 pound bulk mild Italian sausage

1 pound potatoes, scrubbed and diced*

2 cups chicken broth (page 131), divided

1 batch "cheese" base (with cashews or nut-free; pages 110 and 111)

2 big handfuls (about 3¼ ounces) of baby kale or spinach, chopped

½ teaspoon Italian seasoning

½ teaspoon red pepper flakes

Fine sea salt and black pepper

*You may substitute potatoes left over from making Crispy Potato Boats (page 127).

1. Set a large heavy-bottomed pot over low to medium heat. Melt the ghee in the pot, then add the onion and garlic. Break the sausage into pieces with your hands and drop it into the pot. Add the potatoes and ¾ cup of the broth, cover, and simmer over low heat until the potatoes are fork-tender, about 20 minutes.

2. Add the remaining 1¼ cups of broth, "cheese" base, kale, Italian seasoning, and red pepper flakes. Season with salt and pepper to taste. Bring the soup to a simmer, then turn off the heat.

3. Serve hot.

creamy roasted tomato soup

Serves 4 | Prep Time: 20 minutes | Cook Time: 1 hour 15 minutes

This soup is pictured with a drizzle of hot coconut milk and some fresh basil leaves. I like to top mine with crumbled crackers (page 282) as well.

3 pounds tomatoes, seeds removed, quartered (see page 50)

2 tablespoons ghee or avocado oil

1 yellow onion, chopped

1 clove garlic, minced

½ teaspoon Salt Blend (page 117)

¼ cup tomato paste

1 packed tablespoon fresh basil leaves

1 batch "cheese" base (with cashews or nut-free; pages 110 and 111)

1. Set the oven to 400°F. Lightly grease a rimmed baking sheet, then spread the tomatoes evenly on top. Roast until completely softened and wilted, about 1 hour.

2. Set a large heavy-bottomed pot over low to medium heat. Melt the ghee in the pot, then add the onion, garlic, and Salt Blend. Cook until the onion is tender, 5 to 10 minutes.

3. Transfer the onion and garlic to a blender. Add the tomato paste, basil leaves, and roasted tomatoes and puree until smooth. Return the mixture to the pot.

4. Add the "cheese" base to the pot. Bring the soup to a simmer, then turn off the heat.

5. Serve hot.

cream of mushroom soup

Serves 4 | Prep Time: 15 minutes | Cook Time: 15 minutes

This soup is nothing fancy, but the cooking sherry adds a sophisticated flavor that will make you proud to share it with company.

2 tablespoons ghee or avocado oil

1 yellow onion, chopped

16 ounces mushrooms, sliced

Fine sea salt and black pepper

2 tablespoons cooking sherry

2 cups chicken broth (page 131)

1 batch "cheese" base (with cashews or nut-free; pages 110 and 111)

1. Set a large heavy-bottomed pot over low to medium heat. Melt the ghee in the pot, then add the onion and mushrooms and season with salt and pepper. Cook until the mushrooms are tender, about 10 minutes.

2. Add the sherry to deglaze the pan. (Reserve a small amount of the sliced mushrooms to use for garnish, if desired.) Transfer the mushrooms and onion to a high-powered blender. Add the chicken broth and puree until completely smooth.

3. Pour the puree back into the pot and add the "cheese" base. Bring the soup to a simmer, then turn off the heat.

4. Serve hot, garnished with a few mushroom slices, if desired.

broccoli cheese soup

Serves 4 | Prep Time: 15 minutes | Cook Time: 10 to 15 minutes

I use turmeric to support detox. It's also amazing for reducing inflammation. I love that it gives this soup a great cheddar cheese color. Make sure that the kids aren't wearing white, though, because turmeric stains. Top the soup with crumbled crisp bacon if you have some on hand.

1 head broccoli (about 1½ pounds), cut into florets, or 1 (16-ounce) bag frozen broccoli florets

2 tablespoons bacon fat (page 108)

1 yellow onion, finely chopped

2 cloves garlic, minced

1 batch "cheese" base (with cashews or nut-free; pages 110 and 111)

1 tablespoon fresh-squeezed lemon juice

1½ teaspoons turmeric powder

1 teaspoon gluten-free Dijon mustard

2 cups chicken broth (page 131)

Fine sea salt and black pepper

1. Cut the broccoli florets into bite-sized pieces and steam in a steamer pot until just fork-tender.

2. While the broccoli is steaming, set a large heavy-bottomed pot over low to medium heat. Melt the bacon fat in the pot, then add the onion and garlic and cook until the onion is tender, 5 to 10 minutes.

3. Make the "cheese" base according to the directions, but add the lemon juice, turmeric powder, and mustard to the blender with the other ingredients. Pour the puree into the pot with the onion and garlic. Add the broth and stir to combine.

4. Bring the soup to a simmer, then turn off the heat and add the broccoli. Season with salt and pepper to taste.

5. Serve hot.

Note: *This soup is much more cheeselike when made with the "Cheese" Base with Cashews on page 110.*

pho

Serves 4 | Prep Time: 20 minutes | Cook Time: 10 hours

Broth:

3 beef shin bones (about 3 pounds)

Contents of 1 pho spice packet (found at Asian markets) or 6 star anise, 3 cinnamon sticks, 2 teaspoons coriander seeds, 2 teaspoons fennel seeds, and 3 whole cloves

Avocado oil, for the pan

1 yellow onion, cut in half

1 (3-inch) piece fresh ginger, skin scraped off

8 cups water

1 tablespoon apple cider vinegar

1 tablespoon gluten-free fish sauce

½ teaspoon salt

For the bowls:

1 pound sirloin, very thinly sliced against the grain

1 (8.8-ounce) package Thai white rice noodles, 1 (9-ounce) package Cappello's fettuccine, or 1 (12-ounce) package kelp noodles, prepared according to package instructions

Bean sprouts (optional)

Handful of fresh basil leaves, whole or sliced into thin strips

Handful of fresh cilantro leaves, whole or sliced into thin strips

1. Shin bones give up a yucky scum when first heated, so you'll want to get rid of that before putting the bones in the slow cooker. Boil the bones in a pot with enough water to cover. After 10 minutes, discard the scum and water.

2. Meanwhile, toast the spices in a dry medium-sized skillet until fragrant, about 2 minutes. Add them to a 7-quart slow cooker.

3. Add some avocado oil to the skillet that you used to toast the spices and cook the onion and ginger until nicely browned on each side. Add them to the slow cooker.

4. Use tongs to carefully transfer the hot bones to the slow cooker. Add the water, vinegar, fish sauce, and salt. Set the slow cooker to low and cook for 10 hours. (I do this in the garage so that the lovely smell doesn't keep us up all night, stomachs growling.)

5. Remove the bones and strain the broth. Pour the broth into a large pot and bring it to a boil. When the broth boils, turn off the heat and add the sirloin. It will cook instantly.

6. Add some cooked noodles to each serving bowl. Ladle the broth and sirloin over each bowl of noodles. Offer a plate of bean sprouts (if desired), basil, and cilantro for topping each bowl. Eat slowly and enjoy.

Note: *For the white rice noodles, I purchase the King Soba brand (kingsoba.com). I use the kelp noodles from the Sea Tangle Noodle Company (kelpnoodles.com).*

hot & sour soup

Serves 4 | Prep Time: 20 minutes | Cook Time: 15 minutes

My husband, the man behind "Pho Friday" at our house, is also responsible for bringing hot & sour soup into our repertoire, and I am so grateful. There are two reasons why I adore this soup: 1) it's easy to make, and 2) the kids will usually eat it. What more could you ask for?

1 tablespoon ghee or avocado oil

12 ounces cremini mushrooms, sliced

1 (8-ounce) can bamboo shoots

½ to 1 pound thinly sliced pork loin (optional)

1 tablespoon red chili paste

Fine sea salt and black pepper

2 quarts chicken broth (page 131) made with fresh ginger (see Note)

¼ cup coconut aminos

¼ cup apple cider vinegar

½ teaspoon ground white pepper

¼ cup arrowroot or tapioca flour

¼ cup water

2 large eggs, whisked (omit for egg-free)

Sliced green onions, for garnish

1. Set a large heavy-bottomed pot over low to medium heat. Melt the ghee in the pot, then add the mushrooms, bamboo shoots, pork (if using), and chili paste. Add a pinch of salt and pepper, then stir. Cook until the mushrooms are tender, about 10 minutes.

2. Add the broth, coconut aminos, vinegar, and white pepper. Increase the heat to medium-high.

3. In a small dish, whisk together the arrowroot flour and water until well combined. Add the mixture to the pot.

4. When the soup begins to simmer, turn off the heat. Slowly pour the eggs (if using) into the soup while whisking. Taste for seasoning and add more salt if needed.

5. Serve hot, garnished with sliced green onions.

Note: *Make the broth as directed, but add a 2-inch piece of fresh ginger to the slow cooker with the rest of the ingredients. If you forget to add fresh ginger to the slow cooker when making the broth, you may add ¼ teaspoon ginger power to this recipe as a shortcut.*

chapter 11:
Plant Dishes

ranch slaw

Serves 4 | Prep Time: 15 minutes

1 head red cabbage

1 large or 2 small golden beets

4 slices crisp cooked bacon

2 handfuls of watercress

2 green onions

½ to 1 cup Ranch Dressing (page 120), as desired

1. Slice the cabbage into thin strips.

2. Scrub the beet(s), trim both ends, and spiral-slice or shred them.

3. Roughly chop the bacon and watercress.

4. Finely chop the green onions.

5. Layer the cabbage, beets, bacon, watercress, and green onions in a large glass container (or combine in a mixing bowl). Top with the Ranch Dressing.

6. Store in the refrigerator for up to a week.

creamed kale

Serves 4 | Prep Time: 15 minutes | Cook Time: 25 minutes

2 tablespoons bacon fat (page 108), ghee, or avocado oil

2 large bunches of kale, washed, stems removed (see page 50)

1 batch "cheese" base (with cashews or nut-free; pages 110 and 111)

For garnish (optional; omit for nut-free):

2 tablespoons crushed raw macadamia nuts

2 tablespoons sliced almonds

Black pepper

Note: *You may substitute other dark leafy greens. Keep in mind that softer greens like spinach will cook in a fraction of the time.*

1. Place the bacon fat in a 12-inch skillet over low to medium heat. Chop the kale and add it to the pan. If the kale is still wet from washing, it will splatter, so use caution.

2. Cook the kale for about 5 minutes while you puree the "cheese" base. Add the "cheese" base to the kale and simmer, uncovered, for about 20 minutes. The sauce will thicken slightly as it cools.

3. Garnish with crushed macadamia nuts, sliced almonds, and a few cranks of black pepper, if desired.

orange & almond salad

Serves 8 | Prep Time: 5 minutes

Clementines are a great winter fruit and so delicious when combined with almonds in this salad. I also like this salad with some sliced red onion, which I serve on the side so my guests can choose whether to add it or not.

10 ounces baby spring mix

½ to 1 batch Orange & Almond Dressing (page 220), as desired

½ cup sliced almonds, divided

About 1 cup clementine segments, divided

In a large mixing bowl, toss the baby spring mix in the dressing. Fold in half of the almonds and clementine segments. Transfer to a serving bowl and garnish with the remaining almonds and clementine segments.

faux grilled vegetables

Serves 4 | Prep Time: 5 minutes | Cook Time: 20 minutes

I love the flavor that wood chips and smoke give to grilled vegetables. However, I usually just faux grill them in the oven. It's really simple and so yummy.

3 pounds assorted vegetables*

Avocado oil, for brushing

Everyday Seasoning (page 117)

Salad dressing of choice (pages 120 to 125)

*Broccoli, Romanesco, purple asparagus, endive, and yellow cauliflower are shown in the photo below.

1. Set the oven to 400°F and grease a large rimmed baking sheet. Slice the larger vegetables, like broccoli and cauliflower florets, in half.

2. Use a basting brush to apply avocado oil to both sides of the vegetables, then season them on both sides with the Everyday Seasoning. Lay the vegetables on the prepared baking sheet.

3. Cook on the bottom rack of the oven for about 10 minutes per side, until nicely browned.

4. Serve with the dressing of your choice.

brassicas salad

Serves 4 | Prep Time: 10 minutes | Cook Time: 10 minutes

Brassicas (or cruciferous vegetables) act as antioxidants, anti-inflammatories, and liver detoxifiers, among other health benefits. My friend Laura Russell wrote an entire cookbook, titled Brassicas, *about using them without drowning them in cheese.*

I frequently use bok choy and cabbage in this salad because I often have extra on hand after making Curried Chicken & Vegetable Soup (page 202). Feel free to substitute other brassicas, such as Brussels sprouts, broccoli, or cauliflower.

4 big leaves rainbow chard

3 cups sliced cabbage

2 cups chopped bok choy

1 cup chopped onion or leek (white part only)

1 tablespoon bacon fat (page 108)

A few big pinches of fine sea salt

A few cranks of black pepper

¼ to ½ cup Ranch Dressing (page 120), as desired

For garnish (optional):

Handful of toasted sliced almonds (omit for nut-free)

Handful of crumbled crisp-cooked bacon

1. Rinse the chard, remove the stems, and chop the leaves. Set aside. Rinse the cabbage, bok choy, and leek (if using in place of onion) to remove any dirt. Set aside.

2. Place the bacon fat in a 12-inch skillet over low to medium heat. Add the chard, cabbage, bok choy, onion or leek, salt, and pepper and cook for about 10 minutes, stirring occasionally, until tender.

3. Toss the salad in the Ranch Dressing. Garnish with toasted sliced almonds and crisp bacon, if desired. Serve warm or at room temperature.

rainbow beet salad

Serves 6 | Prep Time: 20 minutes | Cook Time: 15 minutes

This slightly cooked Rainbow Beet Salad is as delicious as it is pretty. I say that it serves six people, but that's only if you can keep it away from me . . . .

1 tablespoon avocado oil

1 large or 2 small red beets

1 large or 2 small golden beets

1 fat carrot (ideally 2 inches wide)

Fine sea salt and black pepper

1 apple, cored and chopped

1 blood orange, in sections

2 handfuls of raw or roasted walnut pieces (optional; omit for nut-free)

¼ cup Apple Cider Vinaigrette (page 121), or more as desired

1. Set the oven to 400°F and grease a 10-inch cast-iron skillet with the avocado oil.

2. Peel the beets, then spiral-slice them and add them to the skillet. Trim the ends of the carrot, then spiral-slice it as well, and add it to the skillet. Spread out the beet and carrot noodles so that they cover the bottom of the pan. Season with salt and pepper.

3. Put an oven-safe lid on the skillet and bake until the noodles are slightly softened, about 15 minutes.

4. Top the noodles with the chopped apple, blood orange, walnut pieces, and vinaigrette. Serve at room temperature.

mediterranean zucchini salad

Serves 4 | Prep Time: 15 minutes | Wait Time: 1 to 2 hours

Fish contains selenium, an element needed for detoxification; however, fish also contains mercury, which is undesirable for anyone, but particularly harmful for those with the MTHFR mutation, like my daughter Ashley (see page 8 for a discussion of the MTHFR mutation). Ashley's doctors caution us that no matter how much selenium she gets, she will have trouble excreting heavy metals like mercury. That is why we prefer to eat sardines. Not only are they high in vitamin B12, vitamin D, omega-3 fatty acids, and calcium, to name just a few, but they are also among the least mercury-containing fish in the sea. You can make this salad with Funa Salad (page 228) instead of sardines, if you prefer. I like to eat it with roasted garlic spread over crackers (page 282).

2 green zucchini

2 yellow zucchini

¼ teaspoon fine sea salt

1 cup Caesar Dressing (page 125) or Creamy Italian Dressing (page 124), or as desired

2 (3.75-ounce) cans sardines

Ground black pepper, for serving

1. Scrub the zucchini, then spiral-slice them with the flat blade (or with the comb removed) to create wide, continuous ribbons. Add the spiral-sliced zucchini to a mixing bowl, sprinkle with the salt, and toss to coat. Cover the bowl and let the zucchini sweat for 1 to 2 hours to soften and release some moisture.

2. Squeeze the zucchini in a clean, dry kitchen towel to remove more of the moisture, and discard the liquid in the bowl. Add the zucchini back to the empty bowl and coat in the dressing.

3. Divide the zucchini among four serving bowls and top each portion with half a can of sardines. Serve with pepper for seasoning.

Note: *Remember to plan ahead with this recipe. The zucchini needs 1 to 2 hours to sweat.*

funa salad wraps

Makes about 4 cups salad, enough for about 8 wraps | Prep Time: 20 minutes | Wait Time: overnight

Dried seaweed gives this salad a hint of seafood flavor. The salad is equally good with or without it.

1½ cups raw sunflower seeds

1 cup finely chopped celery

½ cup finely chopped red onion

⅓ cup naturally fermented pickle relish

⅓ cup Paleo-friendly mayonnaise

2 tablespoons fresh-squeezed lemon juice

2 teaspoons dried dill weed

½ teaspoon ground dried seaweed (optional)

Big pinch of fine sea salt

For wrapping:

8 large collard green leaves (1 per wrap)

1. Place the sunflower seeds in a mixing bowl and add enough water to cover, plus 2 inches. Soak the seeds in the refrigerator overnight or for at least 5 hours.

2. Drain the sunflower seeds, rinse in fresh water, and then drain again. Put the seeds in a food processor fitted with the S-blade and process until finely chopped, 5 to 10 seconds.

3. Transfer the seeds to a mixing bowl and add the rest of the ingredients, except for the collard greens. Stir to combine.

4. Bring a medium-sized saucepan of water to a simmer. Rinse the collard greens and remove the stems up to halfway through each leaf (see page 50). Submerge the leaves in the simmering water, one at a time, for about 1 minute.

5. Lay a collard green leaf flat side down. Add a few spoonfuls of salad to the middle. Fold the outsides over the salad, then roll to wrap. (See page 51 for step-by-step photos.) Repeat with the remaining collard greens and salad.

veggie burritos

Makes 2 | Prep Time: 20 minutes | Wait Time: overnight

My husband and kids (and even I occasionally) eat white rice. To make this dish without white rice, substitute cauli-rice. There are multiple recipes for cauli-rice in books and online; to try a spin on this Paleo favorite, search for "Indian 'Couscous'" on my blog, The Spunky Coconut. *And don't forget the coconut aminos—it takes these burritos from good to great!*

½ cup raw sunflower seeds

2 large collard green leaves (1 per burrito)

1 cup shredded carrots

Red onion slices, as desired

1 cup cooked white rice or cauli-rice (see note above)

Fine sea salt

Coconut aminos, for dipping

1. Put the sunflower seeds in a mixing bowl and add enough water to cover, plus 2 inches. Soak the seeds in the refrigerator overnight or for at least 5 hours, then drain.

2. Bring a medium-sized saucepan of water to a simmer. Rinse the collard greens and remove the stems up to halfway through each leaf (see page 50). Submerge the leaves in the simmering water, one at a time, for about 1 minute.

3. Lay a collard green leaf flat side down. Layer the burrito fillings: shredded carrots, onion slices, rice, and drained sunflower seeds. Season with salt to taste. Fold the outsides over the fillings, then roll to wrap. (See page 51 for step-by-step photos.) Repeat with the second collard green leaf and the remaining filling ingredients.

4. Serve the burritos with coconut aminos for dipping.

nacho cheese cauliflower poppers

Serves 4 | Prep Time: 15 minutes | Cook Time: 30 minutes

This is my go-to recipe when I'm craving nachos. Problem solved.

1 cup raw cashews

½ cup water

1 tablespoon fresh-squeezed lemon juice

2 teaspoons gluten-free Dijon mustard

¾ teaspoon fine sea salt

½ teaspoon onion powder

½ teaspoon garlic powder

¼ teaspoon ground cumin

⅛ teaspoon ground black pepper

1 large head cauliflower, cut into bite-sized pieces

1. Set the oven to 400°F and line a rimmed baking sheet or 12-inch cast-iron skillet with unbleached parchment paper.

2. Place the cashews in a high-powered blender or food processor fitted with the S-blade and process until finely ground. Add the rest of the ingredients, except for the cauliflower, and puree until completely smooth.

3. In a mixing bowl, toss the cauliflower in the puree until evenly coated. Spread the coated cauliflower on the prepared baking sheet. Bake for about 30 minutes, until nicely browned.

4. Serve the poppers as soon as they are cool enough to handle.

sun-dried tomato & roasted red pepper dip

Makes 1½ cups | Wait Time: 4 hours | Prep Time: 10 minutes

½ cup raw cashews, soaked in water for at least 4 hours, rinsed, and drained

½ cup roasted red peppers

¼ cup sun-dried tomatoes

2 tablespoons water

1 tablespoon fresh-squeezed lemon juice

⅛ teaspoon garlic powder

Handful of fresh basil leaves

Fine sea salt and black pepper, to taste

For serving:

Peeled and thinly sliced jicama

Cherry tomatoes

1. Place all of the ingredients in a food processor fitted with the S-blade. Puree until completely smooth, about 3 minutes.

2. Serve the dip with sliced jicama and cherry tomatoes.

spinach & artichoke dip

Makes 1½ cups | Wait Time: overnight | Prep Time: 10 minutes

It might surprise you to hear that my kids love this dip, but it's true! I think it's due to the punch of salty flavor that the marinated artichokes add.

½ cup raw cashews, soaked in water overnight in the fridge

2 tablespoons Paleo-friendly mayonnaise

1 tablespoon fresh-squeezed lemon juice

⅛ teaspoon garlic powder

⅛ teaspoon fine sea salt

1 (6½-ounce) jar marinated artichokes, including liquid

1 (10-ounce) package frozen spinach, thawed and squeezed in a kitchen towel to remove as much water as possible

For serving:

Crackers (page 282) or apple slices

1. Rinse and drain the cashews, then place them in a food processor fitted with the S-blade. Add the mayonnaise, lemon juice, garlic powder, and salt and process until mostly smooth.

2. Add the artichokes (including their liquid) and spinach and process again until mostly smooth.

3. Serve the dip with crackers or thinly sliced apples.

roasted garlic bean dip

Makes 1½ cups | Wait Time: overnight | Prep Time: 10 minutes | Cook Time: 45 minutes

We eat beans sometimes. Before you get all bent out of shape about that, read Chris Kresser's article "Are Legumes 'Paleo'? And Does It Really Matter?" (you can find it at http://chriskresser.com/are-legumes-paleo). And by all means, if you don't tolerate properly soaked, home-cooked beans (or any food, for that matter), then you shouldn't eat them.

1 cup dried white beans, soaked in water overnight

2 whole heads garlic

Avocado oil, for drizzling

½ cup (70 g) raw cashews, soaked in water for at least 4 hours, rinsed, and drained

2 tablespoons Paleo-friendly mayonnaise

1 teaspoon fresh-squeezed lemon juice

1 teaspoon gluten-free Dijon mustard

½ teaspoon Salt Blend (page 117)

For serving:
Cucumber slices

1. Rinse the soaked beans and place them in a large saucepan. Cover with cold water and bring to a boil. Reduce the heat to maintain a simmer and continue to cook, with the lid on but slightly ajar, until the beans are completely tender, about 30 minutes. Drain and set aside to let the beans come to room temperature.

2. While the beans are cooking, roast the garlic: Set the oven to 400°F. Cut the top off of each head of garlic and place them in an oven-safe dish with a lid. (I use my oven-safe glass loaf pan, which has its own lid.) Drizzle the tops with avocado oil and roast for about 45 minutes, until the garlic is starting to brown. Remove from the oven and allow to cool until you can easily handle the garlic.

3. Squeeze the roasted garlic cloves from the heads into a food processor fitted with the S-blade. Add the rest of the ingredients, including the cooked beans, and puree until completely smooth, about 3 minutes.

4. Serve the dip with cucumber slices.

sweet potatoes au gratin

Serves 8 | Prep Time: 25 minutes | Cook Time: 50 minutes

1 batch "cheese" base (with cashews or nut-free; pages 110 and 111)

2 teaspoons gluten-free Dijon mustard

¼ teaspoon onion powder

¼ teaspoon garlic powder

⅛ teaspoon smoked paprika

2 pounds sweet potatoes

Ghee or avocado oil, for greasing the baking dish

1. Set the oven to 400°F. Make the "cheese" base according to the directions, but add the mustard, onion powder, garlic powder, and smoked paprika to the blender with the other ingredients. Puree until completely smooth.

2. Peel the sweet potatoes and slice them into ¼-inch rounds. Grease a 2-quart baking dish or Dutch oven with ghee, then pour in some of the sauce. Arrange a layer of the sweet potato rounds in the bottom of the pan, overlapping them slightly. Pour some sauce over the potatoes. Repeat with the rest of the potatoes and sauce, ending with sauce.

3. Cover (if using a baking dish, use a stainless-steel sheet pan turned upside down) and bake for about 50 minutes, until the sweet potatoes are tender.

4. Serve warm.

curry twice-baked potatoes

Serves 2 | Prep Time: 20 minutes | Cook Time: 10 minutes

These spiced potatoes with peas are like deconstructed samosas. They're much easier to make, and they're delicious.

2 Slow Cooker Baked Potatoes (page 126), made with russets

1 cup green peas, room temperature

¼ cup full-fat coconut milk

2 tablespoons melted bacon fat (page 108) or ghee

1½ teaspoons curry powder

½ teaspoon fine sea salt

1. Set the oven (or toaster oven) to 450°F. Slice the baked potatoes lengthwise down the center, going about a quarter of the way down. Carefully scoop out the insides and put the insides in a mixing bowl. Mash the potato with a fork, then add the rest of the ingredients and stir to combine.

2. Spoon the mixture back into the potato "jackets" and load it on top. Bake for about 10 minutes, until nicely browned on top.

3. Serve warm.

mashed potatoes & gravy

Serves 8 | Prep Time: 20 minutes | Cook Time: 30 minutes

Mashed potatoes:

12 large potatoes (about 5 pounds), peeled and cut into chunks

1 cup chicken broth (page 131)

1 cup cashew milk (page 143)

¼ teaspoon garlic powder

1½ teaspoons Salt Blend (page 117)

Ground black pepper

Chopped fresh parsley, for garnish (optional)

Gravy (makes about 3½ cups):

¼ cup ghee

2 tablespoons arrowroot or tapioca flour

1½ cups cashew milk (page 143)

1½ cups chicken broth (page 131)

½ teaspoon Salt Blend (page 117)

¼ teaspoon garlic powder

Ground black pepper, to taste

1. Make the mashed potatoes: In a steamer pot, steam the potatoes until they are fork-tender, about 20 minutes. Transfer the steamed potatoes to a large mixing bowl.

2. In a saucepan, bring the rest of the ingredients for the mashed potatoes, except for the parsley, just to a boil. Pour the liquid over the potatoes and mash with a potato masher. Add more liquid if needed. Garnish with chopped parsley, if desired.

3. Make the gravy: In a saucepan, melt the ghee over medium heat, then whisk in the arrowroot flour. Slowly pour in the cashew milk in increments while whisking, allowing it to thicken before adding more. Continue until all of the milk is incorporated. Add the broth in the same way, whisking to incorporate. Remove the gravy from the heat and whisk in the Salt Blend, garlic powder, and pepper.

4. Serve the gravy hot over the mashed potatoes.

green bean casserole

Serves 8 | Prep Time: 20 minutes | Cook Time: 35 minutes

This was one of the first recipes I created when I found out that I had celiac disease, and over the years it's evolved to become even easier to make. I can't imagine a holiday dinner without it.

2 tablespoons ghee, divided

16 ounces mushrooms, sliced

3 large yellow onions, sliced

Fine sea salt and black pepper

Sauce:

2 tablespoons ghee

2 tablespoons arrowroot or tapioca flour

3 cups cashew milk (page 143) or full-fat coconut milk*

2 teaspoons Salt Blend (page 117)

½ teaspoon garlic powder

¼ teaspoon fine sea salt

2½ pounds (40 ounces) frozen green beans (about 8 cups)

*I prefer this dish with cashew milk, but coconut milk is a good option if you need it to be nut-free.

1. Put two 12-inch skillets over medium heat. Place a tablespoon of ghee in each skillet. Add the sliced mushrooms to one skillet and the sliced onions to the other. Season the mushrooms and onions with salt and pepper. Sauté the mushrooms for about 10 minutes, until they have reduced and are nicely browned. Sauté the onions for about 5 minutes, then reduce the heat to low and continue cooking, stirring frequently, until the onions are caramelized, about 30 minutes.

2. Meanwhile, in a saucepan, make the sauce: Melt the ghee over medium heat, then whisk in the arrowroot flour. Slowly pour in the cashew milk in increments while whisking, allowing it to thicken before adding more. Continue until all of the milk is incorporated. Remove the sauce from the heat and whisk in the Salt Blend, garlic powder, and salt.

3. In a steamer pot, steam the green beans until just tender. Pour out the water and add the strained green beans to the hot empty pot. Add the sautéed mushrooms, caramelized onions, and sauce and stir to combine. (Reserve some of the sautéed onions and mushrooms to garnish the top, if desired.)

4. Transfer to a casserole dish and serve warm, with the reserved onions and mushrooms strewn across the top, if desired.

chapter 12:
Pasta

one-pot pizza pasta

Serves 4 | Prep Time: 20 minutes | Cook Time: 25 minutes

This is a perfect example of how easy it is to replace pasta or grains with vegetables. I know, I know—butternut squash is actually a fruit, but you know what I mean.

1 large butternut squash

1 tablespoon ghee or bacon fat (page 108)

½ teaspoon fine sea salt

½ batch "cheese" base (with cashews or nut-free; pages 110 and 111)

1 cup Pizza Sauce (page 130)

1 cup strained tomatoes

9 ounces mild Italian sausage, cooked and sliced or chopped

2½ ounces pepperoni, sliced

For serving:

Italian seasoning

Red pepper flakes (optional)

1. Peel the butternut squash and cut it in half lengthwise. Remove the seeds, then spiral-slice it to get 7 cups (1¾ pounds) of squash noodles.

2. Place a large pot or 12-inch skillet over medium heat. Melt the ghee in the skillet, then add the squash noodles and salt. Sauté the noodles, stirring frequently, until they have reduced by half, about 5 minutes.

3. Add the "cheese" base, pizza sauce, and strained tomatoes. Stir to combine, then reduce the heat to low. Cover and cook for about 20 minutes, stirring occasionally. The pasta is done when the noodles reach the desired tenderness. Add water if needed to keep the noodles from scorching on the bottom of the pot.

4. Top the noodles with the sliced sausage and pepperoni. Serve garnished with Italian seasoning and red pepper flakes, if desired.

chicken & mushroom alfredo

Serves 4 | Prep Time: 25 minutes | Cook Time: 30 minutes

This creamy pasta is so good. It's like a cross between a casserole and chicken noodle soup. Pure comfort food.

Fine sea salt

2 celery roots (celeriac), each about 4 inches wide, peeled and spiral-sliced

2 tablespoons ghee, divided

1 batch "cheese" base (with cashews or nut-free; pages 110 and 111)

1 tablespoon fresh-squeezed lemon juice

¼ teaspoon onion powder

¼ teaspoon garlic powder

8 ounces mushrooms, sliced

½ batch Easy Chicken (page 126), chopped

Fresh ground black pepper, for serving

1. Sprinkle ½ teaspoon of salt on the celery root noodles. Place a 12-inch skillet over low to medium heat. Melt 1 tablespoon of the ghee in the skillet, then add the noodles. Cook, stirring frequently, until the noodles have reduced by half, about 5 minutes. Reduce the heat to low, cover, and sweat the noodles until they're al dente, about 10 minutes.

2. Add the "cheese" base, lemon juice, onion powder, and garlic powder. Stir to combine. Cover and cook for about 5 minutes, stirring occasionally. The pasta is done when the noodles reach the desired tenderness. Add water if needed to keep the noodles from scorching on the bottom of the pot.

3. While the noodles are cooking, sauté the mushrooms: Place a separate skillet over medium heat. Add the remaining tablespoon of ghee, mushrooms, and a pinch of salt and sauté until the mushrooms are tender, then set aside.

4. Add the chopped chicken and mushrooms to the noodles just before serving. Stir to combine, then serve with fresh ground pepper.

beef stroganoff

Serves 4 | Prep Time: 25 minutes | Cook Time: 30 minutes

When you make this sauce with cashews, it's very creamy and thick. The nut-free sauce (pictured) is thinner and nice as a lighter meal. Substitute more coconut milk for the broth to make the nut-free sauce richer.

½ teaspoon Salt Blend (page 117)

1¼ pounds white-fleshed sweet potatoes, peeled and spiral-sliced (6 cups)

4 tablespoons ghee or avocado oil, divided

1 yellow onion, sliced

8 ounces mushrooms, sliced

Fine sea salt and black pepper

2 cloves garlic, minced

2 tablespoons cooking sherry

1 pound ground beef

Sauce:

½ batch "cheese" base (with cashews or nut-free; pages 110 and 111)

2 teaspoons smoked paprika

1 teaspoon dried dill weed

⅛ teaspoon ground black pepper

1. Sprinkle the Salt Blend on the sweet potato noodles. Place a 12-inch skillet over low to medium heat. Melt 3 tablespoons of the ghee in the skillet, then add the noodles. Cook, stirring frequently, until the noodles have reduced by half, about 5 minutes. Reduce the heat to low, cover, and sweat the noodles until they're al dente, about 5 minutes. Once al dente, slide the pan off the heat and cover to keep the noodles warm while you make the stroganoff.

2. Place the remaining tablespoon of ghee, onion, and mushrooms in another 12-inch skillet over medium heat and season with salt and pepper. Cook until tender, about 10 minutes, adding the minced garlic about halfway through. Add the sherry to deglaze the pan, then transfer the mushrooms and onion to a dish.

3. Return the mushroom skillet to the heat and use it to cook the ground beef. Break up the beef with a spatula and cook until no longer pink. Use a slotted spoon to transfer the beef to the dish with the mushrooms and onion, and discard the fat in the pan.

4. Make the "cheese" base according to the directions, but add the smoked paprika, dill, and pepper to the blender with the other ingredients. Add the puree to a saucepan and bring to a simmer, then turn off the heat.

5. Serve the noodles topped with the beef mixture and sauce.

orange chicken with broccoli

Serves 4 | Prep Time: 20 minutes | Cook Time: 15 minutes

This is what I make when I'm craving Chinese food. It's full of flavor and so satisfying.

Noodles:

½ teaspoon Salt Blend (page 117)

1¼ pounds white-fleshed sweet potatoes, peeled and spiral-sliced (6 cups)

3 tablespoons ghee or avocado oil

Sauce:

1 cup fresh-squeezed orange juice

½ cup chicken broth (page 131)

1 tablespoon apple cider vinegar

1 teaspoon Salt Blend (page 117)

1 teaspoon arrowroot or tapioca flour

2 cloves garlic

1 (1-inch) piece fresh ginger, skin scraped off

1 head broccoli (about 1½ pounds), cut into bite-sized pieces and steamed

½ batch Easy Chicken (page 126), thinly sliced and warmed

For garnish (optional):

Sesame seeds

1. Sprinkle ½ teaspoon of Salt Blend on the sweet potato noodles. Place a 12-inch skillet over low to medium heat. Melt the ghee in the skillet, then add the noodles and cook, stirring frequently, until the noodles have reduced by half, about 5 minutes. Reduce the heat to low, cover, and sweat the noodles until they're al dente, about 5 minutes. Once al dente, slide the pan off the heat and cover to keep the noodles warm while you make the sauce.

2. Make the sauce: Place the orange juice, broth, vinegar, Salt Blend, arrowroot flour, garlic, and ginger in a blender and puree until completely smooth. (If not using a high-powered blender, roughly chop the ginger before adding it to the blender.) Transfer the puree to a saucepan and bring to a simmer, then turn off the heat.

3. Serve the noodles topped with the steamed broccoli, chicken, and sauce. Sprinkle with sesame seeds, if desired.

southwest pasta

Serves 4 | Prep Time: 20 minutes | Cook Time: 25 minutes

½ teaspoon Salt Blend (page 117)

1¼ pounds white-fleshed sweet potatoes, peeled and spiral-sliced (6 cups)

4 tablespoons ghee or avocado oil, divided

1 pound ground beef

Sauce:

1½ cups chicken broth (page 131)

¼ cup sun-dried tomatoes

1½ teaspoons ground cumin

1½ teaspoons chili powder

1 teaspoon Salt Blend (page 117)

1 teaspoon arrowroot or tapioca flour

For garnish:

2 green onions, finely sliced

1. Sprinkle the Salt Blend on the sweet potato noodles. In a 12-inch skillet over low to medium heat, melt 3 tablespoons of the ghee. Add the noodles and cook, stirring frequently, until the noodles have reduced by half, about 5 minutes. Reduce the heat to low, cover, and sweat the noodles until they're al dente, about 5 minutes. Slide the pan off the heat and cover to keep the noodles warm while you prepare the beef and sauce.

2. Place the remaining 1 tablespoon of ghee and the ground beef in another 12-inch skillet. Break up the beef with a spatula and cook until no longer pink. Use a slotted spoon to transfer the beef to a dish.

3. Make the sauce: Place the broth, sun-dried tomatoes, cumin, chili powder, Salt Blend, and arrowroot flour in a blender and puree until completely smooth. Transfer to a saucepan and bring to a simmer, then turn off the heat.

4. Serve the noodles topped with the ground beef and sauce, garnished with sliced green onions.

chicken amatriciana

Serves 4 | Prep Time: 20 minutes | Cook Time: 30 minutes

When my husband and I were dating, there was a charming Italian restaurant within walking distance of my apartment. We would go there for dinner and order Chicken Amatriciana. I always felt so sick after eating the pasta that came with the chicken. What a pleasure it is to be able to eat all of my favorite dishes again, without the pain!

10 ounces bacon, chopped

1 yellow onion, chopped

1½ pounds boneless, skinless chicken breast (about 3 breast halves)

Fine sea salt

Onion powder

Garlic powder

1 (24-ounce) jar strained tomatoes

Noodles:

½ teaspoon Salt Blend (page 117)

1¼ pounds sweet potatoes, peeled and spiral-sliced (6 cups)

3 tablespoons ghee or avocado oil

For garnish (optional):
Fresh basil leaves

1. Place a 12-inch skillet over medium-low heat. Add the bacon and onion and cook until the bacon is nicely browned. Remove the bacon and onion from the pan and set aside. Discard most of the fat, leaving 2 tablespoons in the pan.

2. Sprinkle the chicken on both sides with a few pinches of salt, onion powder, and garlic powder. Place the chicken in the pan and cook for about 1 minute. Flip the chicken over and add the strained tomatoes. Put the bacon and onions on top of the chicken and tomatoes. Reduce the heat to low, cover, and cook until the chicken is done, about 20 minutes.

3. Meanwhile, sprinkle the Salt Blend on the sweet potato noodles. Place another 12-inch skillet over medium-low heat. Add the ghee and noodles and cook, stirring frequently, until the noodles have wilted, about 5 minutes. Reduce the heat to low, cover, and sweat the noodles until they're al dente, about 5 minutes.

4. Serve the noodles topped with the chicken (either sliced, as pictured, or whole breast halves) and sauce mixture from the pan. Garnish with chopped or snipped basil leaves, if desired.

meaty tomato lasagna

Serves 8 | Prep Time: 25 minutes | Cook Time: 55 minutes | Wait Time: 30 minutes

I am so proud of this lasagna. It tastes amazing, and it's free of the unhealthy substitutes commonly found in dairy-free lasagna: tofu and packaged fake cheese. Don't let the watery "ricotta cheese" fool you—it sets up perfectly when baked!

Ghee or avocado oil, for greasing the baking dish

Meat sauce:

1 tablespoon ghee

2 pounds ground beef

4 cups strained tomatoes

1 tablespoon apple cider vinegar

1 tablespoon plus 1 teaspoon Italian seasoning

2 teaspoons fine sea salt

1 teaspoon onion powder

1 teaspoon garlic powder

Ricotta cheese:

1½ cups raw cashews

1½ cups water

2 teaspoons fresh-squeezed lemon juice

1½ teaspoons Salt Blend (page 117)

¼ cup ghee

2 tablespoons arrowroot or tapioca flour

4 large eggs, whisked

Noodles:

1 (12-ounce) package Cappello's fresh grain-free and gluten-free lasagna sheets or 12 ounces butternut squash "noodles"*

*Peel the squash and slice it lengthwise into ⅛-inch-thick strips, as illustrated on page 262. Alternatively, use a julienne slicer to cut the squash into noodles.

1. Set the oven to 350°F. Lightly grease a 13 by 9-inch baking dish with ghee and set aside.

2. Make the meat sauce: Place a 12-inch skillet over low to medium heat. Add the tablespoon of ghee and the beef and cook, breaking up the beef with a spatula, until no longer pink. Add the tomatoes, vinegar, Italian seasoning, salt, onion powder, and garlic powder and stir. Bring the sauce to a simmer, then turn off the heat.

3. Make the ricotta cheese: Place the cashews, water, lemon juice, and Salt Blend in a blender and puree until completely smooth. Heat the ghee in a small heavy-bottomed pot over medium heat, then whisk in the arrowroot flour. Whisk the cashew puree into the arrowroot mixture to thicken, then remove from the heat.

4. When the cheese mixture has cooled to room temperature, add the whisked eggs. (If the mixture is hot, it will scramble the eggs.)

5. To assemble: Arrange a single layer of noodles across the bottom of the prepared dish, followed by a third of the meat sauce. Pour a third of the ricotta cheese over the meat sauce, then repeat the layers twice, ending with ricotta cheese.

6. Bake uncovered for 40 minutes, until the cheese is set. Allow to cool for 30 minutes, then serve.

pumpkin lasagna

Serves 8 | Prep Time: 25 minutes | Cook Time: 45 minutes | Wait Time: 30 minutes

Ghee or avocado oil, for greasing the baking dish

Pumpkin filling:

3 cups pumpkin puree (from 1 [4½-pound] pumpkin or 2 [15-ounce] cans

¼ cup coconut sugar

1 tablespoon ghee

1½ teaspoons ground cinnamon

½ teaspoon fine sea salt

¼ teaspoon ground allspice

Ricotta cheese:

1½ cups raw cashews

1½ cups water

2 teaspoons fresh-squeezed lemon juice

1½ teaspoons Salt Blend (page 117)

¼ cup ghee

2 tablespoons arrowroot or tapioca flour

4 large eggs, whisked

Noodles:

1 (12-ounce) package Cappello's grain-free, gluten-free lasagna sheets or 12 ounces butternut squash "noodles"*

*Peel the butternut squash and slice it lengthwise into ⅛-inch-thick strips, as illustrated. Alternatively, use a julienne slicer to cut the squash into noodles.

1. Set the oven to 350°F. Lightly grease a 13 by 9-inch baking dish with ghee and set aside.

2. Make the pumpkin filling: Puree the filling ingredients in a food processor fitted with the S-blade. Set aside.

3. Make the ricotta cheese: Place the cashews, water, lemon juice, and Salt Blend in a blender and puree until completely smooth. Heat the ghee in a small heavy-bottomed pot over medium heat. Whisk the arrowroot flour into the ghee, then whisk the cashew puree into the arrowroot mixture to thicken. Remove from the heat to cool.

4. When the cashew puree is at room temperature, add the whisked eggs. (If the cashew mixture is hot, it will scramble the eggs.)

5. To assemble: Arrange a single layer of noodles across the bottom of the prepared dish, followed by a third of the pumpkin filling. Pour a third of the ricotta cheese over the pumpkin filling, then repeat the layers twice, ending with ricotta cheese.

6. Bake uncovered for 40 minutes, until the ricotta cheese is set. Allow the lasagna to cool for 30 minutes, then serve.

fettuccine alfredo

Serves 4 | Prep Time: 15 to 25 minutes | Cook Time: 10 to 20 minutes

True story: The first time my thirteen-year-old had (gluten-free) mac-n-cheese made with real cheese, she put down her fork and told me, "Yours is better." What a compliment! Whether you call it mac-n-cheese or fettuccine Alfredo, I hope you love this recipe just as much as my family does.

Sauce:

½ or 1 batch "cheese" base (with cashews or nut-free; pages 110 and 111), depending on type of noodle used

½ or 1 teaspoon fresh-squeezed lemon juice, depending on type of noodle used

Noodles:

2 (9-ounce) packages Cappello's fettuccine or 1¼ pounds white-fleshed sweet potatoes, peeled and spiral-sliced (6 cups)*

½ teaspoon Salt Blend (page 117; if using sweet potato noodles)

3 tablespoons ghee or avocado oil (if using sweet potato noodles)

1 head broccoli (about 1½ pounds), cut into florets

*For egg- and nut-free, use sweet potato noodles.

1. If using Cappello's fettuccine, make a full batch of the "cheese" base and add 1 teaspoon lemon juice to the puree. If using sweet potato noodles, make a half batch of the "cheese" base and add ½ teaspoon lemon juice to the puree.

2. If using Cappello's fettuccine, cook the noodles as directed on the package. If using sweet potato noodles, sprinkle the Salt Blend on the sweet potato noodles. In a 12-inch skillet over low to medium heat, melt the ghee. Add the noodles and cook, stirring frequently, until the noodles have reduced by half, about 5 minutes. Reduce the heat to low, cover, and sweat the noodles until they're al dente, about 5 minutes.

3. Steam the broccoli florets in a steamer pot until just fork-tender.

4. Add the sauce and steamed broccoli to the noodles and stir, then serve.

spaghetti with turkey meatballs

Serves 4 (with leftover meatballs) | Prep Time: 15 to 25 minutes | Cook Time: 25 minutes

This recipe makes enough meatballs for leftovers. Why? Because these meatballs are so good, even without the noodles and sauce. I even eat them straight from the refrigerator. Cut the meatball ingredients in half if you want to make just enough for one meal.

Meatballs:

2 stalks celery, roughly chopped

2 large carrots, roughly chopped

1 teaspoon fine sea salt

¼ teaspoon garlic powder

Handful of fresh parsley

2 pounds ground turkey

¾ cup almond flour or ⅓ cup coconut flour (use coconut flour for nut-free)

2 large eggs, whisked

Red sauce:

4 cups strained tomatoes

1 tablespoon apple cider vinegar

1 tablespoon plus 1 teaspoon Italian seasoning

2 teaspoons fine sea salt

1 teaspoon onion powder

1 teaspoon garlic powder

Noodles:

2 (9-ounce) packages Cappello's fettuccine or 1¼ pounds zucchini, spiral-sliced (6 cups)*

½ teaspoon fine sea salt, if using zucchini noodles

1 tablespoon ghee, if using zucchini noodles

*For nut-free, use zucchini noodles.

1. Set the oven to 350°F. Line a rimmed baking sheet with unbleached parchment paper.

2. Place the celery, carrots, salt, garlic powder, and parsley in a food processor fitted with the S-blade. Process until the celery and carrots are finely chopped. Transfer to a large mixing bowl. Add the ground turkey, almond flour, and eggs and stir until well combined.

3. Use a ¾-ounce (size 40) scoop with a lever or a spoon to make about 40 meatballs. Drop them onto the prepared baking sheet and bake until cooked through, about 25 minutes.

4. While the meatballs are cooking, prepare the sauce: Combine all of the ingredients in a saucepan over medium heat. Bring to a simmer, then remove to the back of the stove to keep warm, with the lid ajar, while you prepare the noodles.

5. If using Cappello's fettuccine, cook the noodles as directed on the package. If using zucchini noodles, sprinkle the salt on the zucchini noodles. Place a 12-inch skillet over low to medium heat. Melt the ghee in the skillet, then add the noodles. Cook, stirring frequently, until the noodles have reduced by half, about 5 minutes. Reduce the heat to low, cover, and sweat the noodles until they're al dente, about 10 minutes.

6. Serve the meatballs with the noodles and sauce.

chapter 13:

Bread & Pizza

sandwich bread

Makes 1 loaf | Prep Time: 15 minutes | Wait Time: 30 minutes | Cook Time: 45 minutes

This bread is hard to resist when it's still slightly warm from the oven. It's an eyebrow-raising kind of yummy. It's also amazing straight from the refrigerator—soft and flexible when sliced for sandwiches—and fantastic toasted or grilled. However you prefer to eat it, this bread is perfect.

1¼ cups warm water

1 teaspoon honey

2 teaspoons active dry yeast

2¼ cups (306 g) Pizza & Bread Mix (page 133)

4 large eggs, room temperature

¼ cup avocado oil

1 tablespoon apple cider vinegar

1. Lay a piece of unbleached parchment paper across an 8½ by 4½-inch loaf pan so that it goes down one of the long sides, across the bottom, and back up the other long side of the pan. Grease the exposed short ends of the pan. Set aside.

2. Pour the warm water into a glass measuring cup with a spout. Add the honey and stir until dissolved. (The honey will activate the yeast.) Mix the yeast into the liquid, then let it sit for 5 minutes. (It should be foamy on top. If it isn't foamy, then either the water was too hot or the yeast is inactive and you will need to try again.)

3. Place the Pizza & Bread Mix in a large mixing bowl. Add the eggs, avocado oil, and vinegar. Finally, add the yeast mixture. Mix with a handheld mixer until just combined.

4. Using a flexible spatula, scoop the dough into the prepared pan and press down firmly. Place the loaf on top of the oven, then turn the oven to 350°F. Let the dough rise for 30 minutes while the oven heats.

5. After 30 minutes, place the pan in the oven and bake for about 45 minutes, until a knife inserted into the middle comes out mostly clean. Let the bread cool in the pan. For neat slices, refrigerate to chill completely before slicing.

6. Store in the refrigerator for up to a week.

Note: *If you've forgotten to take the eggs out of the fridge to come to room temperature, you can hurry up the process by setting them in a bowl of hot tap water for about 10 minutes.*

cinnamon raisin bread

Makes 1 loaf | Prep Time: 15 minutes | Wait Time: 30 minutes | Cook Time: 45 minutes

Like my Sandwich Bread (page 270), this bread is hard to resist warm from the oven. It's also delicious toasted, topped with ghee and cinnamon.

1¼ cups warm water

1 teaspoon honey

2 teaspoons active dry yeast

2¼ cups (306 g) Pizza & Bread Mix (page 133)

4 large eggs, room temperature (see Note, page 270)

¼ cup avocado oil

1 tablespoon coconut sugar

1 tablespoon ground cinnamon

1 tablespoon apple cider vinegar

¾ cup raisins

1. Lay a piece of unbleached parchment paper across an 8½ by 4½-inch loaf pan so that it goes down one of the long sides, across the bottom, and back up the other long side of the pan. Grease the exposed short ends of the pan. Set aside.

2. Place the warm water in a glass measuring cup with a spout. Add the honey and stir until dissolved. (The honey will activate the yeast.) Mix the yeast into the liquid, then let it sit for 5 minutes. (It should be foamy on top. If it isn't foamy, then either the water was too hot or the yeast is inactive and you will need to try again.)

3. Place the Pizza & Bread Mix in a large mixing bowl. Add the eggs, avocado oil, coconut sugar, cinnamon, vinegar, and raisins. Finally, add the yeast mixture. Mix with a handheld mixer until just combined.

4. Using a flexible spatula, scoop the dough into the prepared pan and press down firmly. Place the pan on top of the oven, then turn the oven to 350°F. Let the dough rise for 30 minutes while the oven heats.

5. After 30 minutes, place the pan in the oven and bake for about 45 minutes, until a knife inserted into the middle comes out mostly clean. Let the bread cool in the pan. For neat slices, refrigerate to chill completely before slicing.

6. Store in the refrigerator for up to a week.

pumpkin bread with cream cheese swirl

Makes 2 loaves | Prep Time: 20 minutes | Cook Time: 55 minutes

You can cut the ingredients in half and make just one loaf, but trust me—you're going to want two. Keep the bread in the fridge for up to a week, or freeze individually wrapped slices.

Cream cheese swirl:

½ cup raw cashews

¼ cup unsweetened almond milk

1 tablespoon melted coconut oil or ghee

1 teaspoon vanilla extract

1 large egg white

⅛ teaspoon fine sea salt

Pumpkin bread:

1 cup (136 g) coconut flour, sifted

½ cup (68 g) arrowroot or tapioca flour

1 teaspoon baking soda

1 (15-ounce) can pumpkin puree or 2 cups homemade puree (from 1 [3-pound] pumpkin)

8 large eggs, room temperature (see Note, page 270)

½ cup (80 g) coconut sugar

6 tablespoons melted coconut oil or ghee

2 teaspoons ground cinnamon

2 teaspoons Pumpkin Spice Blend (page 118)

1 teaspoon fine sea salt

¼ teaspoon liquid vanilla stevia

1. Set the oven to 350°F. Line two 8½ by 4½-inch loaf pans with unbleached parchment paper so that it goes down one of the long sides, across the bottom, and back up the other long side of each pan. Grease the exposed short ends of the pans. Set aside.

2. In a mini blender, puree the cream cheese swirl ingredients until completely smooth. Set aside.

3. In a mixing bowl, combine the flours and baking soda with a whisk. Add the rest of the bread ingredients and mix with a handheld mixer until well combined.

4. Transfer just over half of the dough to the lined pans, filling each pan about half full. Using a spoon, do your best to create a channel for the cream cheese in the middle of each pan. Divide the cream cheese swirl evenly between the pans. Add the rest of the dough on top of the cream cheese and smooth out the top. The cream cheese will creep up the sides somewhat—don't worry, the bread will still turn out really yummy.

5. Bake the loaves for about 55 minutes, until a knife inserted into the middle comes out mostly clean. Let the bread cool in the pans, then loosen the ends with a knife. Remove the bread from the pans and serve at room temperature.

6. Store in the refrigerator for up to a week.

banana bread

Makes 2 loaves | Prep Time: 20 minutes | Cook Time: 50 minutes

Dry ingredients:

1 teaspoon sea salt

2 teaspoons ground cinnamon

½ cup (68 g) arrowroot or tapioca flour

1 cup (136 g) coconut flour, sifted

1 teaspoon baking soda

½ cup (80 g) coconut sugar

Wet ingredients:

4 bananas, mashed (about 2 cups)

8 large eggs, room temperature (see Note, page 270)

½ cup melted coconut oil or ghee

Add-ins (optional):

½ cup chopped dark chocolate (80% cacao; about 3 ounces) or chopped raw walnuts (omit walnuts for nut-free)

1. Set the oven to 350°F. Line two 8½ by 4½-inch loaf pans with unbleached parchment paper so that it goes down one of the long sides, across the bottom, and back up the other long side of each pan. Grease the exposed short ends of the pans. Set aside.

2. In a mixing bowl, combine the dry ingredients with a whisk. Add the wet ingredients and mix with a handheld mixer. Fold in the chocolate or nuts, if using.

3. Divide the dough evenly between the prepared pans and smooth the tops with a flexible spatula.

4. Bake the loaves for about 50 minutes, until a knife inserted into the middle comes out mostly clean. Let the bread cool in the pans, then loosen the ends with a knife. Remove the bread from the pans and serve at room temperature.

5. Store in the refrigerator for up to a week.

kalamata focaccia quick bread

Serves 4 | Prep Time: 15 minutes | Cook Time: 15 to 17 minutes

½ cup (68 g) Pizza & Bread Mix (page 133)

1 teaspoon Italian seasoning

⅛ teaspoon garlic powder

¼ cup chopped pitted Kalamata olives (see Note)

1 tablespoon finely chopped sun-dried tomatoes (optional)

¼ cup avocado oil

1 large egg

Extra-virgin olive oil, for serving

1. Set the oven to 350°F and line a baking sheet with unbleached parchment paper.

2. In a mixing bowl, combine the Pizza & Bread Mix, Italian seasoning, and garlic powder with a whisk. Add the olives, sun-dried tomatoes (if using), avocado oil, and egg and mix with a handheld mixer for about 20 seconds. The dough will be very sticky.

3. Press the dough into one solid mass and transfer it to the prepared baking sheet. Use your hands to press it into a 5-inch square or circle. *Optional:* Make an X in the middle for presentation, as shown in the photo, opposite.

4. Bake for 15 to 17 minutes or until the bread is almost firm in the middle when you press it. It's better to undercook it slightly, since it will continue cooking after it comes out of the oven.

5. Enjoy the bread with your favorite extra-virgin olive oil.

6. Store in an airtight container at room temperature for up to 2 days or in the refrigerator for up to a week. If it has been refrigerated, toast the bread to soften it again.

Note: *This bread needs the added moisture from the olives. If they are omitted, the bread will be too dry.*

orange & ginger sweet bread

Serves 4 | Prep Time: 15 minutes | Cook Time: 15 to 17 minutes

This sweet bread is a great fast-and-easy fix when you want something sweet but don't feel up to making a whole cake.

½ cup (68 g) Pizza & Bread Mix (page 133)

¼ cup Orange Chutney (page 136) or chopped kumquats, skin on, seeds removed (see Note)

¼ cup finely chopped crystallized ginger

3 tablespoons coconut oil or palm shortening

1 tablespoon honey

1 large egg

1. Set the oven to 350°F and line a 5-inch square baking dish or a baking sheet with unbleached parchment paper.

2. In a mixing bowl, combine all of the ingredients with a handheld mixer for about 20 seconds. The dough will be very sticky.

3. Press the dough into the lined baking dish, or press it into one solid mass and transfer it to the baking sheet. If using a baking sheet, use your hands to press it into a 5-inch square.

4. Bake for about 20 minutes if using a baking dish or 15 to 17 minutes if using a baking sheet, until it's almost firm in the middle when you press it. It's better to undercook it slightly, since it will continue cooking after it comes out of the oven.

5. Enjoy the bread at room temperature.

6. Store in an airtight container at room temperature for up to 2 days or in the refrigerator for up to a week. If it has been refrigerated, warm the bread to soften it again.

Note: *This bread needs the added moisture from the chutney or kumquats. If omitted, the bread will be too dry.*

Variation: Cherry Chocolate Chip Sweet Bread. *Omit the chutney or kumquats and crystallized ginger. Add 2 tablespoons dairy-free dark chocolate chips, ¼ teaspoon almond or amaretto extract, and ½ cup dried tart cherries that have been soaked in water for 1 hour and then drained.*

crackers

Makes 2 dozen | Prep Time: 15 minutes | Cook Time: 25 minutes

If you were a fan of Ritz Crackers before going Paleo, then you'll love these. They're buttery and crumbly and great in soup or with one of my dips (pages 236 to 238).

Just under 1 cup (138 g) Scone & Pie Crust Mix (page 133)

¼ cup softened ghee or palm shortening

3 tablespoons water

1 tablespoon apple cider vinegar

1 teaspoon Italian seasoning

1. Set the oven to 350°F. Place all of the ingredients in a large mixing bowl. Combine with a handheld mixer until the mixture looks like fine gravel, about 20 seconds.

2. Roll out the dough between two pieces of unbleached parchment paper into a rectangle about ¼ inch thick, or 9 by 11 inches. For a nice rectangular shape, use your hands to press the edges in as you roll. Remove the top piece of parchment and use a pizza wheel to score the dough into 1 by 2-inch crackers, but do not pull the pieces apart yet.

3. By pulling the bottom sheet of parchment paper, carefully slide the dough onto a baking sheet and bake for about 25 minutes, until golden brown. Let cool on the pan.

4. When the crackers are cool, carefully break them apart on the scored lines. Store in an airtight container in the refrigerator for up to 2 weeks.

cracker pizzas

Makes two 7-inch pizzas | Prep Time: 20 minutes | Cook Time: 25 minutes

Cracker crust:

Just under 1 cup (138 g) Scone & Pie Crust Mix (page 133)

¼ cup softened ghee or palm shortening

3 tablespoons water

1 tablespoon apple cider vinegar

1 teaspoon Italian seasoning

Toppings:

16 large fresh basil leaves

½ cup Pizza Sauce (page 130)

8 cherry tomatoes, cut in half

2 to 3 tablespoons diced red onion

Red pepper flakes (optional)

1. Set the oven to 400°F. Cut out two circles of unbleached parchment paper to line the bottoms of two 7-inch springform pans.

2. Place the cracker crust ingredients in a large mixing bowl and combine with a handheld mixer until the mixture resembles fine gravel, about 20 seconds.

3. Divide the crumbly dough evenly between the two prepared pans. Press the dough evenly across the bottom of each pan so that it looks smooth. Run a knife between the crust and the wall of the pan, then remove the wall. Use a chef's knife to score each crust into eight triangular pizza slices, but do not pull apart the triangles yet.

4. Place the pan bottoms on a baking sheet and bake the crusts for about 25 minutes, until nicely browned. Let cool on the pan.

5. When the crusts are cool, carefully separate the triangles. Top each cracker with a basil leaf. Add a teaspoon of pizza sauce on top of the basil. (The basil creates a barrier to prevent the cracker from becoming soggy.) Place a cherry tomato half on top of each dollop of pizza sauce. Sprinkle on the red onion. Garnish with red pepper flakes (if using) and serve. These pizzas are best enjoyed the day they're made.

tomato pizza

Makes one 10-inch deep-dish pizza or two 6-inch thin-crust pizzas | Prep Time: 20 minutes
| Wait Time: 30 minutes | Cook Time: 8 to 12 minutes

*I don't know why I waited so long to try adding yeast to my pizza dough—it makes it taste
just like restaurant pizza. In fact, now that I've perfected this homemade pizza, I can't even
remember the last time we went out for gluten-free pizza! It's a whole new, delicious world.
Also, between you and me, I prefer this crust on the chewier side, so I tend to keep the baking
time at around 8 minutes, even when I'm making a thicker crust.*

Crust:

¾ cup warm water

1 teaspoon honey

2 teaspoons active dry yeast

1½ cups (204 g) Pizza & Bread Mix
(page 133)

¼ cup melted ghee or avocado oil

1 large egg or flax egg (see page
27), room temperature (use flax
egg for egg-free)

1 tablespoon apple cider vinegar

Toppings:

½ cup Pizza Sauce (page 130), or
as desired

¾ cup sliced or diced veggies of
choice

¾ cup sliced or diced cooked
meat of choice

Note: *The crust(s) can be baked
ahead of time.*

1. Place the warm water in a glass measuring cup with a
spout. Add the honey and stir until dissolved. (The honey
will activate the yeast.) Mix the yeast into the liquid, then
let it sit for 5 minutes.

2. Place the Pizza & Bread Mix, ghee, egg, and vinegar in
a mixing bowl. Pour the yeast mixture in last. (It should be
foamy on top. If it isn't foamy, then either the water was
too hot or the yeast is inactive and you will need to try
again.) Mix with a handheld mixer for about 10 seconds.
Press the dough into one mass, then cover the mixing
bowl with a towel and place it on top of the oven.

3. Place a 12-inch cast-iron skillet or pizza stone in the
oven, then turn the oven to 400°F. Let the dough rise for
30 minutes while the oven heats.

4. After 30 minutes, transfer the dough to a piece of
unbleached parchment paper and cover with another
piece of parchment. For a deep dish–style pizza crust,
roll out the dough between the two sheets to a circle 10
inches in diameter, or divide the dough in half and roll out
each crust to 6 inches in diameter. The height of the crust
will double in the oven.

5. Remove the top sheet of parchment paper and top the
crust with the sauce, veggies, and meat. By pulling the
bottom sheet of parchment, carefully slide the pizza and
parchment into the skillet or onto the stone.

6. Bake for 8 to 12 minutes, depending on the thickness of
the crust, then carefully remove the pizza from the oven.
Enjoy right away.

7. Store leftovers in the refrigerator for up to a week.

sausage & egg pizza

Makes one 10-inch deep-dish pizza or two 6-inch thin-crust pizzas | Prep Time: 20 minutes
| Wait Time: 30 minutes | Cook Time: 8 to 12 minutes

Crust:

¾ cup warm water

1 teaspoon honey

2 teaspoons active dry yeast

1½ cups (204 g) Pizza & Bread Mix (page 133)

¼ cup melted ghee or avocado oil

1 large egg, room temperature

1 tablespoon apple cider vinegar

Toppings:

2 tablespoons ghee, softened

4 large eggs

12 ounces breakfast sausage, cooked and chopped, or 8 ounces precooked breakfast sausage, chopped (see Notes, page 322)

Note: *The crust(s) can be baked ahead of time.*

1. Place the warm water in a glass measuring cup with a spout. Add the honey and stir until dissolved. (The honey will activate the yeast.) Mix the yeast into the liquid, then let it sit for 5 minutes.

2. Place the Pizza & Bread Mix, ghee, egg, and vinegar in a mixing bowl. Pour the yeast mixture in last. (It should be foamy on top. If it isn't foamy, then either the water was too hot or the yeast is inactive and you will need to try again.) Mix with a handheld mixer for about 10 seconds. Press the dough into one mass, then cover the mixing bowl with a towel and place it on top of the oven.

3. Place a 12-inch cast-iron skillet or pizza stone in the oven, then turn the oven to 400°F. Let the dough rise for 30 minutes while the oven heats.

4. After 30 minutes, transfer the dough to a piece of unbleached parchment paper. Cover the dough with another piece of parchment. For a deep dish–style pizza crust, roll out the dough between the two sheets to a circle 10 inches in diameter, or divide the dough in half and roll out each crust to about 6 inches in diameter. (It can be difficult to transfer a pizza topped with eggs to the oven if it is larger than 10 inches.) The height of the crust will double in the oven.

5. Remove the top sheet of parchment paper and pinch the edge of the crust slightly to create a well for the eggs. Spread the ghee across the top of the crust, then add the eggs and sausage. By pulling the bottom sheet of parchment, carefully slide the pizza and parchment into the skillet or onto the stone.

6. Bake for 8 to 12 minutes, depending on the thickness of the crust, then carefully remove the pizza from the oven. Enjoy right away.

7. Store leftovers in the refrigerator for up to a week.

greek pizza

Makes one 12-inch pizza or two 7-inch thin-crust pizzas | Prep Time: 20 minutes
| Wait Time: 30 minutes | Cook Time: 8 to 12 minutes

By rolling out this crust on the thinner side, you can fold your slice in half and eat it like pita bread. It's so good!

Crust:

¾ cup warm water

1 teaspoon honey

2 teaspoons active dry yeast

1½ cups (204 g) Pizza & Bread Mix (page 133)

¼ cup ghee or avocado oil, melted

1 large egg or flax egg (see page 27), room temperature (use flax egg for egg-free)

1 tablespoon apple cider vinegar

Sauce:

6 ounces dairy-free coconut yogurt, homemade (page 182) or store-bought

1 clove garlic, minced

¼ teaspoon dried dill weed

Toppings:

¾ cup thinly sliced Easy Chicken (page 126)

½ cup sliced cherry tomatoes

¼ cup finely chopped red onion

¼ cup pitted Kalamata olives

¼ cup chopped green bell pepper

Handful of fresh parsley, chopped

Note: *The crust(s) can be baked ahead of time.*

1. Pour the warm water into a glass measuring cup with a spout. Add the honey and stir to dissolve. (The honey will activate the yeast.) Mix the yeast into the liquid, then let it sit for 5 minutes.

2. Place the Pizza & Bread Mix, ghee, egg, and vinegar in a mixing bowl. Pour the yeast mixture in last. (It should be foamy on top. If it isn't foamy, then either the water was too hot or the yeast is inactive and you will need to try again.) Mix with a handheld mixer for about 10 seconds. Press the dough into one mass, then cover the mixing bowl with a towel and place it on top of the oven.

3. Place a 12-inch cast-iron skillet or pizza stone in the oven, then turn the oven to 400°F. Let the dough rise for 30 minutes while the oven heats.

4. After 30 minutes, transfer the dough to a piece of unbleached parchment paper. Cover the dough with another piece of parchment. Roll it out between the two sheets to a circle 11 or 12 inches in diameter, or divide the dough in half and roll out each crust to 6 to 7 inches in diameter. The height of the crust will double in the oven.

5. Remove the top sheet of parchment paper. Mix the yogurt, garlic, and dill in a small mixing bowl, then spread it across the top of the crust. By pulling the bottom sheet of parchment, carefully slide the pizza and parchment into the skillet or onto the stone.

6. Bake, topped only with the yogurt sauce, for 8 to 12 minutes, depending on the thickness of the crust, then carefully remove the pizza from the oven. Top the pizza with the chicken, tomatoes, red onion, olives, bell pepper, and parsley. Enjoy right away.

7. Store leftovers in the refrigerator for up to a week.

barbecue chicken pizza

Makes one 10-inch deep-dish pizza or two 6-inch thin-crust pizzas | Prep Time: 20 minutes
| Wait Time: 30 minutes | Cook Time: 8 to 12 minutes

Barbecued chicken week makes me so happy. First I make barbecued chicken in the slow cooker (so easy—see page 292), then we have it on salad (page 310), then on potato boats (page 305), and then on this pizza. So much awesome.

Crust:

¾ cup warm water

1 teaspoon honey

2 teaspoons active dry yeast

1½ cups (204 g) Pizza & Bread Mix (page 133)

¼ cup melted ghee or avocado oil

1 large egg or flax egg (see page 27), room temperature (use flax egg for egg-free)

1 tablespoon apple cider vinegar

Toppings:

½ cup Barbecue Sauce (page 129), or as desired

1 cup Slow Cooker Barbecue Chicken (page 298), or as desired

½ red onion, sliced

Handful of fresh cilantro, chopped

Note: *The crust(s) can be baked ahead of time.*

1. Place the warm water in a glass measuring cup with a spout. Add the honey and stir until dissolved. (The honey will activate the yeast.) Mix the yeast into the liquid, then let it sit for 5 minutes.

2. Place the Pizza & Bread Mix, ghee, egg, and vinegar in a mixing bowl. Pour the yeast mixture in last. (It should be foamy on top. If it isn't foamy, then either the water was too hot or the yeast is inactive and you will need to try again.) Mix with a handheld mixer for about 10 seconds. Press the dough into one mass, then cover the mixing bowl with a towel and place it on top of the oven.

3. Place a 12-inch cast-iron skillet or pizza stone in the oven, then turn the oven to 400°F. Let the dough rise for 30 minutes while the oven heats.

4. After 30 minutes, transfer the dough to a piece of unbleached parchment paper. Cover the dough with another piece of parchment. For a deep dish–style pizza crust, roll out the dough between the two sheets to 10 inches, or divide the dough in half and roll out each crust to about 6 inches. The height of the crust will double in the oven.

5. Remove the top sheet of parchment paper and top the crust with the sauce and chicken. By pulling the bottom sheet of parchment, carefully slide the pizza and parchment into the skillet or onto the stone.

6. Bake for 8 to 12 minutes, depending on the thickness of the crust, then carefully remove the pizza from the oven. Top the pizza with the red onion and cilantro. Enjoy right away.

7. Store leftovers in the refrigerator for up to a week.

chapter 14:
Meat Dishes

faux rotisserie chicken with potatoes

Serves 4 | Prep Time: 20 minutes | Cook Time: 4 to 6 hours

This faux rotisserie chicken with potatoes is the epitome of an easy dinner. Just add the potatoes and chicken to the slow cooker in the morning, and most of the work is done for you by the time you get home. What's more, the chicken has all the qualities of an actual rotisserie chicken: It has the same seasoning and perfectly crispy skin, and the meat is melt-in-your-mouth tender. You're going to be a huge fan. To take dinner up a notch, transform the slow-cooked potatoes into chunky mashed potatoes.

2½ pounds russet potatoes (about 6)

1 whole chicken, 3 to 4 pounds

1 tablespoon Everyday Seasoning (page 117)

Chunky mashed potatoes (optional):

Cooked russet potatoes (from above)

½ cup chicken broth (page 131), heated

½ cup cashew milk (page 143), heated (use full-fat coconut milk for nut-free)

¾ teaspoon Salt Blend (page 117)

¼ teaspoon garlic powder

Ground black pepper, to taste

Variation: Brined Chicken Thighs with Potatoes. *Make 3 cups of Poultry Brine, following the recipe on page 128. Soak 8 skin-on, bone-in chicken thighs in the brine for 24 hours, then rinse the chicken. Cook the chicken on top of the potatoes (as directed above) in a slow cooker for 4 hours on high or 6 hours on low. Like the Faux Rotisserie Chicken, you can crisp the skin in the oven afterward.*

1. Scrub the potatoes, poke the tops once with a fork, and lay them in a dry 7-quart slow cooker.

2. Remove the giblets from inside the chicken and use your fingers to separate the skin from the breast. Add about ¼ teaspoon of the Everyday Seasoning to each of the pockets that you created between the breast and the skin. Add the remaining Everyday Seasoning to the outside of the chicken, making sure to cover the breast and legs especially well.

3. Lay the chicken breast side up on top of the potatoes in the slow cooker. Tie the legs together if you like. Cook for 4 hours on high or 6 hours on low.

4. Turn off the slow cooker and allow the chicken to cool slightly. When the chicken is cool enough to move safely, set the oven to 450°F and line a rimmed baking sheet with unbleached parchment paper. Place the chicken breast side up on the baking sheet. Put the chicken in the hot oven for about 10 minutes, until the skin is perfectly golden.

5. Serve the chicken with the slow-cooked potatoes straight from the slow cooker, or use them to make chunky mashed potatoes (to make, proceed to Step 6). (*Note:* Reserve the chicken bones and juices that accumulated in the slow cooker for making chicken broth.)

6. To make the chunky mashed potatoes: While the chicken skin is getting crispy in the oven, place the cooked potatoes in a mixing bowl. Add the broth, cashew milk, Salt Blend, garlic powder, and pepper. Mash with a potato masher until the liquid is incorporated but the potatoes are still slightly chunky. Reheat if needed before serving.

slow cooker barbecue chicken

Makes about 8 cups shredded chicken | Prep Time: 10 minutes | Cook Time: 3 hours

2 cups Barbecue Sauce (page 129)

4 pounds boneless, skinless chicken breast (about 8 breast halves)

Salt Blend (page 117), to season

1. Place a little of the barbecue sauce in the bottom of a 7-quart slow cooker. Season the chicken on both sides with the Salt Blend. Lay the meat in the slow cooker and pour the rest of the barbecue sauce on top. Cook on high for 3 hours.

2. Shred the chicken with two forks. Stir before serving to evenly coat the chicken with the barbecue sauce.

bacon & ranch twice-baked potatoes

Serves 2 | Prep Time: 20 minutes | Cook Time: 10 minutes

My oldest, Zoe, is crazy about these twice-baked potatoes. They're ridiculously good.

2 Slow Cooker Baked Potatoes (page 126)

2 tablespoons melted bacon fat (page 108) or ghee

¼ cup Ranch Dressing (page 120)

4 to 6 slices bacon, cooked until crispy and chopped

⅛ teaspoon ground black pepper

1. Set the oven (or toaster oven) to 450°F. Slice the baked potatoes lengthwise down the center, about a quarter of the way down. Carefully scoop out the insides and add to a mixing bowl. Mash the potato with a fork, then add the rest of the ingredients to the mixing bowl. Stir to combine.

2. Spoon the mixture back into the potato jackets and load it on top. Bake for about 10 minutes, until nicely browned on top.

apple & jicama sandwiches

Serves 2 | Prep Time: 10 minutes

These sandwiches are super easy and super yummy. Assemble them the day you plan to eat them to keep the apples and jicama from getting soggy.

Apple sandwiches:

2 tablespoons sunflower seed butter without added sugar (such as Organic SunButter), or as desired

1 teaspoon honey (optional)

1 teaspoon powdered collagen (see page 26), or more as needed

Pinch of fine sea salt

1 apple

1 teaspoon fresh-squeezed lemon juice or a pinch of ground cinnamon

Jicama sandwiches:

1 jicama, fist-sized or larger

2 romaine lettuce leaves

Gluten-free Dijon mustard or Paleo-friendly mayonnaise (optional; use mustard for egg-free)

¼ pound deli meat of choice*

*If you can't find organic, nitrate-free deli meat, substitute Easy Chicken (page 126), sardines, or Funa Salad (page 228).

1. For apple sandwiches, mix together the sunflower seed butter, honey (if using), collagen, and salt in a small bowl. Add more collagen as needed to thicken. I like the seed butter to be fairly firm so that it doesn't spread or fall out the sides of the sandwich. Turn the apple on its side and slice it into ¼-inch-thick rounds. Use a stainless-steel vegetable cutter to punch a hole in the middle, removing the seeds. Spread the seed butter on the apple slices to create sandwiches. Use a silicone basting brush to brush the apple sandwiches with the lemon juice, or sprinkle the sandwiches with ground cinnamon. (The lemon will prevent browning, and the cinnamon will hide browning.)

2. For jicama sandwiches, peel the jicama, then turn it on its side and slice it into ¼-inch-thick rounds. Place the lettuce on one jicama slice, then spread mustard or mayonnaise (if using) onto the lettuce. Add the deli meat, then the second jicama slice. To serve, cut the sandwich in half as shown, opposite, or leave it whole.

chicken nuggets

Serves 4 | Prep Time: 25 minutes | Cook Time: 20 minutes

One of my kids will eat anything. Like, anything. One will eat whatever she's currently obsessed with eating. Like, the same three things every day for a month. And one of my kids won't eat chicken in any way other than these chicken nuggets. They're that good, you guys, they're that good.

2 cups (224 g) almond flour

2 teaspoons Everyday Seasoning (page 117)

4 large eggs

1½ pounds boneless, skinless chicken breast (about 3 breast halves), cut into strips

½ cup Creamy Honey Dijon Dressing (page 121), for dipping

1. Set the oven to 450°F and line a rimmed baking sheet with unbleached parchment paper.

2. In a mixing bowl, combine the almond flour and Everyday Seasoning with a whisk. In a separate bowl, whisk the eggs.

3. Using a fork, skewer a chicken strip and lower it into the beaten eggs, letting the excess run off. Then put the chicken strip in the flour mixture, spoon the flour over the chicken, and lightly shake off the excess. Dip the chicken in the egg once more, then put it back in the flour again. Place each coated strip on the prepared baking sheet.

4. Bake for about 20 minutes, until nicely browned.

5. Serve with Creamy Honey Dijon Dressing for dipping.

hot dog boats

Serves 4 as a meal, 8 as a snack | Prep Time: 15 minutes

½ cup naturally fermented sauerkraut (such as Bubbies), or as desired

8 nitrate-free hot dogs (such as Applegate), grilled, pan-fried, or boiled

8 Crispy Potato Boats (page 127), hot out of the oven

Naturally fermented pickle relish, to top

Fill each potato boat with sauerkraut and a hot dog. Top with pickle relish.

barbecue chicken boats

Serves 4 as a meal, 8 as a snack | Prep Time: 15 minutes

2 cups (or more) Slow Cooker
Barbecue Chicken (page 298),
warmed

8 Crispy Potato Boats (page 127),
hot out of the oven

1 avocado, sliced

Fill each potato boat with barbecue chicken. Top with
sliced avocado.

taco boats

Serves 4 as a meal, 8 as a snack | Prep Time: 20 minutes | Cook Time: 20 minutes

Fun fact: My husband grew up in rural Pennsylvania, and until we began dating in college, he had never eaten Mexican food. And I had never heard of pirogies. (Right now some of you are Googling pirogies, am I right?)

Taco ground beef:

1 teaspoon avocado oil

1 pound ground beef

½ cup water or chicken broth (page 131)

¼ cup salsa of choice

¼ cup tomato paste

1 tablespoon Easy Taco Seasoning (page 116)

1 batch Guacamole (page 130)

8 Crispy Potato Boats (page 127), hot out of the oven

For garnish (optional):

Chopped fresh cilantro

1. Place a 12-inch skillet over medium heat. Melt the avocado oil in the skillet, then add the ground beef, breaking it up with a spatula, and cook until no longer pink. Add the water, salsa, tomato paste, and Easy Taco Seasoning and stir to combine.

2. Reduce the heat and simmer, stirring occasionally, until the liquid has reduced by half, about 10 minutes.

3. While the sauce is reducing, combine the ingredients for the guacamole.

4. Fill each potato boat with taco ground beef. Top with guacamole and a sprinkle of cilantro (if using) and enjoy.

curry chicken salad wraps

Serves 4 | Prep Time: 20 minutes

When I was growing up, my mom always put curry powder in her chicken salad, and to this day, I never make chicken salad without curry powder. These wraps are great with chips cooked in coconut oil or avocado oil.

½ batch Easy Chicken (page 126), chopped

1½ cups finely chopped celery (about 4 stalks)

½ cup Paleo-friendly mayonnaise

½ cup raisins

½ cup sliced almonds

1 tablespoon packed finely chopped fresh parsley

1 teaspoon curry powder

¼ teaspoon fine sea salt

⅛ teaspoon ground black pepper

For wrapping:
Lettuce or collard leaves

Combine all of the ingredients for the salad in a mixing bowl. Serve wrapped in lettuce or collard green leaves (see pages 50 and 51 for the wrapping technique).

cider cabbage & kielbasa

Serves 6 | Prep Time: 15 minutes | Cook Time: 6 hours

This dish doesn't come out of the slow cooker as pretty as it goes in, but my kids eat it up—it's so delicious! It's one of my most popular easy recipes of all time, and I hope you love it, too. Our tradition is to throw it in the slow cooker the day we go to the pumpkin patch. When we get home, the house smells amazing, and we can't wait to eat.

1 bunch kale, chopped

1 head red cabbage, sliced

1 yellow onion, chopped

2 Granny Smith apples, peeled, cored, and sliced

1 (14-ounce) kielbasa, sliced into ½-inch pieces

½ cup apple cider

1 tablespoon apple cider vinegar

1 tablespoon honey

1 teaspoon Salt Blend (page 117)

Place all of the ingredients in a 7-quart slow cooker—no need to stir. Cook for 6 hours on high. Stir, then serve.

Note: *Some kielbasa can be quite peppery. If you have kids who don't like peppery foods, try bratwurst instead.*

burrito bowl

Serves 4 | Prep Time: 20 minutes | Cook Time: 25 minutes

This burrito bowl is so satisfying, I could eat it every week. But I'm a sucker for Mexican food.

1 batch taco ground beef (page 306)

1 bunch bok choy

½ head cabbage

1 parsnip, peeled

1 tablespoon bacon fat (page 108)

½ red onion, chopped

Fine sea salt and black pepper

For serving:

Salsa of choice

1 batch Guacamole (page 130)

1. Make the taco ground beef, following Steps 1 and 2 on page 306.

2. While the liquid in the taco ground beef is reducing, prep the vegetables: Finely slice the bok choy and cabbage, then rinse and drain them. Spiral-slice the parsnip into noodles, then cut them crosswise into short lengths resembling long-grained rice.

3. Heat the bacon fat in a 12-inch skillet over low to medium heat. Add the bok choy, cabbage, parsnip, red onion, and a pinch of salt and pepper and cook for about 10 minutes, stirring occasionally, until tender.

4. Serve the veggies topped with salsa, taco ground beef, and guacamole.

barbecue chicken salad

Serves 4 | Prep Time: 15 minutes

One of my favorite things about salad is how long it takes to eat. Right? Because dinner usually gets wolfed down in a matter of seconds, but eating a salad takes time. And I love eating. And sitting around eating with my family and friends.

1 head lettuce, chopped or torn into small pieces

⅓ to ½ cup Ranch Dressing (page 120), as desired

3 cups Slow Cooker Barbecue Chicken (page 298)

1 cup cherry tomatoes, sliced

Handful of fresh basil leaves, chopped

Handful of fresh cilantro leaves, chopped

In a mixing bowl, combine the lettuce and Ranch Dressing. Divide the dressed lettuce among four bowls, then top with the barbecue chicken, tomatoes, basil, and cilantro.

antipasto plate

Serves 4 | Prep Time: 15 minutes

My kids eat antipasto plates almost daily, and usually not for lunch. They have them for dinner and even for breakfast! This is just one example of the kinds of foods I put on their plates. They also love a big spoonful of sunflower seed butter with a pinch of salt and honey mixed in, dip (like my Spinach & Artichoke Dip on page 237), and slices of raw goat cheese for my oldest, who can tolerate it. For more on feeding kids, see page 59.

2 pounds assorted veggies, such as celery, carrots, and red bell pepper

1 pound assorted nitrate-free deli meat, such as pastrami and turkey

1 (6½-ounce) jar marinated artichoke hearts

4 naturally fermented pickles

½ (16-ounce) jar roasted red peppers

8 ounces pitted Kalamata olives

8 ounces garlic-stuffed green olives

Clean and prep the veggies as desired, then arrange your assortment on a large platter or divide among individual plates.

fish-n-chips

Makes 6 patties | Prep Time: 10 minutes | Cook Time: 6 minutes

Enjoy this fried fish as soon as it's cool enough to eat. The outsides of these patties are a crunchy, deep-fried kind of heaven, and the insides are just the opposite—tender and moist. They are still good the next day, but they aren't the same. They work without the egg, too; they just won't be as crunchy.

12 ounces canned wild Alaskan salmon, drained

½ cup (74 g) Scone & Pie Crust Mix (page 133)

1½ teaspoons Everyday Seasoning (page 117)

1 tablespoon fresh chopped parsley

1 teaspoon gluten-free Dijon mustard

1 large egg (optional)

1 cup avocado oil

Chips cooked in coconut oil or avocado oil, for serving

1. In a mixing bowl, combine the salmon, Scone & Pie Crust Mix, Everyday Seasoning, parsley, mustard, and egg.

2. Pour the avocado oil into a 12-inch stainless-steel skillet and turn the heat to medium. When the oil begins to shimmer, use a large (⅓-cup) ice cream scoop with a lever or your hands to form balls, then flatten them into patties. Carefully lay the patties in the skillet. Do not disturb them for at least 3 minutes.

3. Cook the patties until nicely browned, then flip and repeat on the second side.

4. Serve with the chips of your choice. (The chips in the photo, opposite, are Jackson's Honest organic sweet potato chips, which are cooked in coconut oil.)

baja drumsticks

Serves 4 | Prep Time: 10 minutes | Cook Time: 50 minutes

These drumsticks can be a little spicy, depending on how much seasoning you use. For less heat, combine equal parts Easy Taco Seasoning and Salt Blend (page 117). We like our drumsticks with salad and Slow Cooker Baked Potatoes (page 126), coated in sea salt and topped with ghee.

Avocado oil, for greasing the baking dish

8 drumsticks

1 teaspoon Easy Taco Seasoning (page 116)

About 1½ cups chicken broth (page 131)

1. Set the oven to 400°F. Lightly grease a 13 by 9-inch baking dish with avocado oil. Place the drumsticks in the prepared dish and sprinkle them on all sides with the Easy Taco Seasoning.

2. Fill the baking dish with ½ inch of broth and bake for 50 minutes, until the drumsticks are cooked through. Remove from the oven and carefully spoon the broth over the drumsticks.

3. Enjoy the drumsticks hot, or cold from the fridge.

taco rice skillet

Serves 4 | Prep Time: 15 minutes | Cook Time: 15 minutes

3 parsnips, peeled

1 tablespoon ghee or bacon fat (page 108)

1 pound ground beef

2 bell peppers, any color, chopped

½ cup salsa of choice

¼ cup Easy Taco Seasoning (page 116)

For serving:

Sliced avocado

Sliced lime

1. Spiral-slice the parsnips into noodles, then cut them crosswise into short lengths resembling long-grained rice. Set aside.

2. Place the ghee in a 12-inch skillet over medium heat. Add the ground beef, breaking it up with a spatula. Add the chopped peppers, salsa, Easy Taco Seasoning, and parsnip "rice" and stir to combine.

3. Reduce the heat to low and cook, stirring occasionally, until the meat is fully cooked.

4. Serve with avocado and lime slices.

individual pot pies

Serves 6 | Prep Time: 30 minutes | Wait Time: 30 minutes | Cook Time: 50 minutes

I make these mainly for myself, because pot pie is one of my favorite things in the whole world.

Crust:

1 batch Savory Pie Crust (page 134)

¼ cup water

Filling:

1 tablespoon ghee or avocado oil

2 cups finely chopped carrots (about 3 large carrots)

2 cups finely chopped celery (about 6 stalks)

2 cups finely chopped yellow onion (about 1 large onion)

½ teaspoon Salt Blend (page 117)

1 batch Easy Chicken (page 126), chopped

1 batch "cheese" base (with cashews or nut-free; pages 110 and 111)

1½ cups full-fat coconut milk

⅛ teaspoon ground black pepper

1. Make the pie crust dough according to the directions, but add the water to the mixing bowl with the other ingredients. Place a piece of unbleached parchment paper on top of a large cutting board. Press the dough together, place it on top of the paper, and lay another sheet of parchment on top. Roll the dough between the sheets to about 10 by 14 inches. Place the board of dough in the freezer and set a timer for 30 minutes.

2. Meanwhile, set a large heavy-bottomed skillet over low to medium heat. Add the ghee, carrots, celery, onion, and Salt Blend. Cook until almost tender, about 20 minutes. Transfer to a large mixing bowl and add the chicken.

3. Make the "cheese" base according to the directions, but add the coconut milk and pepper to the blender with the other ingredients. Pour one-quarter of this sauce mixture into the bowl with the chicken and vegetables and stir to coat. Divide the filling among six 14-ounce soufflé ramekins. Pour the rest of the sauce into the ramekins to just cover the filling.

4. After 30 minutes, remove the dough from the freezer and set the oven to 350°F. Use a cookie cutter or wide-mouth mason jar lid to cut out 6 circles of dough. *Optional:* Press a mini cookie cutter, like the heart shown in the photo, opposite, into the middle of each circle for presentation. Use a large spatula to transfer the cut dough to the ramekins.

5. Place the ramekins on a rimmed baking sheet and bake for about 30 minutes, until the crust is golden. Let the pot pies cool slightly before serving.

6. Store leftovers in the fridge for up to a week.

curried turkey meatloaf

Makes 2 loaves | Prep Time: 20 minutes | Cook Time: 55 minutes

This meatloaf was inspired by a meatloaf I used to get at the hot bar at the Boulder Whole Foods. It was my favorite thing to eat there. I wonder if they still have it?

Meatloaf:

2 stalks celery, roughly chopped

2 large carrots, roughly chopped

1 teaspoon fine sea salt

1 teaspoon minced garlic

1 teaspoon minced fresh ginger

½ teaspoon curry powder

2 pounds ground turkey

⅓ cup (50 g) coconut flour

2 large eggs, whisked

Curry sauce:

2 tablespoons ghee or avocado oil

2 teaspoons arrowroot or tapioca flour

1 (13½-ounce) can full-fat coconut milk

1 tablespoon coconut aminos

1 teaspoon curry powder

½ teaspoon fine sea salt

1. Set the oven to 350°F and grease two 8½ by 4½-inch loaf pans.

2. Place the celery, carrots, salt, garlic, ginger, and curry powder in a food processor fitted with the S-blade. Process until finely chopped, then transfer to a large mixing bowl. Add the ground turkey, coconut flour, and eggs and combine with your hands.

3. Divide the mixture evenly between the loaf pans, pack it down, and smooth the tops. Bake for 50 minutes or until cooked through, then remove from the oven and let the loaves rest while you make the sauce.

4. To make the curry sauce: Melt the ghee in a saucepan over medium heat, then whisk in the arrowroot flour. Slowly pour in the coconut milk while whisking, allowing it to thicken before adding more. Continue until all of the milk is incorporated. Turn off the heat and add the coconut aminos, curry powder, and salt. Whisk to combine.

5. Slice the meatloaf and serve with the curry sauce.

holiday turkey

Serves 8 | Prep Time: 10 minutes | Wait Time: 24 hours plus 30 minutes | Cook Time: 2 hours

This is how I make Thanksgiving easier: by asking for my turkey in parts. It's easier to brine turkey parts (less equipment and monitoring), and the parts cook in a fraction of the time that it takes to cook a whole bird. Try this recipe and enjoy all the compliments for making the best Thanksgiving turkey ever!

6¾ cups Poultry Brine (page 128), cooled

12 to 14 pounds turkey parts

1 batch Tart Cranberry Sauce (page 137), for serving

1. Place the turkey parts in your largest pot, or use large mixing bowls with lids. Pour the brine evenly over the turkey parts. Add more water as needed to completely cover the turkey. Refrigerate for 24 hours.

2. Rinse the turkey and discard the brine. Let the turkey come to room temperature. Set the oven to 325°F.

3. Lightly grease your largest baking dish and place the turkey parts inside. Bake for 1½ to 2 hours or until a thermometer reads 170°F when inserted into the largest section of thigh.

4. Let the turkey rest, covered, for 30 minutes, so that the juices are reabsorbed. Serve with Tart Cranberry Sauce.

holiday stuffing

Serves 8 | Prep Time: 25 minutes | Cook Time: 45 minutes

I always make this stuffing to satisfy my bread-eating family and friends, who adore it, thereby keeping our holiday table gluten-free. Gotta love that.

20 slices gluten-free sandwich bread, homemade (page 270) or store-bought (see Notes)

Ghee or avocado oil, for greasing the baking dish

1 onion, diced

12 ounces breakfast sausage, cooked and chopped, or 8 ounces precooked breakfast sausage, chopped (see Notes)

2 large carrots, chopped

3 stalks celery, chopped

2 handfuls of fresh parsley

1 teaspoon Salt Blend (page 117)

½ teaspoon Everyday Seasoning (page 117)

1½ cups Chicken broth (page 131)

2 large eggs

1. Set the oven to 325°F, then toast the bread on both sides, being careful not to let it burn. Increase the oven temperature to 350°F and lightly grease a 13 by 9-inch baking dish with ghee.

2. In a food processor fitted with the S-blade, pulse the toasted bread in four batches until you have fine crumbs. Transfer the breadcrumbs to a large mixing bowl.

3. In a skillet, sauté the onion, sausage, carrots, and celery until the vegetables are almost tender. Add the sautéed veggies to the food processor, along with the parsley, Salt Blend, and Everyday Seasoning. Pulse to finely chop. Add the veggie mixture to the breadcrumbs.

4. Whisk together the broth and eggs, then pour over the rest of the ingredients and stir to combine.

5. Spread the mixture in the prepared baking dish and bake for about 40 minutes, until slightly darker.

Notes: *My recipe for homemade sandwich bread is both nut-free and gluten-free. If you are using store-bought gluten-free bread, check the ingredients carefully to make sure that it does not contain nuts, if that is a concern.*

For its quality and convenience, I use fully cooked frozen Applegate breakfast sausage links.

swedish meatballs

Makes about 50 | Prep Time: 25 minutes | Cook Time: 25 minutes

What makes Swedish meatballs Swedish? It's the allspice, so don't leave it out! Lingonberry sauce is traditionally served with Swedish meatballs, but I haven't been able to find it without added sugar. For an all-fruit alternative, I like to use Bionaturae's bilberry fruit spread.

2 cups almond or cashew flour

½ yellow onion, chopped

¼ cup melted ghee or avocado oil, plus more for greasing the pan

Handful of fresh parsley leaves

2 teaspoons chopped fresh rosemary

2 teaspoons fine sea salt

1 teaspoon ground allspice

1 teaspoon garlic powder

¼ teaspoon ground black pepper

1 pound ground beef

1 pound ground pork

2 large eggs, whisked

1. Set the oven to 400°F. Grease a broiler pan or rimmed baking sheet with ghee.

2. Place the flour, onion, ghee, parsley, rosemary, salt, allspice, garlic powder, and pepper in a food processor fitted with the S-blade. Process for about 1 minute, until well combined, then transfer to a large mixing bowl.

3. Add the meat and eggs to the flour mixture and combine with your hands. Use your hands or a ¾-ounce (size 40) scoop with a lever to form 1½-inch meatballs. Drop the meatballs onto the prepared pan and bake for about 25 minutes, until cooked through.

chapter 15:

Cakes & Cookies

black-bottom cupcakes

Makes 12 | Prep Time: 20 minutes | Cook Time: 25 minutes

These cupcakes combine two of my most popular chocolate recipes: Chocolate Swirl Cheese Danish Cake, which is featured in my book The Paleo Chocolate Lovers' Cookbook, *and Paleo Chocolate Cake, which is posted on my blog,* The Spunky Coconut. *If you prefer, you can cut the sweetener further by using ¼ cup of honey and 1 cup of applesauce.*

Cream cheese filling:

1½ cups raw cashew pieces

¾ cup unsweetened almond milk

¼ cup plus 2 tablespoons melted coconut oil

3 tablespoons honey

3 teaspoons vanilla extract

2 egg whites

Dry ingredients:

¾ cup (62 g) cocoa powder (sift if lumpy)

⅓ cup (48 g) coconut flour, sifted

⅓ cup (48 g) tapioca or arrowroot

½ teaspoon baking soda

¼ teaspoon fine sea salt

Wet ingredients:

5 large eggs

¾ cup unsweetened applesauce

½ cup honey

1 tablespoon vanilla extract

¼ teaspoon liquid vanilla stevia

¼ cup melted coconut oil

1. Set the oven to 325°F and line a 12-well muffin pan with unbleached paper liners.

2. In a blender, puree the ingredients for the filling until completely smooth. Set aside.

3. Place the dry ingredients in a large mixing bowl and whisk to combine. In a separate mixing bowl, combine the wet ingredients with a handheld mixer, adding the melted coconut oil last, just before mixing. Add the dry ingredients to the wet, then mix again.

4. Fill the muffin cups two-thirds full with the batter. Use the back of a spoon to spread the batter the rest of the way up the walls of each cup, creating a well in the center. Fill the wells with the cream cheese.

5. Bake the cupcakes for about 25 minutes, until the tops are just set. Remove from the pan and let cool on the counter.

6. Store in an airtight container in the refrigerator for up to a week.

harvest cupcakes

Makes 17 | Prep Time: 35 minutes | Cook Time: 30 minutes

These cute cupcakes can be made with stevia or honey or a combination of the two, depending on your needs.

Dry ingredients:

⅔ cup (96 g) coconut flour, sifted

¼ cup (34 g) arrowroot or tapioca flour

1 tablespoon ground cinnamon

1 teaspoon baking soda

¼ teaspoon fine sea salt

¼ teaspoon ground allspice

Wet ingredients:

3 cups shredded carrots (4 to 5 carrots)

5 large eggs, room temperature

½ cup full-fat coconut milk

½ cup unsweetened applesauce or honey (I like using half of each)

½ teaspoon liquid vanilla stevia (optional)*

¼ cup melted coconut oil

Add-ins:

1 cup raisins

1 cup chopped raw walnuts (optional; omit for nut-free)

Frosting:

1 batch Orange Frosting (page 334)

1 tablespoon India Tree blue decorating sugar (optional)

*If you omit the stevia, use ½ cup honey and no applesauce.

1. Set the oven to 350°F and line 17 wells of two standard-size muffin pans with unbleached paper liners.

2. Place the dry ingredients in a mixing bowl and whisk to combine. In a separate large mixing bowl, combine the wet ingredients, adding the melted coconut oil last, and mix with a handheld mixer. Add the dry ingredients to the wet ingredients, then mix again until well combined. Fold in the raisins and chopped walnuts (if using).

3. Use a large (⅓-cup) ice cream scoop with a lever to transfer the batter into the muffin cups. Using a scoop makes the tops nice and round, and it's much faster than using a spoon.

4. Bake the cupcakes for about 30 minutes, until a knife inserted into the middle comes out mostly clean. Remove from the pan and let cool on the counter.

5. Trim off a corner of a sturdy plastic food storage bag and insert a Wilton #1M Open Star Tip into the hole in the bag. Transfer the frosting to the corner that has the tip. Twist the bag and pipe the frosting onto the cupcakes. Top each cupcake with a pinch of decorating sugar (if using).

6. Store in an airtight container at room temperature for up to 2 days, or refrigerate for up to a week.

Note: *The large (#1M) Open Star Tip is the only tip I ever use, which keeps things easy. I think it gives the prettiest ribbonlike shape to my frosting, and even a beginner cake decorator (like myself) can use this tip to create nice effects. I got mine at a craft store, but they are also available online.*

basic white frosting

Makes 1½ cups

Basic white frosting is typically made of a ratio of 1 cup fat (butter or shortening) to 3 to 4 cups confectioners' sugar. Three to four cups of confectioners' sugar? Like, whoa. I can't get on board with that. I insist that my treats be as healthy as possible. I originally developed this recipe for The Paleo Chocolate Lovers' Cookbook. *It is the base for the naturally colored frostings on the following pages.*

1 cup palm shortening

½ cup honey

⅓ cup (42 g) coconut flour, sifted

⅛ teaspoon fine sea salt

⅛ teaspoon liquid vanilla stevia

Place all of the ingredients in a mixing bowl and combine with a handheld mixer.

Note: *The frosting pictured was made with vanilla bean seeds, which are not included in this recipe. If you are not using this as the base for the naturally colored frostings that follow, you can add the contents of one fresh vanilla bean.*

naturally colored frostings

Each recipe makes 1 cup

Each of these naturally colored frostings uses 1 cup of Basic White Frosting (opposite), which is enough to frost a single-layer 7-inch cake. If you are making all five colors, such as for the Rainbow Cake on page 341, you will need to make a triple batch of the white frosting.

Tips for Making Naturally Colored Frosting

· *My frostings have the least amount of (natural) sweetener you will find anywhere, making them the healthiest possible frostings. One batch of my frosting contains ½ cup of honey, whereas typical frostings contain 3 CUPS or more of (refined) powdered sugar.*

· *Some people say that you can add baking soda to the purple (cabbage) coloring and make blue. However, when I tried it the frosting came out more silver than blue.*

· *I was excited when I came up with the idea of using spirulina powder to make green frosting one day, because I've heard mixed reviews about using juiced spinach, which is a common way to make a naturally colored green frosting. Plus, by using spirulina powder I save myself some time!*

· *Turmeric powder will also work for yellow frosting. I haven't used it because I am worried that my kids (or their friends) will be able to taste it, so I simply lighten my orange frosting (made with goji berries) with white frosting instead. If you use turmeric, keep in mind that it stains.*

· *Beet powder is the only natural food coloring I use that we can taste, which is why I cover it up with almond extract, and then it's yummy. Beet powder will clump over time. You don't want beet-flavored lumps in your frosting, so grind the powder before adding it if it gets lumpy. You can find beet powder at health food stores and online.*

pink frosting

1 cup Basic White Frosting (opposite)

2 teaspoons beet powder

¼ teaspoon almond extract*

*For nut-free, substitute a natural fruit extract, such as those available from Olive Nation.

In a mixing bowl, combine all of the ingredients with a handheld mixer.

orange frosting

¼ cup plus 2 tablespoons goji berries

¼ cup plus 2 tablespoons water

1 cup Basic White Frosting (page 332)

1 tablespoon coconut flour, sifted

1. In a small bowl, soak the goji berries in the water for about 20 minutes.

2. Puree the berries and water in a mini blender or food processor.

3. Place a fine-mesh sieve over a mixing bowl. Pour the goji berry puree into the bowl, pressing the puree against the sieve to extract as much juice as possible. Scrape the back of the sieve with a flexible spatula to get as much juice as possible into the bowl. Discard the seeds left in the sieve.

4. Add the frosting and coconut flour to the bowl and combine with a handheld mixer until smooth.

yellow frosting

¾ cup Basic White Frosting (page 332)

¼ cup Orange Frosting (page 334)

In a mixing bowl, combine the ingredients with a handheld mixer.

blue-green frosting

1 cup Basic White Frosting (page 332)

1 tablespoon spirulina powder

1 teaspoon fresh-squeezed lemon juice

In a mixing bowl, combine all of the ingredients with a handheld mixer.

purple frosting

½ small head red cabbage

1 cup Basic White Frosting (page 332)

1 tablespoon coconut flour, sifted

1. Roughly chop the cabbage and put it in a small pot. Add water to almost cover the cabbage and bring to a boil. Cover and allow to boil for 20 minutes.

2. Use a slotted spoon to remove the cabbage from the water. Lower the heat and simmer, uncovered, to reduce the liquid to about 1 tablespoon. Keep a close eye on it so you don't accidentally reduce it to nothing and burn the pot.

3. Transfer the reduced liquid to a small jar and put it in the fridge to cool.

4. Place the cooled cabbage liquid, frosting, and coconut flour in a mixing bowl and combine with a handheld mixer until smooth.

mint chocolate christmas cake

Serves 9 | Prep Time: 40 minutes | Cook Time: 40 minutes

This has become one of our favorite holiday cakes. It's based on the first egg- and nut-free cake that I ever created. I called it Fudge Cake, and you will see why when you eat this cake. I make it almost every year for my girls' combined birthday party because they request it, and because it's allergen-free for the kids at the party who have egg or nut allergies!

Dry ingredients:

½ cup (46g) cocoa powder (sift if lumpy)

½ cup (68 g) coconut flour, sifted

½ cup (80 g) coconut sugar

¼ cup (30 g) ground golden flax seeds

¼ cup (34 g) arrowroot or tapioca flour

1 teaspoon baking soda

Wet ingredients:

1 cup water

½ cup unsweetened applesauce

1 teaspoon vanilla extract

¼ teaspoon liquid vanilla stevia

¼ cup melted coconut oil

Frosting:

½ batch Basic White Frosting (page 332)

1 batch Blue-Green Frosting (page 334)

½ teaspoon mint extract, divided

1 candy cane*

*In December you can find organic candy canes, free of corn syrup and artificial colors and flavors, at health food stores. They can also be found online. TruJoy is the brand I used for the cake pictured. Always check ingredients for your food sensitivities.

1. Set the oven to 325°F and line an 8-inch square baking dish with unbleached parchment paper. Pinch the corners to help the paper stay in place. Set aside.

2. Place the dry ingredients in a mixing bowl and whisk to combine. In a separate large mixing bowl, mix the wet ingredients with a handheld mixer, adding the melted coconut oil last, just before mixing. Add the dry ingredients to the wet ingredients, then mix again. The batter will look almost doughlike.

3. Transfer the thick batter to the prepared baking dish. Use a flexible spatula or wet hands to spread the dough evenly and pack it down.

4. Bake the cake for about 40 minutes, until a knife inserted into the middle comes out mostly clean. Let cool, then remove from the pan. Cut the parchment paper in half and center the pieces side by side on top of a serving plate. Place the cake on top of the paper. This makes it easier to remove the paper after frosting the cake.

5. Make the frosting as directed, but add ¼ teaspoon mint extract to each color. Use a small flexible spatula to draw a tree shape with white frosting, then frost the background and sides of the cake with the white frosting. Place the blue-green frosting in one corner of a sturdy plastic food storage bag. Cut ⅛ inch off that corner of the bag. Twist the bag and pipe the frosting in short lengths inside the tree shape to mimic the boughs of a pine tree.

6. Crush the candy cane with the back of a spoon. Use the bigger candy cane pieces to decorate the tree, then sprinkle the finer crumbs over the background like snow.

7. Store in an airtight container at room temperature for up to 2 days, or refrigerate for up to a week.

coconut cake

Serves 10 | Prep Time: 40 minutes | Cook Time: 30 minutes | Wait Time: 1 hour

Unlike typical "coconut cakes" found in restaurants and bakeries, which are made of wheat flour and artificial flavoring, mine is the real deal. Made with only coconut flour, this delicious nut-free white cake actually IS a coconut cake.

Dry ingredients:

½ cup (68 g) coconut flour, sifted

¼ teaspoon baking soda

¼ teaspoon fine sea salt

Wet ingredients:

¾ cup egg whites (from about 6 large eggs)*

2 tablespoons honey

¼ cup water

⅛ teaspoon liquid vanilla stevia

¼ cup melted coconut oil, plus more for greasing the pan

Frosting:

2 batches Basic White Frosting (page 332)

1 cup unsweetened coconut flakes, toasted

*Save the yolks for making Coconut Custard (page 357). If you prefer a yellow cake, use ¾ cup whole eggs instead of egg whites.

1. Set the oven to 325°F. Line the bottom only of a 7-inch springform pan with unbleached parchment paper, then grease the walls with coconut oil.

2. Place the dry ingredients in a mixing bowl and whisk to combine. In a separate large mixing bowl, mix the wet ingredients with a handheld mixer, adding the melted coconut oil last, just before mixing. Add the dry ingredients to the wet ingredients, then mix again until well combined.

3. Transfer the batter to the prepared pan. If the batter is thick when you transfer it, use a wet flexible spatula to press it into place.

4. Bake the cake for about 30 minutes, until a knife inserted into the middle comes out mostly clean. The cake will continue cooking slightly after it comes out of the oven. Let cool in the pan.

5. Run a knife around the outside of the pan to loosen the cake, then remove the wall. Freeze the cake for about 1 hour to make slicing easier. Use a long chef's knife to carefully cut the cake in half horizontally so that it is half as tall (for a total of two thin layers).

6. The frosting should be just spreadable. If it's too soft, put it in the fridge to firm up for about 30 minutes. Place a cake layer on a serving plate and frost the top. Place the second cake layer on top and then frost the sides and then the top. Press the toasted coconut onto the sides and sprinkle it on top.

7. Store in an airtight container at room temperature for up to 2 days, or refrigerate for up to a week.

rainbow cake

Serves 12 | Prep Time: 1 hour | Cook Time: 30 minutes | Wait Time: 1 hour

I created this white cake for maximum contrast to the rainbow of frosting. And since I wanted to make a Rainbow Cake for my kids' joint birthday party, it had to be nut-free because some of the children attending the party are allergic to nuts. Although it's possible to be allergic to any food, including coconut, coconut is not actually a nut, but a type of fruit called a drupe.

Dry ingredients:

1½ cups (170 g) coconut flour, sifted

¾ teaspoon baking soda

¾ teaspoon fine sea salt

Wet ingredients:

2¼ cups egg whites (from about 16 large eggs)

¾ cup water

¼ cup plus 2 tablespoons honey

¼ teaspoon plus ⅛ teaspoon liquid vanilla stevia

¾ cup melted coconut oil*, plus more for greasing the pans

Frosting:

1 batch Purple Frosting (page 334)

1 batch Blue-Green Frosting (page 334)

1 batch Yellow Frosting (page 334)

1 batch Orange Frosting (page 334)

1 batch Pink Frosting (page 333)

*To make the cake slightly less coconut-flavored, substitute melted palm shortening for the coconut oil.

1. Set the oven to 325°F. Line the bottoms only of three 7-inch springform pans with unbleached parchment paper, then grease the walls with coconut oil.

2. Place the dry ingredients in a mixing bowl and whisk to combine. In a separate large mixing bowl, mix the wet ingredients with a handheld mixer, adding the melted coconut oil last, just before mixing. Add the dry ingredients to the wet ingredients, then mix again until well combined.

3. Divide the batter evenly among the prepared pans. If the batter is thick when you transfer it, use a wet flexible spatula to press it into place.

4. Bake the cakes for about 30 minutes, until a knife inserted into the middle comes out mostly clean. The cakes will continue cooking slightly after they come out of the oven. Let cool in the pans.

5. Run a knife around the outside of the pan to loosen each cake, then remove the wall. Freeze the cakes for about 1 hour to make slicing easier.

6. Use a long chef's knife to carefully cut each cake in half horizontally so that it is half as tall (for a total of six thin layers). Trim the edges of five of the cakes for presentation purposes. Save the sixth cake layer for another use or give it to a friend.

7. The frosting should be just spreadable. If it's too soft, put it in the fridge to firm up for about 30 minutes. Place one cake layer on a cake plate and spread the purple frosting over it. Lay the next cake layer on top and spread the blue-green frosting over it. After adding the following cake layer, spread the yellow frosting, then

repeat the process with the orange frosting and lastly the pink frosting. If needed at any time during assembly, refrigerate the cake to keep it firm.

8. Refrigerate the cake until 2 hours before you plan to serve it. Enjoy it at room temperature.

9. Store in an airtight container at room temperature for up to 2 days, or refrigerate for up to a week.

no-bake coconut fig bites

Makes about 8 | Prep Time: 20 minutes | Wait Time: overnight

1 packed cup (8 ounces) stemmed and chopped sun-dried and unsulfured figs

1 cup (70 g) unsweetened shredded coconut

2 teaspoons ground cinnamon

1 teaspoon grated orange zest (optional)

⅛ teaspoon fine sea salt

1. Place the chopped figs in a food processor fitted with the S-blade and process until a ball forms. Add the rest of the ingredients and process again until well combined.

2. Use your hands or a ¾-ounce (size 40) scoop with a lever to form 1½-inch balls. Place them on a baking sheet and refrigerate overnight to set.

3. Store in the refrigerator. The bites will keep for at least a week.

crunchy arrowroot cookies

Makes 12 | Prep Time: 20 minutes | Cook Time: 15 minutes

My Australian and British readers have long been asking me for crunchy "arrowroot biscuits." This recipe is for them. Even if you're not an Aussie or a Brit, though, I think you will enjoy these cookies.

¾ cup (90 g) almond flour

½ cup (68 g) arrowroot or tapioca flour

¼ cup (40 g) coconut sugar, ground into a powder

¼ teaspoon fine sea salt

½ cup palm shortening

1 large egg

1 teaspoon vanilla extract

1. Set the oven to 350°F and line a baking sheet with unbleached parchment paper.

2. In a mixing bowl, combine the flours, powdered coconut sugar, and salt with a whisk. Add the shortening, egg, and vanilla and mix with a handheld mixer until well combined.

3. Use a ¾-ounce (size 40) scoop with a lever or a spoon to drop 12 cookies onto the prepared baking sheet, spacing them about 2 inches apart to allow for spreading. Do not flatten the cookies.

4. Bake for about 15 minutes, until the edges of the cookies are nicely browned. Let cool on the baking sheet.

5. Store at room temperature, lightly covered with a cloth napkin, for up to 5 days.

chocolate hazelnut cookies

Makes about 2 dozen | Prep Time: 20 minutes | Cook Time: 24 minutes

I'm crazy for the combination of chocolate and hazelnut. If you are, too, then also check out my famous homemade Nutella recipe, which you can find on my blog, The Spunky Coconut. *What's nice about these cookies is that you don't have to dry the pulp before making them!*

1 heaping cup hazelnut pulp, left over after making Hazelnut Coffee Creamer (page 114)

½ cup (46 g) cocoa powder (sift if lumpy)

¼ cup (34 g) coconut flour, sifted

½ teaspoon baking soda

½ cup chopped raw hazelnuts

½ cup honey

¼ cup softened ghee or coconut oil

¼ cup dairy-free chocolate chips (70% cacao)

¼ teaspoon liquid vanilla stevia

1. Set the oven to 325°F and line a baking sheet with unbleached parchment paper.

2. Place all of the ingredients in a large mixing bowl. Combine with a handheld mixer for about 20 seconds, until well combined.

3. Use your hands or a ¾-ounce (size 40) scoop with a lever to form 1½-inch balls of dough. Drop the balls onto the prepared baking sheet, spacing them about 2 inches apart. Wet your hands and use your palms to flatten the cookies. They won't spread in the oven.

4. Bake for about 24 minutes, until slightly darker in color. Let cool on the baking sheet for about 5 minutes, then transfer to wire racks to finish cooling.

5. Store at room temperature, lightly covered with a cloth napkin, for up to 2 days. Refrigerate to keep for up to a week, or freeze for up to a month.

no-bake strawberries & cream chocolate-covered cookies

Makes about 6 | Prep Time: 20 minutes | Wait Time: 2 hours

Truth be told, my kids ate only the chocolate-covered halves of these cookies the first time I made them. Now I drizzle the chocolate back and forth across the tops of the cookies and they eat the whole thing.

¼ cup plus 2 tablespoons freeze-dried strawberries

½ cup raw cashew butter, room temperature, plus more as needed

⅛ teaspoon fine sea salt

2 ounces dairy-free dark chocolate (70% cacao)

1. In a coffee grinder or Magic Bullet blender, grind the freeze-dried strawberries to a powder, then transfer the powder to a mixing bowl. Add the cashew butter and salt, then combine with a handheld mixer. If the dough is too dry and crumbly and does not hold together, add another spoonful of cashew butter and mix again. Chill the dough in the refrigerator for 1 hour.

2. Use your hands or a ¾-ounce (size 40) scoop with a lever to form 1½-inch balls of dough. Flatten each ball between your palms and lay it on a sheet of unbleached parchment paper. Freeze for at least 1 hour.

3. Place the chocolate in a double boiler and melt over low heat (see page 46 for how to create a double boiler setup). When the chocolate is just melted, remove from the heat. Take the cookies out of the freezer and use a silicone basting brush or small knife to coat half of each cookie in melted chocolate.

4. Store in the freezer. (The cookies can also be stored in the fridge, but they're better frozen!) They will melt at room temperature.

cookie dough bites

Makes about 15 | Prep Time: 30 minutes | Wait Time: 2 hours

Some people turn to ice cream when they're having one of those days. I've always been a cookie dough person myself. Ice cream is more of an everyday food for me. Funny and true.

1 cup (112 g) almond flour

½ cup (68 g) coconut flour, sifted

¼ cup (30 g) ground golden flax seeds

1 teaspoon baking soda

¼ teaspoon fine sea salt

½ cup unsweetened applesauce

1⅓ cups (8 ounces) dairy-free chocolate chips (70% cacao), divided

¼ cup melted coconut oil or ghee

¼ cup honey

1 tablespoon vanilla extract

1. Line a baking sheet with unbleached parchment paper.

2. Place the flours, ground flax seeds, baking soda, and salt in a mixing bowl and whisk to combine. Add the applesauce, ⅓ cup of the chocolate chips, coconut oil, honey, and vanilla and mix with a handheld mixer until well combined.

3. Use a ¾-ounce (size 40) scoop with a lever or a spoon to make about 15 bites. Place them on the prepared baking sheet and freeze for at least 2 hours.

4. To make the dipping chocolate, place the remaining 1 cup of chocolate chips in a double boiler and melt over low heat (see page 46 for how to create a double boiler setup). When the chocolate is just melted, remove from the heat. Insert a toothpick into the bottom of a bite of frozen cookie dough, then dip it into the melted chocolate. Let the excess chocolate run off, then slide the bite off the toothpick onto the lined baking sheet. Repeat with the rest of the bites until all of them are coated.

5. Store in the freezer for up to 2 weeks. Enjoy cold, straight from the freezer.

sunbutter fudge

Makes 30 pieces | Prep Time: 20 minutes | Cook Time: less than 5 minutes | Wait Time: overnight

I used to make this fudge with twice as much honey. When I cut the honey in half, my kids didn't even notice. They love it just as much as ever. This is one of the healthiest treats in this book, and it's also one of the easiest to make.

1 cup sunflower seed butter without added sugar (such as Organic SunButter)

½ cup plus 1 teaspoon melted coconut oil, divided

¼ cup honey

¼ teaspoon fine sea salt

1½ ounces dairy-free dark chocolate (70% cacao)

1. Line an 8 by 6-inch glass dish with unbleached parchment paper. Pinch the corners to help the paper stay in place.

2. In a bowl, combine the sunflower seed butter, ½ cup of the coconut oil, honey, and salt. Pour the mixture into the prepared dish. If the mixture is very runny, refrigerate it until it firms up slightly.

3. Place the chocolate and the remaining 1 teaspoon of coconut oil in a double boiler over low heat (see page 46 for how to create a double boiler setup). When the chocolate is just melted, remove from the heat and pour the chocolate into a small glass measuring cup with a spout. Let it come to room temperature.

4. Pour the chocolate in lines across the top of the fudge. Drag a toothpick through the chocolate in a serpentine line in the opposite direction. Refrigerate overnight, until solid, then slice into 30 pieces.

5. Store in the fridge for up to 2 weeks.

chapter 16:

Puddings & Pies

coconut custard

Serves 3 | Prep Time: 20 minutes | Cook Time: 30 minutes

Coconut oil, for greasing the ramekins

3 large eggs

6 large egg yolks

¼ cup honey

¼ teaspoon fine sea salt

2¾ cups full-fat coconut milk

⅛ teaspoon liquid vanilla stevia

For serving:

Fresh berries

1. Set the oven to 325°F and grease three 14-ounce ramekins with coconut oil.

2. Place the whole eggs, egg yolks, honey, and salt in a deep mixing bowl. Set aside.

3. Combine the coconut milk and stevia in a saucepan over medium heat. When it comes to a boil, remove the pan from the heat.

4. Very slowly pour the coconut milk mixture into the egg mixture while whisking continuously. Continue until all of the milk is incorporated.

5. Pour the custard evenly into the prepared ramekins. Place the ramekins on a rimmed baking sheet and carefully transfer to the oven. Bake for about 30 minutes, until the custard is just set in the middle. Let cool.

6. Serve at room temperature or chilled, with fresh berries.

7. Store covered in the refrigerator for up to a week.

peach cobbler

Serves 8 | Prep Time: 20 minutes | Cook Time: 20 minutes

Ghee or coconut oil, for greasing the pan

6 cups sliced fresh peaches (about 3 pounds)

Crumble topping:

1 batch Chocolate Chip Scone dough (page 176), chocolate chips omitted

1 teaspoon ground cinnamon

1. Set the oven to 350°F and grease a deep 9-inch ceramic pie pan or 8 by 8-inch glass baking dish with ghee or coconut oil. Place the sliced peaches in the dish.

2. Make the crumble topping: Prepare the dough for the Chocolate Chip Scones according to the directions, but omit the chocolate chips and add 1 teaspoon of ground cinnamon.

3. Sprinkle the crumble topping over the peaches. Bake for about 20 minutes, until the topping is starting to brown. Serve warm.

4. Store covered in the refrigerator for up to a week.

strawberry pudding

Serves 6 | Prep Time: 10 minutes | Wait Time: 6 hours

¼ cup water

1 tablespoon grass-fed gelatin

1½ cups full-fat coconut milk

1¼ cups pureed strawberries, divided

½ cup packed soft pitted Medjool dates (about 8)

Pinch of fine sea salt

1. Bring the water to a boil in a small saucepan. Transfer the boiling water to a mug and immediately stir in the gelatin until completely dissolved.

2. Place the gelatin mixture, coconut milk, 1 cup of the strawberry puree, dates, and salt in a food processor fitted with the S-blade. Puree, being sure to hold down the lid firmly for the first 10 seconds to prevent spilling. Continue to puree for about 5 minutes, until completely smooth.

3. Divide the pudding evenly among six small bowls and refrigerate until set, about 6 hours. Top each bowl with a spoonful of the remaining strawberry puree.

4. Store covered in the refrigerator for up to a week.

banana carob pudding

Serves 6 | Prep Time: 10 minutes | Wait Time: 6 hours

I wish I had tried carob sooner. Now that I've been using it awhile, I don't think of it as a replacement for chocolate, although I'm sure it makes a good substitute. It has its own unique flavor and sweetness that the kids and I really love.

¼ cup water

1 tablespoon grass-fed gelatin

1½ cups full-fat coconut milk

1 cup mashed banana (about 2 bananas)

½ cup packed soft pitted Medjool dates (about 8)

1 tablespoon carob powder

Pinch of fine sea salt

For garnish:

Banana slices

1. Bring the water to a boil in a small saucepan. Transfer the boiling water to a mug and immediately stir in the gelatin until completely dissolved.

2. Place the gelatin mixture, coconut milk, mashed banana, dates, carob powder, and salt in a food processor fitted with the S-blade. Puree, being sure to hold down the lid firmly for the first 10 seconds to prevent spilling. Continue to puree for about 5 minutes, until completely smooth.

3. Divide the pudding evenly among six small bowls and refrigerate until set, about 6 hours. Garnish with banana slices.

4. Store covered in the refrigerator for up to a week.

strawberry cheesecake

Serves 8 | Prep Time: 25 minutes | Cook Time: 28 minutes | Wait Time: 3 hours plus overnight

For me, giving up dairy was harder than giving up gluten. Then, in 2005, I was given a raw food cookbook, and I learned how to make cheesecake using cashews and coconut. I was so happy! I experimented with raw cheesecake recipes of my own, using fewer cashews and more coconut, until I finally nailed it with this version. I think you will find my cheesecake as delicious as my family does. For a raw crust substitute, use the No-Bake Pumpkin Pie crust on page 376.

½ batch Sweet Pie Crust (page 135)

Cream cheese layer:

¾ cup full-fat coconut milk

½ cup (70 g) raw cashews, soaked in water for at least 3 hours, rinsed, and drained

¼ cup honey

1 teaspoon vanilla extract

½ cup melted coconut oil

Strawberry layer:

12 ounces fresh strawberries, plus more for garnish

¼ cup water

1 teaspoon fresh-squeezed lemon juice

1 teaspoon agar powder

For garnish:

Fresh whole strawberries

1. Set the oven to 350°F and line the bottom of a 7-inch springform pan with unbleached parchment paper.

2. Make the pie crust dough as directed, then press it into the bottom of the prepared springform pan. Bake for about 18 minutes, until golden. Set aside to cool.

3. Make the cream cheese layer: Place the cream cheese ingredients in a blender in the order listed, adding the melted coconut oil last, just before blending. Puree until completely smooth. When the crust is cool, pour the cream cheese layer into the crust and refrigerate until set, at least 3 hours. Rinse the blender jar.

4. Make the strawberry layer: In the blender, puree the strawberries, water, and lemon juice until smooth. In a small heavy-bottomed pot, simmer the strawberry puree, uncovered, for about 10 minutes. Turn off the heat and whisk in the agar powder until completely dissolved.

5. When the cream cheese layer has set, pour the strawberry layer over it and refrigerate overnight.

6. Run a knife between the cheesecake and the wall of the pan to loosen it, then remove the wall. Transfer the cheesecake to a plate and top with fresh strawberries. Serve cool or at room temperature.

7. Store covered in the refrigerator for up to a week.

Variation: Pumpkin Spice Cheesecake. *Add 2½ teaspoons Pumpkin Spice Blend (page 118) to the cream cheese layer and omit the strawberry layer.*

apple pie

Serves 8 | Prep Time: 30 minutes | Cook Time: 25 minutes

If you've been a fan of The Spunky Coconut *for a long time, then you may know that the way to my husband's heart is apple pie. Ever since he was little, he's requested apple pie (never cake!) for his birthday. Last year we got a big box of organic apples from Mom's Country Orchards in Oak Glen, California, and he made so many of these apple pies.*

½ batch Sweet Pie Crust (page 135), for decorative leaf-shaped cutouts

1½ teaspoons water

1 batch Sweet Pie Crust (page 135)

Filling:

3 Gala apples, peeled and sliced into ¼-inch strips

1 tablespoon ghee or coconut oil

Big pinch of fine sea salt

1 cup unsweetened applesauce

¼ to ½ cup coconut sugar, depending on tartness of apples

1 tablespoon arrowroot or tapioca flour

2 teaspoons ground cinnamon

Special equipment:

Leaf-shaped cookie cutter

1. Make the half batch of pie crust dough, but add 1½ teaspoons of water. Place the dough between two pieces of unbleached parchment paper and roll it out to ¼ inch thick. Freeze the rolled-out dough for 30 minutes.

2. Make the full batch of pie crust dough and press it into the bottom and up the sides of a 9-inch pie pan as directed; set aside.

3. Set the oven to 350°F. Combine the apples, ghee, and salt in a small heavy-bottomed pot. Cover and cook over low to medium heat, stirring occasionally, until the apples are just tender.

4. Meanwhile, in a mixing bowl, combine the applesauce, coconut sugar, arrowroot flour, and cinnamon. Add the applesauce mixture to the pot with the apples and stir to combine. Pour the filling into the crust.

5. After the rolled-out dough has been in the freezer for 30 minutes, take it out. Use a leaf-shaped cookie cutter to create pie crust leaves, then arrange the leaves on top of the filling.

6. Bake the pie for 18 minutes, until golden. Allow to cool, then slice and serve.

7. Store covered in the refrigerator for up to a week.

mock key lime pie

Serves 8 | Prep Time: 25 minutes | Cook Time: 18 minutes | Wait Time: 3 hours plus overnight

We all have our favorite pies, and this one is Zoe's favorite. It's also one of the prettiest pies, in my opinion, which makes it great for parties.

1 batch Sweet Pie Crust (page 135)

Mock Key lime filling:

½ cup water

1 tablespoon grass-fed gelatin

¾ cup full-fat coconut milk

½ cup fresh-squeezed lime juice

¼ cup honey

Small handful of spinach

⅛ teaspoon fine sea salt

1 batch Whipped Coconut Cream (page 366)

For garnish (optional):

Thin lime slices

1. Set the oven to 350°F. Make the pie crust as directed, then bake for about 18 minutes, until golden. Set aside to cool.

2. Make the filling: Bring the water to a boil in a small saucepan. Pour the boiling water into a mug and immediately stir in the gelatin until completely dissolved.

3. Place the gelatin mixture, coconut milk, lime juice, honey, spinach, and salt in a blender and puree until completely smooth. Pour the filling into the cooled crust and refrigerate until set, at least 3 hours.

4. When the lime layer is set, top it with a thick layer of Whipped Coconut Cream and refrigerate overnight.

5. Slice the pie and enjoy. Garnish with thin slices of lime, if desired.

6. Store covered in the refrigerator for up to a week.

whipped coconut cream

Makes about 2 cups | Wait Time: overnight | Prep Time: 10 minutes

2 (13½-ounce) cans full-fat coconut milk with guar gum, refrigerated for 24 hours (see Note)

2 tablespoons honey

1 teaspoon vanilla extract

Several drops of liquid vanilla stevia, to taste (optional)

2 tablespoons water, if needed

1 teaspoon grass-fed gelatin, if needed

1. Open the cans of coconut milk, skim off the cream that has separated and risen to the tops of the cans, and transfer the cream to a mixing bowl. Discard the water.

2. Add the honey, vanilla, and stevia to the bowl with the coconut cream and mix with a handheld mixer until just combined.

3. If the whipped cream does not appear thick (like whipped cream should) after mixing, then boil the water. Transfer the boiling water to a mug and immediately stir in the gelatin until completely dissolved. Add the gelatin mixture to the whipped cream and combine with the mixer. Refrigerate the whipped cream to set if needed.

Note: *Coconut milk containing guar gum, such as Native Forest or Thai Kitchen brand, tends to separate more easily into coconut cream and water, and the whipped coconut cream tends to be more stable, which is why I recommend it. However, this recipe can be made with gum-free coconut milk. If you use gum-free coconut milk, see the "How to Make Coconut Cream Tutorial" on my blog, The Spunky Coconut. (To find it, click on the recipe index, then use the search field.)*

banana chocolate cream pie

Serves 8 | Prep Time: 20 minutes | Cook Time: 18 minutes | Wait Time: overnight

1 batch Sweet Pie Crust (page 135)

Filling:

About 4 bananas, plus more for garnish

⅓ cup (30 g) cocoa powder (sift if lumpy)

¼ cup packed soft pitted Medjool dates (about 4)

2 teaspoons vanilla extract

¼ teaspoon ground cinnamon

⅛ teaspoon fine sea salt

½ cup melted coconut oil

1. Set the oven to 350°F. Make the pie crust as directed, then bake for about 18 minutes, until golden. Set aside to cool.

2. Make the filling: In a blender, puree the bananas until you have 2 cups of pureed bananas. Then add the rest of the ingredients in the order listed, adding the melted coconut oil last, just before blending. Puree until completely smooth.

3. Pour the filling into the cooled crust and refrigerate overnight.

4. Serve topped with sliced bananas.

5. Store covered in the refrigerator for up to a week.

blueberry pie

Serves 8 | Prep Time: 20 minutes | Cook Time: 25 minutes | Wait Time: overnight

I wouldn't list blueberries as one of my favorite fruits, but this IS my favorite pie. Go figure!

1 batch Sweet Pie Crust (page 135)

Filling:

5 cups frozen blueberries, not thawed

¼ cup coconut sugar

2 tablespoons arrowroot or tapioca flour

2 teaspoons agar powder

For serving:

Whipped Coconut Cream (page 366)

1. Set the oven to 350°F. Make the pie crust as directed, then bake for about 18 minutes, until golden. Set aside to cool.

2. While the crust is baking, make the filling: Put the blueberries and coconut sugar in a medium-sized heavy-bottomed pot. Simmer over low to medium heat for about 10 minutes, until hot.

3. Use a slotted spoon to remove the blueberries from the juices in the pot and put them in a mixing bowl. Simmer the juices for another 10 minutes to reduce slightly.

4. Turn off the heat and whisk the arrowroot flour and agar powder into the blueberry juices until dissolved. (The mixture will begin to thicken right away.) Add the thickened sauce to the blueberries in the mixing bowl and stir well to combine.

5. Pour the filling into the cooled crust and refrigerate overnight.

6. Serve the pie with Whipped Coconut Cream.

7. Store covered in the refrigerator for up to a week.

strawberry rhubarb pie

Serves 8 | Prep Time: 20 minutes | Cook Time: 18 minutes | Wait Time: overnight

There are two recipes that I remember my grandmother Sitti making: ratatouille and strawberry rhubarb pie. I was a big fan of both dishes. She would be so proud that I make this pie today.

1 batch Sweet Pie Crust (page 135)

Filling:

10 ounces fresh rhubarb, sliced (about 2 cups)

10 ounces frozen whole strawberries (about 2 cups), not thawed

½ cup coconut sugar

1 teaspoon ground cinnamon

⅛ teaspoon fine sea salt

2 tablespoons arrowroot or tapioca flour

2 teaspoons agar powder

For serving:

Whipped Coconut Cream (page 366)

1. Set the oven to 350°F. Make the pie crust as directed, then bake for about 18 minutes, until golden. Set aside to cool.

2. While the crust is baking, make the filling: Put the rhubarb, strawberries, coconut sugar, cinnamon, and salt in a medium-sized heavy-bottomed pot. Simmer over low to medium heat for 5 to 10 minutes, until the rhubarb has softened.

3. Turn off the heat and stir the arrowroot flour and agar powder into the filling mixture until dissolved. Pour the filling into the cooled crust and refrigerate overnight.

4. Serve the pie with Whipped Coconut Cream.

5. Store covered in the refrigerator for up to a week.

salted caramel pecan pie

Serves 8 | Prep Time: 20 minutes | Cook Time: 20 minutes | Wait Time: overnight

There's no need to compromise on healthy ingredients around the holidays. Using whole foods like dates and nuts is a fast and easy way to make pecan pie without corn syrup or wheat flour. Trust me: This pie is amazing!

Crust:

1 cup (134 g) raw cashews, soaked in water for 3 hours, rinsed, and drained

1 tablespoon coconut oil or ghee, plus more for greasing the pan

1 tablespoon honey

1 teaspoon vanilla

½ cup (35 g) unsweetened shredded coconut

Filling:

1 cup packed soft pitted Medjool dates, soaked in 1 cup water for 3 hours (save the soaking water)

¼ cup coconut oil or ghee

1 tablespoon vanilla

¼ teaspoon fine sea salt

2 cups salted roasted pecans, plus more for garnish

1. Set the oven to 400°F and grease a 9-inch glass pie pan with coconut oil.

2. Make the crust: Puree the cashews, coconut oil, honey, and vanilla in a food processor fitted with the S-blade for about 1 minute. Add the shredded coconut and puree until the mixture forms a ball. Using wet hands, press the crust into the prepared pie pan.

3. Make the filling: Place the dates (including the soaking water), coconut oil, vanilla, and salt in a blender and puree until smooth. Fold in the pecans, then pour the filling into the unbaked crust. Garnish the top of the pie with more pecans.

4. Bake the pie for 10 minutes, then reduce the oven temperature to 350°F and bake for 10 more minutes, until the crust is golden. Allow the pie to cool on the counter, then refrigerate overnight.

5. An hour before serving, take the pie out of the fridge to bring it to room temperature.

6. Store covered in the refrigerator for up to a week.

chocolate pecan pie

Serves 8 | Prep Time: 25 minutes | Cook Time: 20 minutes | Wait Time: overnight

Crust:

1 cup (134 g) raw cashews, soaked in water for 3 hours, rinsed, and drained

1 tablespoon coconut oil or ghee, plus more for greasing the pan

1 tablespoon honey

1 teaspoon vanilla extract

Big pinch of fine sea salt

½ cup (35 g) unsweetened shredded coconut

Filling:

½ cup packed soft pitted Medjool dates, soaked in 1 cup water for 3 hours (save the soaking water)

¼ cup coconut oil or ghee

1 tablespoon vanilla extract

¼ heaping teaspoon fine sea salt

6 ounces dairy-free dark chocolate (70% cacao), melted in a double boiler (see page 46)

2 cups salted roasted pecans, plus more for garnish

1. Set the oven to 400°F and grease a 9-inch glass pie pan with coconut oil.

2. Make the crust: Puree the cashews, coconut oil, honey, vanilla, and salt in a food processor fitted with the S-blade for about 1 minute. Add the shredded coconut and puree until the mixture forms a ball. Using wet hands, press the crust into the prepared pie pan.

3. Make the filling: Place the dates (including the soaking water), coconut oil, vanilla, salt, and melted chocolate in a blender and puree until smooth. Fold in the pecans, then pour the filling into the unbaked crust. Garnish the top of the pie with more pecans.

4. Bake for 10 minutes, then reduce the oven temperature to 350°F and bake for 10 more minutes. Allow to cool on the counter, then refrigerate overnight.

5. An hour before serving, take the pie out of the fridge to bring it to room temperature.

6. Store covered in the refrigerator for up to a week.

no-bake pumpkin pie

Serves 8 | Prep Time: 20 minutes | Wait Time: 6 hours

You can easily make this pie nut-free by making it without a crust—something I do often. I love to use stevia because it keeps the amount of sweetener (in this case, dates) to a minimum. However, you can add another ¼ to ½ cup of dates and omit the stevia if you prefer.

Crust:

1 cup raw walnut pieces

¼ cup packed soft pitted Medjool dates (about 4)

1 teaspoon ground cinnamon

Pinch of fine sea salt

Filling:

1½ cups full-fat coconut milk

1 cup pumpkin puree

½ cup packed soft pitted Medjool dates (about 8)

1 teaspoon Pumpkin Spice Blend (page 118)

½ teaspoon fine sea salt

¼ teaspoon liquid vanilla stevia

¼ cup water

1½ tablespoons grass-fed gelatin

1. Make the crust: In a food processor fitted with the S-blade, puree the crust ingredients for about 20 seconds, until very fine. Transfer the mixture to a 7-inch springform pan and pack it down into the bottom.

2. Make the filling: Rinse the bowl of the food processor, then add the coconut milk, pumpkin puree, dates, Pumpkin Spice Blend, salt, and stevia and puree, being sure to hold down the lid firmly for the first 10 seconds to prevent spilling. Continue to puree for about 5 minutes, until completely smooth.

3. Meanwhile, bring the water to a boil in a small saucepan. Transfer the boiling water to a mug and immediately stir in the gelatin until completely dissolved. Add the gelatin mixture to the food processor and puree to combine.

4. Pour the filling over the crust in the springform pan and refrigerate until set, about 6 hours.

5. To serve, run a knife between the pie and the wall of the pan, then remove the wall. Run the knife between the crust and the bottom of the pan to loosen it, then use a spatula to transfer the pie to a plate or cake stand. The pie is best enjoyed at room temperature.

6. Store covered in the refrigerator for up to a week.

appendix:

Natural Living

This book isn't just about food. It's about my family's lifestyle, the health challenges we have faced, how we've overcome those challenges, and what you can do to prevent your family from having the same issues.

Natural living—from using homemade deodorant to home birthing—is as important to my family as the way we eat. It also goes hand in hand with Paleo. Paleo isn't just a way of eating; it's a lifestyle. The Paleo lifestyle emphasizes nature: being outside, playing, and getting your hands dirty. Moreover, Paleo is about getting rid of the junk. Not just junk food, but junk products of all kinds, from chemical household cleaners and toxic cookware and food storage containers to toxic makeup, skincare products, and deodorant.

This appendix is meant to complement the core of this book—the kitchen organization and meal-planning tips and my go-to, family-favorite recipes. In this section I will give you some practical information about how to take Paleo to the next level, beyond the kitchen to your medicine cabinet and broom closet and even to family planning. The simple use of lavender and chamomile for stress and insomnia, or the use of zinc and rash guards for sunblock, are just a sample of what you'll find in the following pages.

natural cleansers

- Use only natural and biodegradable laundry detergent and cleaning supplies (I buy them from Tropical Traditions).

- Use old-fashioned homemade cleansers instead of store-bought cleaning products. Here are two of my favorites:

  - White vinegar is fantastic for cleaning glass and mirrors. I put a quarter-sized amount on a clean, dry washcloth, then add a little water, wring it out, and voilà! Inexpensive and effective. Vinegar is also a great natural weed killer! Just make sure not to get it on the plants you want to keep.

  - Peroxide will remove blood from clothing or bedding and prevent staining if you use it right away. Apply the peroxide (undiluted) directly to the area, then rub if needed.

natural remedies

I'm a big fan of natural remedies. Here are the natural remedies that my family uses:

Acid reflux: Lemon juice, unfiltered apple cider vinegar (with the mother), green juice

Allergic reaction: Benadryl, though not a natural remedy, can save a person's life if he or she has an allergic reaction. I keep it on hand for emergencies only; fortunately, I've never had to use it.

Anxiety or panic attacks: Peppermint oil applied to the temples, homeopathic motion sickness remedy such as Highland's (take as directed)

Cold or flu: At the first sign of cold or flu, vitamin C, vitamin D, probiotics, electrolytes (two good sources are coconut water [preferably fresh or raw] and maple water), bone broth and pho (pages 131 and 212), elderberry syrup, rose hip tea

Bee sting: Apis homeopathic (take as directed)

Bruising: Arnica homeopathic (take as directed)

Burns: After the burn has cooled, apply lavender essential oil, aloe, or coconut oil

Chicken pox: Rhus Tox homeopathic (take as directed)

Congestion: Peppermint oil and a few drops of eucalyptus oil mixed with olive oil (rubbed on the chest), neti pot (must use water that has been boiled)

Constipation: Magnesium citrate supplements, vitamin C supplements (I prefer the MegaFood brand), enema

Cough: A few drops of eucalyptus oil mixed with olive oil (rubbed on the chest), warm air humidifier, elderberry syrup (use as directed)

Cuts: Lavender essential oil or coconut oil, applied a few times per day

the benefits of krill and coconut oil

In addition to following a grain-free and dairy-free diet and a detox program, I attribute krill oil and coconut oil to Ashley's success. Krill oil contains phospholipids, which cross the blood-brain barrier, helping to repair heavy metal damage. Coconut oil is made up of medium-chain triglycerides, mainly lauric acid, which is also found in human milk. Lauric acid improves nutrient absorption and digestive function and regulates blood sugar. It also protects against bacteria and viruses.

Detox: Activated charcoal (take as directed), vitamin C, probiotics (I prefer Klaire Labs brand, Therbiotic Complete capsules, and VSL#3 capsules), electrolytes (two good sources are coconut water [preferably fresh or raw] and maple water), bone broth and pho (pages 131 and 212), rose hip tea (because it's very high in vitamin C)

Diarrhea: Activated charcoal, Arsenicum album homeopathic (take as directed)

Earache: Mullein garlic ear oil, warmed by placing the dropper in a glass of hot water and then dropped into the ear

Fever: Ferrum phosphoricum homeopathic (take as directed), washcloth of room-temperature water for forehead, room-temperature bath if necessary

Headache: Peppermint oil on the temples, Meriva curcumin phytosome supplements (take as directed)

Infection: Rose hip tea, Biocidin (from Bio-Botanical Research, Inc.; take as directed), oil of oregano supplements (take as directed)

Liver detox: Dark greens, beets, turmeric, apples, grapefruit, carrots, avocados, members of the brassicas genus of plants (such as cabbage, broccoli, and cauliflower), lemon juice, lime juice

Menstrual problems, fertility problems, PMS: Evening primrose oil supplements, raspberry leaf tea and/or supplements

Nausea: Peppermint oil on the temples, crystallized ginger (consume a few pieces), activated charcoal (take as directed)

Sleep problems: A few drops of lavender oil on the neck, magnesium citrate capsules or powder added to warm water, chamomile tea

Sore throat: Oil of oregano supplements, Monolauren, Biocidin (from Bio-Botanical Research Inc.; take as directed)

Soreness: Arnica homeopathic cream (apply as directed)

supporting gut health

Supporting gut health is about more than just taking probiotics, which my family does. (We have used Klaire Labs and VSL#3 probiotics.) The second most important thing you can do for your gut is to avoid refined sugars, processed foods, and refined vegetable oils. Eat lots of leafy greens and make your own yogurt (page 182) and broth (page 131)—both are so much easier than you might think. It's all about planning!

recipe index

Staples

108	112	114	116	118	120
bacon fat	coconut porridge mix	hazelnut coffee creamer	my go-to seasonings	pumpkin spice blend	salad dressings

128	129	132	134	135	136	137
poultry brine	barbecue sauce	baking mixes	savory pie crust	sweet pie crust	orange chutney	tart cranberry sauce

Drinks

138	143	144	146	148	149
strawberry rose hip jam	cashew milk	detox piña colada	magenta ginger juice	chilled dandelion mocha	eggnog

Breakfast Anytime

150	152	157	158	160	162
tea	molten chocolate	crepes	best-ever pancakes	bagels	mini boulder cream donuts

   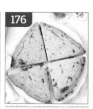

165	166	168	170	172	174	176
cherry almond bars	cheese danish	pumpkin cinnamon rolls	strawberry rhubarb gummies	cherry muffins	blueberry muffins	chocolate chip scones

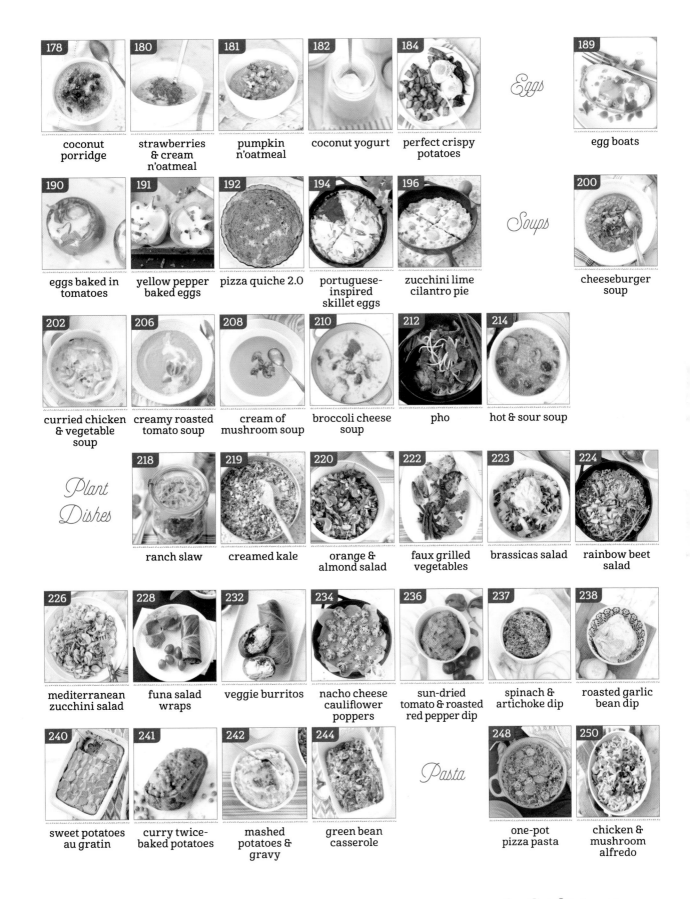

178 coconut porridge

180 strawberries & cream n'oatmeal

181 pumpkin n'oatmeal

182 coconut yogurt

184 perfect crispy potatoes

Eggs

189 egg boats

190 eggs baked in tomatoes

191 yellow pepper baked eggs

192 pizza quiche 2.0

194 portuguese-inspired skillet eggs

196 zucchini lime cilantro pie

Soups

200 cheeseburger soup

202 curried chicken & vegetable soup

206 creamy roasted tomato soup

208 cream of mushroom soup

210 broccoli cheese soup

212 pho

214 hot & sour soup

Plant Dishes

218 ranch slaw

219 creamed kale

220 orange & almond salad

222 faux grilled vegetables

223 brassicas salad

224 rainbow beet salad

226 mediterranean zucchini salad

228 funa salad wraps

232 veggie burritos

234 nacho cheese cauliflower poppers

236 sun-dried tomato & roasted red pepper dip

237 spinach & artichoke dip

238 roasted garlic bean dip

240 sweet potatoes au gratin

241 curry twice-baked potatoes

242 mashed potatoes & gravy

244 green bean casserole

Pasta

248 one-pot pizza pasta

250 chicken & mushroom alfredo

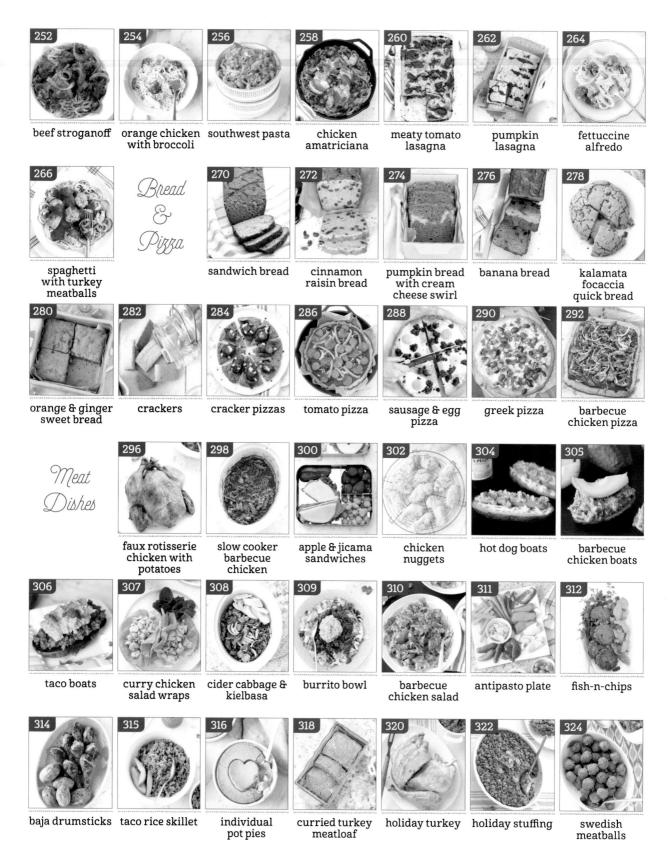

252 beef stroganoff

254 orange chicken with broccoli

256 southwest pasta

258 chicken amatriciana

260 meaty tomato lasagna

262 pumpkin lasagna

264 fettuccine alfredo

266 spaghetti with turkey meatballs

Bread & Pizza

270 sandwich bread

272 cinnamon raisin bread

274 pumpkin bread with cream cheese swirl

276 banana bread

278 kalamata focaccia quick bread

280 orange & ginger sweet bread

282 crackers

284 cracker pizzas

286 tomato pizza

288 sausage & egg pizza

290 greek pizza

292 barbecue chicken pizza

Meat Dishes

296 faux rotisserie chicken with potatoes

298 slow cooker barbecue chicken

300 apple & jicama sandwiches

302 chicken nuggets

304 hot dog boats

305 barbecue chicken boats

306 taco boats

307 curry chicken salad wraps

308 cider cabbage & kielbasa

309 burrito bowl

310 barbecue chicken salad

311 antipasto plate

312 fish-n-chips

314 baja drumsticks

315 taco rice skillet

316 individual pot pies

318 curried turkey meatloaf

320 holiday turkey

322 holiday stuffing

324 swedish meatballs

Cakes & Cookies

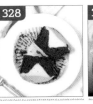
328 black-bottom cupcakes

330 harvest cupcakes

332 basic white frosting

333 naturally colored frostings

336 mint chocolate christmas cake

338 coconut cake

341 rainbow cake

344 crunchy arrowroot cookies

346 chocolate hazelnut cookies

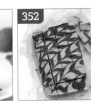
348 no-bake chocolate-covered cookies

350 cookie dough bites

352 sunbutter fudge

Puddings & Pies

357 coconut custard

359 banana carob pudding

360 strawberry cheesecake

362 apple pie

364 mock key lime pie

366 whipped coconut cream

367 banana chocolate cream pie

368 blueberry pie

370 strawberry rhubarb pie

372 salted caramel pecan pie

374 chocolate pecan pie

376 no-bake pumpkin pie

nut-free recipes

egg-free recipes

kids' favorite recipes

general index

with gratitude

To my family: I love you so much and I'm so grateful to have you.

To my friends Rina and Elana: Thank you so much for all your help and support. I love you so much.

To my readers, who made this book possible: I love you. Thank you so much for sharing your lives with me, and for being a part of mine.

To my publisher, Erich, and his team at Victory Belt: Thank you so much for making this book with me. I love you guys. And to all my editors at Victory Belt, especially Holly and Pam: I couldn't have done it without your help.

To all my friends in the real food community: You mean so much to me. I feel so blessed to call you friends.

my other publications

Hungry for more? Check out my blog, *The Spunky Coconut,* and my other cookbooks, listed below!

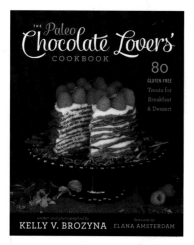

The Paleo Chocolate Lovers' Cookbook

This book features 80 gluten-, grain-, and dairy-free recipes for the health-conscious chocolate lover, including recipes for breakfast and even dinner! For this book I created delicious chocolate treats made with coconut and ground nut flours. And, using dates and small amounts of the herbal sweetener stevia in these nutrient-dense baked goods, I show you how to keep the honey and coconut sugar to a minimum.

Recipes include savory dishes like Chili with Roasted Butternut Squash, Cocoa and Spice-Rubbed Ribs, and Oven-Roasted Barbecue Drumsticks, along with numerous sweet treats, such as Chocolate Crepe Cake with Coconut Cream, White Chocolate Dipped Macadamia Biscotti, homemade (dairy-free, low-glycemic) chocolate bars, Chocolate Swirl Cheese Danish Cake, Lava Cakes, Dark Chocolate Hazelnut Cookies, White Chocolate Truffles, Cherry Cordial Fudge, and more.

This book also details the components of chocolate: the importance of organic and fair-trade chocolate, frequently asked questions about chocolate, and a side-by-side comparison of store-bought dark chocolate bars.

Dairy-Free Ice Cream

In this book you will find all of your favorite ice cream flavors free of dairy, gluten, grains, soy, and refined sugar. Chapters include Cool Tips for Perfect Ice Cream, A History of Dairy-Free Ice Cream, The Classics, Coffee & Tea Ice Cream, Yogurt Pops & Sorbet, Ice Cream Cakes & Sandwiches, and Toppings.

For both health and personal reasons, eliminating dairy has improved the lives of so many people. With *Dairy-Free Ice Cream,* you can not only enjoy every flavor of ice cream again, but also avoid refined sugars, harmful oils, soy, preservatives, and other common ingredients found in store-bought dairy-free ice cream. Making your own dairy-free ice cream is affordable, healthy, and fun for the whole family. Delight guests at your next birthday party with ice cream sandwiches or build-your-own sundaes!